SECOND EDITION

D0220967

Patients' Rights, Law and Ethics for Nurses

SECOND EDITION

Patients' Rights, Law and Ethics for Nurses

Paul Buka

University of West London, UK

CRC Press
Taylor & Francis Group
Boca Raton London New York

CRC Press is an imprint of the
Taylor & Francis Group, an **informa** business

CRC Press
Taylor & Francis Group
6000 Broken Sound Parkway NW, Suite 300
Boca Raton, FL 33487-2742

© 2015 by Taylor & Francis Group, LLC
CRC Press is an imprint of Taylor & Francis Group, an Informa business

No claim to original U.S. Government works

Printed on acid-free paper
Version Date: 20140528

International Standard Book Number-13: 978-1-4822-1739-1 (Paperback)

Visit the Taylor & Francis Web site at
http://www.taylorandfrancis.com

and the CRC Press Web site at
http://www.crcpress.com

Printed and bound in the United States of America by Edwards Brothers Malloy on sustainably sourced paper.

This second edition is dedicated to all of our families.
They provided support and encouragement for this project.

CONTENTS

Today's healthcare users are more informed of their rights and their expectations may be high. The second edition of this book will focus on the rights of the patients and how these relate to nursing. With improved healthcare provision, it is inevitable that people are living longer. There are clearly resources issues.

Since the implementation of the Human Rights Act 1998, in 2000, the United Kingdom has seen changes, with a political drive toward partnership and patient-centred care. Nurses are more autonomous in their practice and more accountable. Expectations of quality care are on the rise; this is likely to be linked to increased complaints and potential litigation.

Nurses owe their patient a duty of care in ethics and law and should recognize and safeguard these rights. Aspects of current policy including legislation are there to facilitate this. Ethical principles have something positive to offer as they are universally acknowledged and fundamental to every patient's basic rights; nevertheless, the law takes precedence.

This book lays no claim to providing all the answers, the domain or function of a standard comprehensive legal textbook; rather, it aims to provide a framework, with an outline of the ethical and legal frameworks within which care is delivered, with key principles which aim to blend together law and ethics as they define the fiduciary relationship and patients' rights. It could be argued that ethics informs the law while the latter regulates citizens and healthcare professionals' conduct. Key aspects of the law herein are based mainly on United Kingdom law. The author and contributors recognize that while key legislation is of United Kingdom origin, wherever practicable, every effort will be made to highlight only key distinctions between English and Scots law. Due to the nature and size of this book, a comprehensive and detailed analysis would not be practicable. Furthermore, occasionally there may also be specific references with relevance to Scotland and Northern Ireland.

In healthcare provision, it is no longer possible to stipulate a 'formal' code of professional conduct which is not based on law and ethics. Gone are the days when nurses could claim immunity from accountability or prosecution on the basis that they were following medical instructions or 'the doctor's orders'. With a more advanced and wider scope of practice comes a higher level of accountability. It is hoped that by challenging nurses and raising awareness of legislation and ethical implications, nurses will improve their rationale for their decision-making and care provision. Knowledge and application of ethical principles as well as the law defining patients' rights are essential for nurses, thus enabling them to put the patient at the centre of decision-making.

ACKNOWLEDGEMENTS

I thank all those involved in the preparation and production process for this second edition, especially my commissioning editors, Jo Koster and Naomi Wilkinson, for their patience and invaluable support, as well as my original project editor, Clare Patterson, for helping me to start off the process for the first edition.

I acknowledge the valuable contributions to this project from Sue Watkinson and Kathy Chambers with respect to Chapter 2 and the first edition Chapter 4 – now Chapter 3 (respectively).

I continue to draw inspiration from my academic colleagues, friends and of course my students (past and present) who gave me some encouragement and challenges on their journeys to become nurses. I appreciate the invaluable critical reviews from my fellow academics, Davidson Chademana, Ganapathy Ganesalingam and Swapna Williamson, who helped me with ideas for improving the focus for the second edition. Importantly, I must not forget to include key clinical reviews provided by Laura Carlin, a senior staff nurse with many years of clinical practice, for kindly assisting with painstaking and constructive reviews.

On a personal note, a big thank you to all my family, and especially my wife, Carol, without whom this project would not have been possible. Carol was always patient enough to give honest opinions and dedicate many hours to proofreading as well as putting up with the 'at times' messy paperwork. Finally, but not least, my gratitude would not be complete without acknowledging both of our wonderful sons, Sandy (for the original concept for the cover design) and TG (for being who he is). They have both supported and provided some encouragement – as always.

AUTHOR AND CONTRIBUTORS

Paul Buka, MIHM, MSc (Leicester), PGCE, LL.B (Hons), FETC (City and Guilds, 7307), HNC (Public Admin), RN, RNT is a senior lecturer in adult nursing at the University of West London, London, UK. Prior to the start of his nurse training, he read philosophy. As a senior nurse in clinical practice, Buka developed a keen interest in legal studies and progressed to read law up to the postgraduate level, specializing in healthcare law and ethics as well as criminal justice (specialist area: domestic violence). He taught law in higher education, and has several years of teaching in nursing, specializing in healthcare law and ethics. Buka has other publications in this area.

Kathleen Chambers, RN, RM, RMN, Cert Ed, BSc, MA is a retired senior lecturer in the Faculty of Health and Human Sciences at the University of West London, London, UK. Her specialist clinical interests are neonatal nursing and child law. She earned an MA in childcare law and practice from the University of Keele. Chambers has considerable experience in teaching child law and child protection within pre- and post-registration nurse education (first edition).

Sue Watkinson, BA, RN, OND (Hons), PGCEA, MSc, PhD is a retired senior lecturer in the Faculty of Health and Human Sciences at the University of West London, London, UK. Her specialist clinical interest is in ophthalmic nursing and she has published extensively within this field. Dr. Watkinson earned an MSc in educational studies and PhD in education from the University of Surrey. She has considerable experience in teaching research, ethics and philosophy within pre- and post-registration nurse education.

TABLE OF CASES

TABLE OF STATUTES

STATUTES

STATUTORY INSTRUMENTS

EU AND INTERNATIONAL LEGISLATION

DIRECTIVES

1 CONCEPT OF LAW AND HUMAN RIGHTS

INTRODUCTION

The law will be introduced first on the assumption that law is more definitive in comparison to any other discipline regulating human behaviour. The significance of ethics and how it underpins the law should not be underestimated, and this will be highlighted throughout the chapters. The terms 'patient' or 'user' will be used interchangeably.

Most children's first experience of 'the law' or 'legislation' may relate to 'rules' which may be disciplined and ingrained in their memory as they grow up (and they may face a dichotomy of 'dos' or 'don'ts'). They will learn how to comply with rules either based on love or respect for parents and authority and rules or adversely, based on fear (of consequences) for breaching those rules. As they grow up, people may turn out to have learnt some moral values, a way of life which respects society's rules, or not knowing any different, they may deviate from expected norms of behaviour and go on to breach rules which others may consider as sacrosanct. Such experience is relevant for the beginnings of morality, moral values and the law. Morals for most, on the other hand, would accept that all persons are equal and therefore entitled to protection under the law

(Harris, 1985). However, there may be potential abuses of human rights based on law and morality, and governmental rules may be reprehensive (Wacks, 2012).

Given the challenge which citizens may face in attempting to define 'a concept of law', any such attempt may produce a variety of definitions. Without a clear definition of law, it is difficult to provide clarity in this area when individual laws are applied to a given context.

The concept of law is abstract but the impact of legislation is very real, with a presence all around us. This is not helped by the fact that in both Parliament (as a law-making body) and the courts it is not always easy for the judges to match the intention of Parliament with preceding case law. For most people the meaning of 'legal concepts' may be shrouded in mystery and be open to subjective interpretations and argument. This may present difficulties as miscarriages of justice and grounds for appeal result. In jurisprudence, legal principles may be the basis of arguments resulting in legal disputes, and challenges to a superior court. The application of law can be difficult to grasp or justify, as in interpreting laws, lower courts try to find a judicial precedent (principle), which represents previous authoritative case law which binds a court of the same or lower-level decision of a lower court. Stare decisis (Latin: 'stand by the decision') is a legal phrase referring to the obligation of courts to honor past precedents (Civil Liberty, About. com, http://civilliberty.about.com/od/historyprofiles/g/stare_decisis.htm, accessed March 2014).

As suggested by Aquinas (1225–74) in *Summa Theologiae* (McDermott, 1997), individuals have a free will or the power to choose to follow or adopt as their own individual standards of morality. Morality or behaviour influenced by a 'moral fibre' may have been influenced by psychosocial factors such as religion, culture upbringing and education of individual experience. In morals, there will be variables, highlighting similarities as well as differences, depending on certain local, national or international values. These are also influenced by religion, culture and social environment which all shape the development of a given society. As people may choose individual morality, there is a need for asserting order and harmony. This should be the role of the state, through all its three arms: the legislature (Parliament), the executive (government) and the judiciary (courts). The last branch acts as guardian of the rule of law by interpreting the will of Parliament as well as developing the principles of case law.

From a nursing perspective, ethical beliefs of an individual nurse may influence their conduct on issues such as compassion and empathy toward their patients and how they should treat them with dignity and respect. This may be evident if and when ethical dilemmas arise in healthcare provision. Nurses and healthcare professionals must follow the dictates of the law. The rule of law is necessary in order to establish a system of governance and to prevent chaos in a given society.

There are, however, exceptions to the rule. A nurse who is a conscientious objector may resort to their 'conscience' for guidance, or may indeed be exempt from participating in certain procedures. Current provisions for abortion and human fertilization and embryology allow conscientious objection. Section 4 of Abortion Act 1967 defines conscientious objection to participation in treatment as such:

> *(1) Subject to subsection (2) of this section, no person shall be under any duty, whether by contract or by any statutory or other legal requirement, to participate in any treatment authorised by this Act to which he has a conscientious objection.*

The principle of law was applied in the following:

Doogan and Anor v NHS Greater Glasgow and Clyde Health Board [2013] ScotCS CSIH 36 (24 April 2013)

A senior nurse (Band 7) midwife (supervising junior midwives) sought clarification on whether conscientious objection on religious grounds included 'the entitlement to refuse to delegate, supervise and/or support staff in the participation in and provision of care to patients undergoing termination of pregnancy or feticide throughout the termination process'.

Held: This right did not extend to conscientious objection for staff supervising staff who are participating in terminations of pregnancy.

Abortion Act 1967 is not applicable to Northern Ireland.

Furthermore, Articles 38(1–2) of Human Fertilization and Embryology Act 1990 provide for healthcare professionals such as nurses and midwives the right to conscientious objection:

> *(1) No person who has a conscientious objection to participating in any activity governed by this Act shall be under any duty, however arising, to do so.*
>
> *(2) In any legal proceedings the burden of proof of conscientious objection shall rest on the person claiming to rely on it.*

'Conscientious objection' is acceptable on the grounds of religion or individual moral values where procedures aimed at achieving conception and pregnancy are concerned.

An individual nurse may, however, choose to act contrary to professional standards of ethics and standards or morality (*R v Allitt*, 1992 [2007] EWHC 2845 (QB)) (see Chapter 3), while also disregarding the law as well as 'accepted' societal norms – hence the overlap. This may harm the patient in their care. The question posed is whether it is the norm for professionals to identify their own individual morality with 'professional ethics', which happens to be embodied in the law, in the form of the NMC Code of Conduct (2008).

For the patient, however, the more vulnerable they may be, the more likely they are to have those basic human rights undermined (Article 3 of the Human Rights Act 1998). Where there is a lack of clarity, rights therefore may at times need to be defined, asserted or protected – by the law. The nurse, on the other hand, has nothing to fear so long as they are acting within the confines of the law. They need to be aware that they are expected (by the Nursing and Midwifery Council (NMC) or in court of law) not only to be aware of patients' rights but also to safeguard those rights, and report this as necessary. This is part of their duty of care (NMC, 2010). There may be situations where colleagues or others within a caring relationship with a patient may indeed undermine these rights. Hence, it is important that the nurse be aware of how the law defines patients' rights (which include human rights and how ethics may influence clinical decisions in the clinical practice and how those rights relate to the law). Ethics is a product of society, and individual morals or ethical values vary and may influence opinions and legal decisions on crucial ethical issues such as human fertilization, abortion, capacity and withdrawal of treatment and end of life decisions. Judges who sit in judgement where moral issues and ethical dilemmas arise may be influenced by their own personal ethical values as they 'wrestle' with their conscience on matters of law and ethics when they deliberate. This is clear from the judicial deliberations in ruling in the landmark withdrawal-of-treatment case, the Tony Bland case (*Airedale NHS Trust v Bland* [1993] AC 789 HL) (see Chapter 9).

The concept 'law' or 'legal' applies to a system of rules which set standards of conduct and which are applicable to a group or groups of people. The law defines people's rights and obligations. For a law to be effective, it should be enforceable, with consequences for failure to compliance. One important element is that law derives from an authoritative source in order to give it efficacy. Like ethics, 'law develops continually in response to social, political and economic conditions, and any attempt to divide up its history must largely be arbitrary' (Smith, 1962, p. 3). The law should be accessible to all citizens in its application and key characteristics of the law are that it

- must have certainty with an identity,
- is impersonal,
- is applicable universally (for all citizens) or to a specified group of people,
- creates rights as well as corresponding obligations.

Development of law can be seen in society's attempt to establish order, in the ancient codification of law by Hammurabi (ca. 1792–50 bc), of Mesopotamia; Hammurabi's Code was a systematic code of laws (with 282 articles in total). The aim of the code was to regulate human conduct, both in private and in public; nevertheless, this was mostly meting out justice on an 'eye for an eye' basis. The following aspects of the code are examples of the application of this principle:

> 218. *If a physician make a large incision with the operating knife, and kill him, or open a tumour with the operating knife, and cut out the eye, his hands shall be cut off....*
> 221. *If a physician heals the broken bone or diseased soft part of a man, the patient shall pay the physician five shekels in money....*
> 229. *If a builder build a house for someone, and does not construct it properly, and the house which he built fall in and kill its owner, then that builder shall be put to death.*
> ***http://www.lawbuzz.com/ourlaws/hammurabi/***
> ***hammurabi.htm***

In democratic societies, there are recognized channels for individuals to seek redress and/or to assert their rights. It is possible that there are vulnerable patients who may not be aware of or able to define duties and assert their rights or may simply think that 'it is not worth the hassle' to complain. Hence, it is important that nurses are aware of patients' rights and how to safeguard these patients (NMC, 2010). Laws evolve in response to the needs of society and they survive or become obsolete depending on customary usage; otherwise, they become obsolete through time. In some nations, 'good' laws may be seen as immutable, being frameworks for all other laws to follow; one example is the bill of rights (presently not in the United Kingdom constitution). Other laws may be subject to review as time moves on, in any given society or within a group of people with a common interest. While most laws are promulgated by democratically elected government, laws may nevertheless be imposed from a superior order such as the dictate of an autocratic ruler as they deem fit. In a theocracy, which advocates for a divine right, there are those who may learn to give laws their pre-eminence in the belief that all laws come from a divine source, through a theocratic authority. As a representative of (theocratic) authority, some rulers have been known in history to abuse the rights of their subjects. Acceptable forms of authority in a democracy emanate from elected representatives. The judiciary should be an arm of the government for safeguarding and defining the rights of citizens. In comparison, most people would also accept that in the scientific world there are accepted laws of nature which if breached may have disastrous consequences.

The law may be invoked not only to define rights and create obligations, but also to define sanctions against those who may fail to comply with its dictates; the link between ethics and law is easy to see. This is highlighted in the following:

R v *Instan* [1893] I QB at 453

D lived with her aunt, who developed gangrene in her leg and became totally dependent and unable to call for help. The defendant failed to feed her aunt or to call for medical help, even though she remained in the house and continued to eat her aunt's food. The aunt's dead body was found in the house decomposing for about a week.

Held: The defendant had a duty to supply her deceased aunt with sufficient food to maintain life. In addition, the death of her aunt had been accelerated due to her neglect of this duty of care.

In the same case, it was noted furthermore that nevertheless, breach of ethical principles does not necessarily have a legal basis:

> *It would not be correct to say that every moral obligation involves a legal duty; but every legal duty is founded on a moral obligation. A legal common law duty is nothing else than the enforcing by law of that which is a moral obligation without legal enforcement.*
> **Lord Chief Justice Coleridge, CJ at 453, R v Instan [1893]**

Albert Dicey (1835–1922), a classical jurist and legal philosopher, contributed to the debate on the objectives of the law (in regulating human conduct) in society and gives it pre-eminence over other disciplines such as natural law and ethics. Central to his belief is the suggestion that for it to work, there is a need for the law to be impartial. His central argument was that this would protect the human rights of citizens (Dicey, 1950). Aspects of law such as human rights, criminal law, employment law, contract and the law of torts take human rights and ethical principles such as fairness and discrimination on board. In the aftermath of the Second World War, a consensus to protect human rights emerged and the United Nations Universal Declaration of Human Rights 1948 (Ghandi, 2013) was proclaimed by the General Assembly of the United Nations on 10 December 1948 (the basis for the European Convention on Human Rights).

Everyone's right to life shall be protected by law. No one shall be deprived of his life intentionally save in the execution of a sentence of a court following his conviction of a crime for which this penalty is provided by law.

Article 2(1) of the European Convention on Human Rights 1950

This puts basic human rights at the centre of governing and protecting citizens from arbitrary actions by other, more powerful citizens who may choose to usurp their rights. This was central to a framework for human rights to which signatories signed up. The United Kingdom enacted the Human Rights Act 1998 which received royal assent on 9 November 1998, 25 years after Britain became a signatory of the then European Economic Community (EEC), on 1 January 1973. This statute came into force on 2 October 2000, aiming to give effect in UK law the rights established in the European Convention on Human Rights 1950. The relevant aspects will be explored below. The key issue is citizens' ability to access justice and recourse to the law as morals need the law. It could also be argued that the law likewise needs morality.

THINKING POINT

One winter Sunday morning on a busy acute medical 24-bed mixed ward for older people, the Band 6 staff nurse in charge of the long-day shift was Anna (not her real name), who had been qualified for five years. She normally coped very well but recently she had been increasingly working under considerable pressure due to staff shortages. On the day in question, the experienced trained staff nurse in overall charge of the ward was Anna, being supported by Simon (not his real name), who had qualified within the last year and had worked with Anna as her preceptor. His actions gave Anna cause for concern as he claimed to have given intravenous (IV) antibiotics, which she had checked but not witnessed him draw up or give for a number of patients for the medicines round on that morning, but this was difficult to prove and check as the patients in question were poorly and were not in a position to corroborate this. Anna was surprised at the speed with which this had been completed. Other staff members had occasionally expressed minor concerns informally about his practice; however, no one was prepared to substantiate any issues of concern because 'he was a very dedicated nurse'. There had been other

(Continued)

occasions when Anna had some uncertainty about Simon's practice, including poor communication skills and poor documentation. Without any conclusive evidence, she could not verify that the medications had been administered. Incidentally, on the day in question the condition of one of the patients (an 87-year-old man) under Simon's care had deteriorated rapidly and he passed away, unexpectedly. The patient was not for active resuscitation and the death was recorded as due to natural causes since the patient had co-morbidities including diabetes and renal failure, as well as dementia and pneumonia.

Anna subsequently met with Simon, who admitted in private having omitted medication and falsified patients' records and entered intravenous antibiotics medications as having been administered when in fact he had not. Concerned about the potential reflection on her practice and supervisory skills, she told him she would not report him but he must never mention this to anyone.

When one of the experienced healthcare assistants subsequently made a complaint to the ward manager, Simon was suspended from duty pending further investigation. Anna went off sick following the initial investigation.

- Consider the term 'human rights' and define what the patient's rights were in this scenario.
- What legal (and professional) implications can you identify with reference to Anna and Simon's conduct?
- Revisit the above scenario when you complete the section on 'duty of care' (below).

SOURCES OF LAW

The laws of most countries originate from two main sources:

- Primary sources,
- Secondary sources.

Primary sources of law are international treaties, the European Parliament and the United Kingdom (UK) Parliament and assemblies (pertaining to their respective laws). These are in the form of statute law.

Secondary sources are all other multiple sources. France is one of those countries with their laws codified; the United Kingdom laws have experienced more fluidity in their development. Delegated legislation such as byelaws are laws made by bodies such as local authorities (while government agencies and arms-at-length government bodies work with government departments) and what used to be called quasi-non-governmental organizations (QUANGOs) and statutory instruments, which is supportive legislation which is enabled by a parent statute from which it is derived. Additionally, byelaws are from professional bodies established by royal charter, such as the Nursing and Midwifery Council (NMC). Another important source is common law, when the courts develop principles of law based on previous decisions of the same or higher court. This is considered to be authoritative and binding toward a current decision.

The European Parliament has authority to legislate for UK law – by virtue of accession and membership of the European Union (EU) (Blair, 2010). There are four main political institutions of the EU:

- *Council of Ministers*: This is composed of representative ministers from each member state. This is the most effective group as the law-making body of the EU.
- *Commission*: This is the administrative arm of the EU and is composed of technocrats and administrators who are responsible for drafting legislation. This is the equivalent of the civil service with the function of supporting the Council of Ministers. It is headed by an unelected president.
- *Assembly*: This is also known as the European Parliament. Unlike the UK Parliament, this body has no law-making powers. Its main function is to debate on topics of interest to the EU, which may be contemporary to and of interest to Europe. Its consensus-based recommendations will be the basis for recommendations or guidelines for ministers on the Council of Ministers when legislating. They may also influence governments as they relay decisions to influence their own national parliaments. The assembly is also responsible for electing officials such as judges.
- *European Court of Justice*: This is the highest court in the EU, which should not be confused with the European Court of Human Rights. Sometimes known as the Court of Justice of the European Communities, it is based in Luxembourg. While each EU state has a sovereign jurisdiction of its different legal systems, this court is responsible for adjudicating between the EU and member states or in an interstate dispute on the interpretation of European law, for example:
  - between the European Commission and a member state which fails to implement a European Union directive,
  - between the European Commission and a member state, claiming that the European Commission has acted ultra vires, outside its jurisdiction,

- between national courts from member states asking for clarification on the validity of specific EC legislation (subject to Article 189/EC, which defines the method extent and application of the European laws).

Judges, on the basis of representation of member states, normally serve for a renewable term of six years.

Additionally, on specific human rights issues, the European Court of Human Rights in Strasbourg was established for addressing human rights, currently under the Human Rights Act 1998. Cases may be launched on an appeal basis or may go directly to this court. There are three classifications of EU laws:

- Regulations, which are binding to member states, and must be applied directly in their entirety.
- Directives, which must bring into line national laws, subject to an agreed timetable for the implementation. An example is the (EU) Data Protection Directive 1995, which had as its main aim protection of personal information and harmonization of privacy laws within the EU. In the UK, the result was the Data Protection Act 1998.
- Decisions, which are the legal decisions (or case law) of the European Court of Justice. This effectively modifies the constitutional principle that Parliament can make or unmake any laws based on a majority vote.

European laws are equally binding and applicable to all countries of the United Kingdom. The law can be changed by the UK Parliament subject to the EU European Court of Justice's interpretation.

The Roman invasion of Western Europe, as a whole, left Latin terminology still dominant in legal principles and use of terminology. In contrast to English common law, Scots law has developed its own unique ways, e.g. in law of delict; as well as influences from a number of sources, there are some principles rooted in the Roman-Dutch law traditions (which affected Scots law through trading and the links with scholars studying law there mainly through links with the Kirks in the seventeenth and eighteenth centuries). French law had also played a part in the development of Scots law, following the signature of the 'Auld Alliance' between John Balliol of Scotland and Philip IV of France (1295). This alliance was against Edward I of England. Scottish jurists went across to be educated in France.

In comparison, English private law has stronger roots in the feudal system, with the influence of the church in both traditions in areas such as family, succession and property laws. Finally, institutional writers like Professor Erskine's Institutes (1730) and Viscount Stair's Institution (1773) also provided a unique source for Scotland, and are often quoted as authority in Scots law. The Union of Crowns (1603) influenced both countries, with more similarities between the two systems, though nevertheless distinct principles in some areas.

In 1707, following the Union of Parliaments, the House of Lords became the final court of appeal for all cases including Scottish cases, with the result that English law could be applied to Scottish cases and vice versa (the Acts of Union, 1706 and 1707). In criminal law, however, appeals continue to be heard under the Scottish High Court of Justiciary (criminal appeal court) sitting as the final court.

DUTY OF CARE

The 'duty of care' principle has evolved from a moral sense of responsibility or obligation. The difference is that apart from social isolation, ethics alone may not be sufficient to enforce the duty of care or to impose sanctions for breach. The law, on the other hand, should be systematic and clearly defined. In criminal law, the state is responsible for prosecuting a wrongdoer, while in tort law (delict in Scotland) (which includes civil actions against clinical negligence), the personal injury action is initiated by the wrongdoer and/or their representatives (Elliott and Quinn, 2009).

The following landmark House of Lords case originating in Scotland defined the duty of care while establishing the 'neighbour principle'. This is still good law today in the United Kingdom as well as being consistently applied to clinical negligence cases in other common law systems worldwide.

The term 'duty of care' has developed with a moral influence to it. It is the basis of our obligations toward others with whom we may have a relationship,

---

Donoghue v Stevenson HL [1932] HL All ER Rep1

The claimant had gone to a café with a friend, who had bought her ice cream and a drink of ginger beer. The café owner poured some of the drink over her ice cream, and she consumed it. When she poured the rest of it she found the decomposing remains of a dead snail. The claimant became unwell as a result. She could, however, not claim against the manufacturer in contract law as she had no contract with him.

Held: The claim for damages for negligence (in tort) against the manufacturer was entitled to succeed despite not having contractual rights.

with the following definition being generally accepted as a foundation in tort/delict law (and applied to clinical negligence):

> *You must take reasonable care to avoid acts or omissions which you can reasonably foresee would be likely to injure your neighbour.*
>
> **Lord Atkins, at p. 580,**
> **Donoghue v Stevenson** *HL [1932]*

The principle that a manufacturer who allows a defective product to leave their possession for distribution for sale owes a duty of care to their ultimate consumer is now applicable to the healthcare relationship. In response to the question 'who is my neighbour?', the House of Lords established the so-called 'neighbour principle' in the above case: 'persons who are so closely affected by my act that I ought reasonably to have them in my contemplation as being affected when I am directing my mind to the acts or omissions which are called in question' (Lord Atkins, at p. 580, *Donoghue* v *Stevenson* [1932]). This is applicable to clinical practice in that the question of duty of care may arise when there is an allegation of negligence, and where care is said to have fallen below certain specific standards. On the basis of this principle and the relationship of trust, there is little difficulty for the courts to establish that a healthcare professional who is responsible for treating a patient owes them a duty of care not to harm them as well as to avoid omissions, which may cause them (patients) harm. As citizens, nurses have their own rights and obligations arising from the law of the land. The obligations are based on the common law a healthcare provider owes the user or patient a duty of care. Consider Beauchamp and Childress's (2012) four principles of ethics (Chapter 2).

The law of tort or delict, which deals with claims in damages for personal injury, has certain requirements to be met before a victim of clinical negligence can raise a claim for damages in court. They are called 'hurdles' which they need to overcome before negligence is established:

- The plaintiff or victim is owed a *duty of care* by the particular defendant or defender (Scotland). This is to prevent unwarranted and frivolous claims, which may be unrelated to the alleged injury, and to limit the claims, as the nurse cannot be expected to owe a universal duty of care to all and sundry fitting into the category of 'patient', but only to those in their care.
- The plaintiff should have proof of *breach of that duty by the defendant*. There must be a sufficient degree of proximity in their relationship. This could be the most difficult aspect to prove.

- The plaintiff suffered harm as a result of the alleged breach of the duty of care.
- Did the alleged breach cause the harm in question (a *causal nexus*), i.e. in the chain of causation or affected by the actions of the defendant?
- In the mind of the defendant, there should be reasonable foreseeability (or as common sense predicts), and this pertains to the *limitation of damages*. This is a matter in the public interest to limit frivolous claims and prevent floodgates.

The law provides for the right of the defendant to be heard and counter-argue their case in their own defence (Hodgson and Lewthwaite, 2007). One example is the response that a victim caused or contributed to the injury.

The aim is to seek damages in compensation (or reparation) for the harm (or personal injury) they (victim) may have suffered as a result of the wrongdoer's (defendant, or defender in Scots law) negligent actions or omissions. The aim of tort or delict is to make reparation or restitution (Scots law) for any harm done. A patient who suffers harm as result of healthcare professional negligence is entitled to damages in compensation for personal injury. The main hurdle for the litigant is proving the causation by the defendant. 'Quantum' or 'quantification' is a term used for measure of damages by the courts. Several categories may be included, with the main ones in tort being classed under the headings of general speculative or special damages. Very rarely, exemplary (punitive) damages may be awarded, for example, in cases where the courts feel the importance of making a public statement, in order to prevent something from happening again. Such damages are not awardable to the victim.

General damages: 'If the victim sought a money award for pain and suffering, mental anguish, and loss of consortium, these would be classified as general damages' (*Free Dictionary*, accessed 2013). Examples of headings for the injury the claimant received are pain, loss and suffering, and loss of amenity.

Special damages: These are compensatory and are 'designed to return persons to the position they were in prior to the alleged injury'. For example, if a person was injured in a surgical operation, 'the victim could seek damages that would cover medical expenses … and the loss of earnings now and in the future' (*Free Dictionary*, accessed 2013). This would also include nursing home care and adaptations to living accommodations.

THINKING POINT

Mrs. X was an 85-year-old widow on an orthopaedic trauma ward, and had just had hip surgery following a fall and a resultant fractured neck of femur. Prior to this she had lived on her own in a two-bed roomed bungalow, and was self-caring apart from home help once a week to help with shopping. She suffered from mild dementia, but was normally independent. Post-operatively her condition deteriorated rapidly; she stopped eating and became more confused, and she died 10 days post-operatively, amongst other things as a result of a chest infection, with a further infection in the wound (the consultant surgeon had refused to prescribe more antibiotics on the grounds that the patient was 'old', giving orders to 'just keep her comfortable').

- Her children often found that their mother (who was by then doubly incontinent) had been covered in excrement for some time and on asking, the response the nurse gave was that they were 'busy' and short staffed due to sickness.
- According to the patient's records, the dressing had not been changed for three days (when the care plan was meant to be renewed daily) – this was obvious from the state.
- There had been no documentation of observations for about five days, even if they informed the nurse.
- Their mother advised them that she was constantly in pain; she had told the nurse, but nothing had been done.
- Additionally, they were concerned about their mother's nutrition as when they visited, she was given no help with meals. They were more concerned with what was happening in their absence.

1. Based on the NMC Code of Conduct, define 'duty of care'.
2. Consider the complaints procedure used in your workplace and the role of the Care Quality Commission.

On completion of the section of 'Duty of Care', revisit the above thinking point and apply and reflect on duty of care.

More recently the duty of care and the neighbour principle in the *Donoghue* case have been applied in the following case:

Johnson v Fourie [2011] EWHC 1062 (QB)

A patient underwent cosmetic surgery then suffered from severe disfigurement and disablement due to the surgeon's negligent action. The surgeon admitted liability.

Held: Negligence by the surgeon had been proven. The litigant was awarded damages with a total of nearly £6 million being awarded.

CLASSIFICATION OF LAW

This section provides a brief overview of breaches of law and explores specifically the issue of liability in law and ethics.

There are different ways of classifying law in the United Kingdom. For both Scots law and English law the overall classification is similar, with differences in terminology used, e.g. the law of torts in England and its equivalent, delict in Scots law. One classification can be divided into two main branches, public law which is within the public domain and private law which has been developed for the benefit of the private individual. Examples of public law are criminal, administrative law, health and safety law. The private law blanket would include examples such as family law, law of trusts and law of torts, which includes the tort of negligence.

HUMAN RIGHTS AND LEGAL OBLIGATIONS

To the question on the justification of human rights, several responses have been put forward by ethical theorists in their search for moral philosophy (these will be examined in more detail in Chapter 2). The articles, found in the schedule, stipulate these rights. The Human Rights Act 1998 is applicable to criminal and civil law (Hodgson and Lewthwaite, 2007). The most important principle embodied in this piece of legislation (Leckie and Pickersgill, 2000) is that 'everyone's right to life shall be protected by the law' (Article 2, European Convention on the Protection of Human Rights and Fundamental Freedoms 1950). The European convention may be used to apply human rights, by state versus state or individual versus state, in the European Court of Human Rights (ECHR) (De Than and Shorts, 2013). The United Kingdom is signatory to the human rights legislation and provides for human rights through the Human Rights Act 1998. As signatory to European legislation, the United Kingdom now must subscribe to provisions of the Human Rights Act (HRA) 1998 which give the UK courts power to implement it.

The general categories of rights under the HRA (1998) are classified as follows (Ministry of Justice, 2006):

- *unqualified/absolute rights*, which cannot be amended – Articles 2, 3, 4(1) and 7;
- *qualified rights*, which may be modified by the state in extreme circumstances, e.g. in a state of emergency – Articles 4(2), 5, 6 and 12;

- *limited rights*, which are subject to limitation by the state depending on society's needs – Articles 8, 10 and 11.

Relevant aspects of the articles affect the way we care for patients. Since 2 October 2000, public bodies and local authorities now have a duty to safeguard individual rights and these can be enforced in UK courts (Makkan, 2000). Judges also have the power to refer to Parliament for clarification of the intention of legislature, if the law is uncertain. Some of the aspects of the Human Rights Act affecting patient care are as follows:

Article 2 – Right to life. Everyone's right to life shall be protected by law. No one shall be deprived of his life intentionally save in the execution of a sentence of a court following his conviction of a crime for which this penalty is provided by law.

Article 3 – Prohibition of torture. No one shall be subjected to torture or inhuman or degrading treatment or punishment. An example of an alleged breach of this article is illustrated in the following case:

NHS Trust A v *M* and *NHS Trust B* v *H* [2001] Fam 348

A hospital sought permission to discontinue artificial hydration and nutrition to a patient who in 1997 had been diagnosed as being in a 'permanent vegetative state'. The court held that Article 2 imposed a positive obligation to give treatment where that is in the best interests of the patient – but not where it would be futile. Discontinuing treatment would not be an intentional deprivation of life under Article 2, and provided that withdrawing treatment was in line with a respected body of medical opinion, and that the patient would be unaware of the treatment and not suffering, there would be no torture under Article 3.

Environmental Law Centre, http://www.elc.org.uk/pages/lawarticleshra.htm#2 (accessed 2 June 2013).

Article 8 – Right to respect for private and family life. Everyone has the right to his private and family life, his home and his correspondence. There shall be no interference by a public authority with the exercise of this right except such as is in accordance with the law. This is consistent with the patient's right of autonomy consent to treatment and informed choice.

Article 14 – Outlaws discrimination. Under the Equality Act 2012, this may be on various grounds such as age, gender and sexuality.

Article 17 – Prohibition of abuse of rights. Nothing in this convention may be interpreted as implying for any state, group or person any right to engage in any activity or perform any act aimed at the destruction of any of the rights and freedoms set forth herein or at their limitation to a greater extent than is provided for in the convention.

The United Kingdom courts may in the first make a declaration of human rights and award damages, if infringement has been proven, or opt to make a declaration only if they feel that damages are not warranted. For any cases which do not fall within the provisions of the 1998 Act, the court will apply existing domestic law.

The Human Rights Act 1998 gives effect to the convention rights by requiring the United Kingdom courts to interpret the law in compatibility with this statute. UK courts also have a duty to refer the matter to Parliament if there is conflict with existing legislation, thus enabling them to make a 'declaration of incompatibility' and apply UK legislation, even if this is in breach of European legislation (Welch in Addis and Morrow, 2005). The onus is on Parliament to decide on amending the existing legislation in question, in order to bring it into line with European legislation. A claimant may appeal or take their case directly to the European Court of Human Rights (ECHR) in Strasbourg. The extent of the human rights applies to public bodies only and does not cover private organizations. While patient A, in an NHS trust hospital, may be able to raise an action subject to the HRA 1998 Act, patient B in a private hospital would not be entitled to do so. The statute also covers those in employment who may wish to litigate against an employer. Thus, the act creates both civil and criminal rights. Membership of the EU has made it possible for the 18 rights outlined in the Human Rights Act schedule to be enforceable in United Kingdom courts normally within three months if this is for a declaration of rights only. If, however, a complainant is seeking damages for breach of human rights, they must file the case within a year of the date of the alleged incident. However, a patient resorting to litigation should be aware that the time limit for litigation under the HRA varies depending on the brief (the document stating the facts and points of law of a client's case).

Subject to the Limitation Act 1980 and the Prescription and Limitation (Scotland) Act 1973, a litigant seeking redress normally has a three-year limitation, at the discretion of the courts.

THINKING POINT

Joe assists the gastroenterologist, in an endoscopy unit, where he has worked for the past 12 years, having been a Band 6 staff nurse for the last 6 years. He is aware of his responsibilities and role but recently the department has been at times stretched due to staff shortages, barely coping. He is concerned that patients may be put at risk as the trust has now asked them to carry out 18 per cent more cases than the previous year, in order to meet their contract and government targets. Recently, a near-miss incident highlighted some issues, where a patient was found choking and aspirated before this was rectified; there were not enough nurses on the floor as the nurses were forced to do work which would normally be undertaken by porters, as their only allocated porter was overwhelmed. The one nurse looking after two patients, having been busy with another patient, had not noticed that the other patient who had been sick was 'aspirating'. Fortunately and by chance, Joe was passing when he read the warning signs and reacted quickly to assist the patient and called for help, thus avoiding a dangerous situation.

1. Are you aware of the local guidelines for reporting near misses and actual untoward incidents within your department?
2. What risk assessments would you need to carry out?
3. Consider your local policy on risk assessment.

LITIGATION AND COMPENSATION SYSTEMS

Until the enactment of the Crown Proceedings Act 1947, the crown or the government, as its representative, could not be sued. Following removal of crown immunity, it is now possible for the crown to have liability in tort/delict, with a government minister having nominal liability (Cracknell, 2004). In fact, to the present day, subject to Section 40(1) of the above act, the queen cannot be made personally liable in tort. Additionally, judges cannot be sued for action in the process of dispensing their duties.

With modern-day advancements in medicine, patients have also come to have raised expectations (Davies, 2001). In addition, due to current policy standards, any high expectations on the quality of care may be reinforced.

The time limit requirement is that court proceedings must be issued within three years of the victim first being aware of having suffered an injury. A victim claiming damages must also establish (on a balance of probabilities) the facts, which can be 'hurdles' in the progress before the courts can award damages for personal injury in tort (McHale and Tingle, 2001). Some claims fall short of the requirements at the initial hurdles as it can be difficult to prove clinical negligence at times, especially where there are latent complications of a clinical event, which may surface a long time after. It has been suggested that it is likely that most victims of clinical negligence may not bother to bring an action for personal injury, with only a relatively small proportion doing so, and about 76 per cent of these were unsuccessful (Mason et al., 2010). Latent claims may be allowed at the discretion of the court.

Litigation usually involves an uphill struggle and most victims cannot afford the hassle, time and money to fight a case. In order to recover damages, a claimant must establish on a balance of probabilities that the defendant's negligence had a material effect on the outcome of the disease. The burden of proof (on a balance of probabilities) lies with the victim.

For healthcare professionals who hold themselves out as having a specialist skill, they will be judged by the standards of a reasonably competent healthcare professional. The standard of care expected by the courts is that of the 'reasonable' clinician based on peers, which is the higher rather than the lower one, and the *Bolam* test, established in *Bolam v Friern Hospital Management Committee* [1957] 1 WLR 582. The following case illustrates this point in issue:

Wilsher v Essex Area Health Authority [1987] QB 730.CA, 1988 AC 1074

The plaintiff was born prematurely. Subsequently the defendant negligently gave the plaintiff excess oxygen. A catheter was wrongly inserted into his vein on two occasions instead of his artery and as a result, he developed an incurable eye condition. The court accepted that his blindness could have been caused by one of any other conditions found in premature babies. The hospital admitted only negligence in general on that basis, but the court upheld the objective standard in respect of a junior doctor who could not argue his inexperience as a reason to avoid liability.

Held: The hospital was liable.

Davies (2001) acknowledges that there are potential difficulties in accessing evidence, which is mainly retained in clinical records. The reality of the matter is that over many years, witnesses may move, forget what happened, change their mind or die before the case comes to court. Delays may work against a victim. The Access to Health Records Act 1990 gives a patient or their representative a right to access non-computerized clinical records, with the Data Protection Act 1998 regulating computerized ones.

The NHS litigation authority

Established in 1995, this is a voluntary National Health Service (NHS) scheme, with the main aim of indemnifying NHS organizations in the event of claims. Foundation trusts may choose to opt out of this scheme since one change is the introduction of the National Clinical Assessment Service (NCAS) on 1 April 2013, which acts as the operating division of the NHS Litigation Authority (NHSLA). It is responsible for representing the NHS organizations such as trusts. It receives and manages a pool of contributions from each organization while also providing risk management by monitoring the level and the nature of claims.

Their key role includes the following functions:

- managing claims to ensure consistency across the NHS;
- advising the Department of Health on current and projected costs of claims through risk management;
- managing cases centrally and monitoring compliance across NHS bodies in relation to the Human Rights Act 'by providing a central source of information on relevant case-law development, to provide mechanisms for the proper, prompt and cost-effective resolution of dispute' (http://www.nhsla.com/FHSAU/Pages/Home.aspx, accessed June 2013);
- providing advice on litigation in clinical negligence, human rights, equal pay, discrimination and claims involving NHS bodies in England.

The claims they manage may also be non-clinical, e.g. where there is third-party injury.

Available evidence suggests that the level of claims is on the rise:

- In 2004–05, 5,609 claims of clinical negligence and 3,766 claims of non-clinical negligence against NHS bodies were received by the NHSLA.
- This compares with 6,251 claims of clinical negligence and 3,819 claims of non-clinical negligence in 2003–04.

The annual accounts for the NHSLA showed that clinical negligence claims for the year 2011–12 totalled around £1.2 billion.

The NHSLA works with the National Institute for Health Care Excellence (NICE). Its functions can be summarized as to 'contribute to the incentives for reducing the number of negligent or preventable incidents' (http://www.nice.org.uk/usingguidance/benefitsofimplementation/nhsla.jsp).

In Scotland, the Central Legal Office deals with complaints. For 2009–10, £35 million was paid out for clinical negligence.

Systems of compensation

The main UK system of compensation for personal injury has always been adversarial in that the victim must prove fault or negligence. Under the 'fault system', the blame or fault must be established or proven for the claim to be successful. From a clinical negligence victim's perspective, the process of seeking compensation can be protracted and difficult as the onus on them to establish negligence may be difficult. Unlike in criminal law where the evidence must be proved 'beyond reasonable doubt', the victim is only required to provide the court with evidence 'on a balance of probability'. This lower standard of proof is applicable to civil law cases. While a few cases will settle out of court, the reality for most people is that they will find litigation costs prohibitive and may not bother pursuing what may be a legitimate claim.

Another factor which may put off a potential litigant is delays which may be involved in the conditional or 'no-win no-fee' system that has been introduced. This means that the lawyers get about 12 per cent legal fees plus costs, which include expert witnesses and court fees. The victim may still find themselves having to pay the legal costs for the other side if they lose unless they are covered by insurance. The difficulty with this scheme is that due to the financial risk factor for victim legal counsel, lawyers will be reluctant to take on a case unless they are guaranteed of its success. There may be issues in the no-win no-fee system, where a claimant will only pay if they win. The problem is that not many lawyers are willing to take the risk of such cases unless they are confident of winning. Since 2011, there have been some changes to the limit of legal fees that lawyers can charge:

> *The proportion of any damages that can be taken by lawyers will be capped at 25%.*
> *The justice secretary said he believed 'no win, no fee' was one of the reasons for recent increases in the cost of car insurance, and he hoped the planned changes would help drive premiums down.*
> *He also estimated they would save the NHS about £50m a year.*

> *According to the Ministry of Justice, in 2008–09 the health service*
> *paid out £312m in damages but £456m in legal costs.*
> **BBC News, 29 March 2010,**
> **http://www.bbc.co.uk/news/uk-12890256**

In England and Wales, the NHS redress scheme was introduced by the NHS Redress Act 2006, as amended in 2010, and this scheme works with the NHS Litigation Authority. The scheme aims to compensate patients on low claims of up to £20,000 initially. This came into force in April 2012 and is expected to give some help to patient claims and avoid delays. It is observed that this limit set by the government is nowhere near the typical levels of damages awarded by the courts for claims in clinical negligence cases.

> *Other key elements of the NHS Redress Scheme include the following:*
>
> - *Provision for patients to receive redress in the form of care.*
> - *A duty on all scheme members to appoint an appropriate person responsible for learning from mistakes.*
> - *A more proactive approach to clinical negligence, with the onus no longer on the patient to initiate a claim. All scheme members will be required to review.*
>
> **DH, 2005, http://www.dh.gov.uk/PublicationsAndStatistics/**
> **PressReleases (accessed 2 June 2013)**

In contrast, other countries such as Scandinavia and New Zealand have a 'no fault' system which makes it easier and quicker for the litigant; nevertheless, the damages awarded are much less than those in the fault system.

NURSING REGULATION AND LAW

The NMC was established under the Nursing and Midwifery Order 2001 ('the order') and came into being on 1 April 2002. Before this, in 1983, the United Kingdom Central Council for Nursing, Midwifery and Health Visiting (UKCC) had been set up, with its main objective as one of maintaining a register of UK nurses, midwives and health visitors, as well as providing guidance to registrants; professional misconduct issues with national boards (with a remit for nurse education) were created for each of the UK countries.

With increased autonomous practice and accountability, the days of the nurse who was subservient to the 'doctors' orders' are now behind us.

Nurses function more and more autonomously but more importantly, collaboratively within a multidisciplinary team setting. This collaboration includes the doctor, who is a key member of the team, with the patient at the centre of treatment. The concepts of scope of practice and account-ability are such that it is inevitable for nurses to have more regulation in a climate of more awareness of patient rights in the face of increased litigation.

> *Nursing encompasses autonomous and collaborative care of indi-viduals of all ages, families, groups and communities, sick or well and in all settings. Nursing includes the promotion of health, pre-vention of illness, and the care of ill, disabled and dying people. Advocacy, promotion of a safe environment, research, participation in shaping health policy and in patient and health systems manage-ment, and education are also key nursing roles.*
> ***http://www.icn.ch/about-icn/icn-definition-of-nursing/***
> ***(last updated 12 April 2010)***

Likewise, it was important that nurses would be represented by pro-fessional nurses in regulating the profession. The concept of democratic representation is applicable to professional bodies such as the Nursing and Midwifery Council (NMC, 2008), who are professionally representative of nurses, with the legal authority created by royal charter to regulate stan-dards of professional behaviour for nurses (Hinchcliff et al., 2008). This is in addition to their contractual obligations to fulfil their role under employment law (Sargeant, 2008).

It is possible for nurses to appeal to the High Court against an NMC decision (in this case against being struck off). In *Kituma v Nursing and Midwifery Council* (Rev 1) [2009] EWHC 373 (Admin) (9 March 2009), where a midwife performed an episiotomy contrary to established proce-dure trust policy, it was held that due to the harm suffered by the patient and the failure to follow procedure trust policy by the appellant, the appeal was entitled to fail.

The International Council of Nurses (ICN) provides additional guid-ance on professionalism for nurses:

> *[ICN] is a federation of more than 130 national nurses associations (NNAs), representing the more than 13 million nurses worldwide. Founded in 1899, ICN is the world's first and widest reaching inter-national organization for health professionals. Operated by nurses and leading nurses internationally, ICN works to ensure quality*

nursing care for all, sound health policies globally, the advancement of nursing knowledge, and the presence worldwide of a respected nursing profession and a competent and satisfied nursing workforce.
http://www.icn.ch/about-icn/about-icn/

CONCLUSION

A clearer concept of law is essential in providing for the needs of the patient more effectively. The issue of patients' rights is fundamental to nurses' understanding of their clients' needs. The Human Rights Act 1998 and other key statutes are necessary for defining these rights. The full effect of human rights legislation has yet to be tested. For example, breach of the patient's right of choice may result in infringement of other statutory provisions with not only breach of indictable criminal offences but also attraction of civil action with damages for compensation for personal injury. Most patients are now more aware of their rights than ever, and litigation or the threat of it is real. Should a patient ever become a victim of negligence, the trust between them and other healthcare professionals (they may meet in the future) may be eroded. Instead, where partnership and transparency are present, healthcare professionals should work together and in collaboration – with the patient at the centre of decision-making. On the other hand, a significant number of patients are vulnerable, especially if they lack the mental capacity to assert their rights.

Those rights may be open to abuse, by those purportedly representing or advocating for them. What is needed is a balance between the interests of the patient, those of other stakeholders, and those of healthcare professionals; the provisions of the law must be followed. Whatever clinical decision-making, whether it be by family members, patients' carers, healthcare professionals or the courts, there is need to place the patient at the centre of decision-making and to respect the patient's human rights and, where capacity is lacking, to always act in the patient's best interests.

REFERENCES

Addis M, Morrow P, eds. *Your rights: the liberty guide to human rights.* London: Liberty, 2005.

BBC News. 29 March 2010. http://www.bbc.co.uk/news/uk-12890256.

Beauchamp T, Childress F. *Principles of biomedical ethics*, 7th ed. Oxford: Oxford University Press, 2012.

Blair A. *The European Union since 1945*, 2nd ed. Harlow: Pearson Education Limited, 2010.

Code of Hammurabi. http://www.lawbuzz.com/ourlaws/hammurabi/hammurabi.htm (accessed 1 June 2013).

Cracknell DG, ed. *Obligations: the law of tort*, 3rd ed. London: Old Bailey Press, 2004.

Davies M. *Medical law*, 2nd ed. London: Blackstone Press, 2001.

De Than C, Shorts E. *Human rights*, 3rd ed. Harlow: Pearson Education Limited, 2013.

DH. *The NHS redress scheme.* 2005. http://www.dh.gov.uk/Publications AndStatistics/PressReleases (accessed 16 July 2006).

Dicey A. *Law of the constitution*, 9th ed. London: Macmillan, 1950.

Elliott C, Quinn F. *Tort law*, 7th ed. Harlow: Person Longman, 2009.

Environmental Law Centre. http://www.elc.org.uk/pages/lawarticleshra.htm#2 (accessed 23 May 2006).

The free dictionary. http://legal-dictionary.thefreedictionary.com/Special+ damages (accessed June 2013).

Ghandi S. *International human rights documents*, 8th ed. Blackstone's Statutes. Oxford: Oxford University Press, 2013.

Harris J. *The value of life: an introduction to medical ethics.* London: Routledge and Kegan Paul, 1985.

Hinchcliff S, Norman S, Schrober J. *Nursing practice and healthcare*, 5th ed. London: Arnold, 2008.

Hodgson J, Lewthwaite J. *Tort Law*, 2nd ed. Oxford: Oxford University Press, 2007.

International Council for Nurses. http://www.icn.ch/about-icn/about-icn/ (accessed July 2013).

Leckie D, Pickersgill D. *Human Rights Act explained.* Norwich: Stationery Office, 2000.

Makkan S. *The Human Rights Act 1998.* London: Callow Publishing, 2000.

Mason JK, McCall RA, Laurie GT. *Law and medical ethics*, 8th ed. London: Butterworths, 2010.

McDermott T, ed. *Summa Theologiae: a concise translation.* Notre Dame: Christian Classics, Ave Maria Press, 1997.

McHale J, Tingle J. *Law and nursing.* Oxford: Butterworth Heinemann, 2006.

Ministry of Justice. *Making sense of human rights: a short introduction.* 2006. www.justice.gov.uk/aboutdocs/act-studyguide.pdf.

NHS Litigation Authority. http://www.nhsla.com/home.htm (accessed 25 June 2013).

NMC. *Raising and escalating complaints: guidance for nurses and midwives.* NMC, 2010. www.nmc-uk.org/raisingconcerns.

NPSA. 2006. www.npsa.nhs.uk (accessed 25 June 2006).

Nursing and Midwifery Council (NMC). *The code: standards of conduct, performance and ethics for nurses and midwives.* London: NMC, 2008. www.nmc-uk.org.

Reid K, Zimmerman R, eds. *A history of private law in Scotland*. Oxford: Oxford University Press, 2000.

Sargeant M. *Employment law*, 4th ed. Harlow: Longman, 2008.

Smith TB. *Scotland: the development of its laws and constitution*, 2nd ed. London: Stevens and Sons, 1962.

Wacks R. *Understanding jurisprudence: an introduction to legal theory*, 3rd ed. Oxford: Oxford University Press, 2012.

2 ETHICS AND PATIENTS' RIGHTS

Sue Watkinson

INTRODUCTION

In this chapter, the term 'ethics' will be considered in the same way that the meaning of the term 'law' was considered and discussed at some length in Chapter 1. Some definitions of the term 'ethics' will be offered and four main approaches to ethics will be outlined to provide the reader with a basis for understanding a subsequent and more detailed discussion on the relevance of ethics for practice. A brief review of the philosophical dimension on ethical theories provides some insight into how the concepts of 'ethical values' and 'human rights' have emerged, and enhance the reader's appreciation of the significance of the relationship between ethics and patients' rights. The areas of rights and freedom of choice, necessity and the greater good principle, ethical decision-making frameworks, and ethics and the therapeutic relationship will subsequently be discussed. Thinking points have been included to engage the reader in some ethical thinking and decision-making related to the ongoing discussion.

WHAT IS 'ETHICS'?

In its broadest context, ethics is the study of human conduct (Thompson, 2008a, p. 4). It is a general term for what is often described as the science of morality. Indeed, the Western tradition of ethics is sometimes called moral philosophy. Thompson (2008b, p. 121) specifically defines 'ethics' as the study of how people behave – what they do, the reasons they give for their actions and the rationale behind their decisions. In other words, ethics implies a rational and systematic study of moral issues. Thompson (2008a, pp. 3–4) further suggests that ethics is not simply concerned with average standards of behaviour, but rather that it is about the quest to find what is right and good, and the best way to live. It is about wanting to find a basis for the values by which to live, on the assumption that justice and happiness will follow.

Approaches to ethics

The main approaches to ethics may be categorized as

- descriptive ethics,
- normative ethics,
- meta-ethics,
- applied ethics.

Descriptive ethics examines the moral choices and values that are held in a particular society. For example, some societies impose the death sentence for certain crimes while others do not. It is closely related to sociology and moral psychology in that it describes the way people in different societies behave. It also examines the background influences on what people do. The key feature of all descriptive ethics is that it does not examine or question issues of right or wrong. It simply states what the case is (Thompson, 2008a).

Normative ethics examines the norms by which people make moral choices (Thompson, 2008a). In other words, it examines issues of right and wrong, and how people justify the decisions they make when faced with situations of moral choice. Normative ethics may also be called 'moral philosophy', since it is the rational examination of morality (Thompson, 2008a). It involves questions about one's own duty, in other words, what one 'ought' to do. These are referred to as deontological questions. It also asks questions about the values expressed through moral choices, in other words, what constitutes the 'good' life. These are sometimes referred to as axiological questions. Normative ethics takes a statement about behaviour and asks, 'Is it right to do that?' For example, is it right to allow euthanasia? Here, one is asking about the norms of behaviour and the basis upon which people decide right from wrong.

Meta-ethics is a discussion of the meaning of moral language and how it can be justified (Thompson, 2008b). Instead of asking 'Is it right?', the question asked is 'What does it mean to say that something is right?', or 'What am I doing when I make that sort of statement?' Meta-ethics represents a response to the viewpoint that all moral propositions are meaningless. It is basically attempting to find out what people do mean (Thompson, 2008b).

Applied ethics examines moral choices that are made in the light of ethical theories (Thompson, 2008b).

ETHICS – ITS RELEVANCE FOR PRACTICE

From an examination of these definitions and ethical approaches, the relevance of 'ethics' for professional practice becomes clearer. It is about making judgements that are considered to be in the best interests of the individual. Applied ethics is particularly important for practicing nurses as it allows the testing of ethical theories by applying them to practical situations to see whether they work and provide reasonable outcomes.

Judgement

Judgement can be viewed from many standpoints. Rowson (1990) points out that people make judgements about what is right and wrong from the standpoints of law, morality, visual taste and what is effective in practical terms. He further points out that we are all called upon to judge behaviour from the following standpoints (Rowson, 1990, p. 6):

- law,
- social etiquette,
- professional codes or professional etiquette,
- religious beliefs,
- visual and 'aesthetic' sense,
- what is most practical,
- morality.

For the practicing nurse the most important reference viewpoint is that of the Nursing and Midwifery Council (NMC) Code of Conduct (Nursing and Midwifery Council, 2008). For example, a nurse ought to refuse to 'accept delegated functions without first having received instruction in regard to those functions and having been assessed as competent'. For instance, a junior nurse who has been requested by a senior nurse to perform a wound dressing on a patient with a leg ulcer should refuse if she has not been previously supervised and deemed competent in the application of her knowledge of the principles of asepsis to the skill of undertaking an aseptic wound dressing.

Ethics is an integral part of decision-making within professional practice. Practicing nurses are involved on a daily basis in difficult decision-making regarding the management of their patients. However, what makes this process difficult is the application of moral views since morality is becoming increasingly more complex within a multicultural, postmodern world. Coverston and Rogers (2000) point out that the latter is exemplified by complex change related to vast increases in information and technology, and exposure to diverse people and ideas. Practicing nurses encounter patients from many different cultural backgrounds, and this constant exposure to cultural and individual differences should heighten their awareness and knowledge of different values and beliefs.

Values

Ethical decisions are based in values, and if there is no concordance in values, or agreement as to which values take precedence over others, then a problem arises as to how to make a decision. As previously mentioned, the NMC Code of Conduct (Nursing and Midwifery Council, 2008) serves as a framework for decision-making. It may be regarded as an interpretative framework. In applying this concept of an interpretative framework, it might be argued that professional practice is subjective since an individual interpretation is involved, which is based on both individual and professional values and belief systems (Watkinson, 1999). As a result, practicing nurses continue to encounter many ethical dilemmas that arise from a conflict between personal and professional values and beliefs. The problem is that such frameworks are protected by professional validation and are seldom questioned or challenged (Watkinson, 1999). Professional practice is underpinned by the concept of holism. However, can the practice of holistic individualized care ever become the reality when working with such professional frameworks, or do such frameworks constrain that possibility? The practicing nurse is not a pure, objective and impersonal being since she is involved in the process of human judgement that can be fallible and open-ended (Watkinson, 1999). Personal confusion and dualistic thinking may result, thus negating the possibility of solving personal or professional dilemmas. However, thinking and reasoning about the moral dimensions of practice will help the development of more effective ethical decision-making skills in the best interests of patients. Consider the following scenario.

Case study

A mental health nurse working within a forensic mental healthcare setting is utilizing the Roper, Logan and Tierney model of nursing as a basis for her healthcare decision-making. She identifies the problem of poor personal hygiene in a male client displaying psychotic symptoms and with a strong tendency to aggressive and violent behaviour. The nurse knows that physical intervention to improve the client's personal hygiene by arranging for him to be physically assisted to have a bath or wash would be a correct decision to make within the guiding framework of the nursing model. However, she decides instead to simply discuss with the client the need to improve personal hygiene.

Would you consider the mental health nurse's decision-making to be right or wrong in this situation?

PHILOSOPHICAL DIMENSION ON ETHICAL VALUES AND HUMAN RIGHTS

At this stage in the discussion a brief review of the main philosophical ethical theories will provide some insight into how the concepts of 'ethical values' and 'human rights' have been formed. For the nurse practitioner, a knowledge and understanding of these concepts will further enhance an appreciation of the significance of the relationship between ethics and patients' rights.

Ethical theory is defined as 'the study of the nature and justification of general ethical principles that can be applied to moral problems, and attempts to provide a more rigorous systematic approach to how decisions are made' (Keatings and O'Neil Smith, 2009, p. 13). The two most common theories are teleological theory and deontological theory.

Teleological theory is also called utilitarianism or consequentialist theory. This theory was advanced by Jeremy Bentham (1748–1832), a teleological ethicist, and is about judging whether the consequences of actions are good or bad. John Stuart Mill (1806–73) also contributed to this theory by emphasizing the balance between the benefits and risks to people, associated with a certain action. Mill argued that if actions lead to the best outcome for the highest number of people, they are perceived as the best actions. The two approaches to utilitarianism either consider particular acts in relation to particular circumstances (act utilitarianism), or formulate rules of conduct that determine what is right or wrong in general (rule utilitarianism) (Keatings and O'Neil Smith, 2009). Thus, decision-making about nursing practice has 'utilitarian moral justification' if it produces good consequences for the care of patients and is beneficial for the care of future patients. The NMC Code of Conduct (Nursing and Midwifery Council, 2008) is a good example of rule utilitarianism.

Both act and rule utilitarianism, however, contain flaws associated with predicting the future. Individuals can use their life experiences to attempt to predict outcomes, but no individual can be certain that his or her predictions will come true. Consider the following example:

THINKING POINT

A staff nurse was working the late shift on a male surgical ward. It was 3 pm and Wayne, a 19-year-old patient, admitted for elective surgery on his left leg following a motorbike accident a few months ago, had only just arrived back from theatre. He was received by the staff nurse, who was aware that Wayne had been sent to theatre early that morning having been fasted from 12 pm the previous day. A little while later, Wayne asked the staff nurse for something to eat as he was very hungry. Lunch had finished and the supper trolley was not due to arrive until 6 pm. Meanwhile Wayne was given some toast to eat. However, shortly afterwards he complained again of hunger.

The staff nurse decided to look in the ward kitchen and found a spare chicken and vegetable pie left over from lunchtime. She quickly reheated the pie in the microwave oven and then served it to a grateful Wayne, who devoured it with relish. Unfortunately, 24 hours later, Wayne was beginning to show the signs and symptoms of salmonella poisoning.

From this scenario, it can be seen that despite the staff nurse's best intentions, her actions failed to benefit the patient, and in fact, caused harm and a great deal of suffering. As a professional practitioner, taking the risk of reheating a meal that had already been kept in an ambient temperature for a period of time was unethical.

Preference and interest utilitarianism

These approaches represent more modern developments of utilitarianism theory. They can also be seen to be the basis for the development of the concept of human rights since they seek to examine the 'interest' of 'preferences' of everyone concerned with a particular situation, and are very much based on the rights of and autonomy of individuals.

As Thompson (2008a) points out, a key problem with utilitarian arguments is that utilitarianism itself does not define the nature of 'good'. Therefore, people might have different ideas about what constitutes their benefit, advantage or happiness in respect of their race, culture, gender or sexual orientation. However, while it is important to consider what is in people's interest, it is also important to recognize that what is in the interests of one person may not be in the interests of another. Nevertheless, within a democratic society the political situation has to reflect the right of all individuals to express their own preferences, rather than have other people's ideas of a benefit, advantage or happiness imposed on them. Preference utilitarianism was a form introduced by Hare (2001), who argued that it was important to consider individuals' preferences, except where those preferences came into direct conflict with the preferences of others. The aim is to maximize the chances of satisfying everyone's preferences.

Deontological theory

This was first associated with the moral philosophy of Immanuel Kant (1724–1804) in the late eighteenth century. Deontological theories assert that individuals have a special status, and because of that status, they are owed a respect that must not be violated regardless of consequences (Furrow, 2005). Respect for persons and their rights and duties are the building blocks of moral reasoning.

One weakness of this theory, however, is that there is no rationale or logical basis for deciding an individual's duties. Consider the following example: A student nurse may decide it is her duty always to arrive early for her college course lecture. Although this appears to be a noble duty, there is no way of knowing her reasons for choosing to make this her duty. The reason perhaps could be that she always has to sit in the same chair in the front row of the classroom.

Other weaknesses of deontology include the fact that sometimes an individual's duties are in conflict, and that deontology is not concerned with the welfare of others. Consider the same example again: If the student nurse who must arrive early for her college course lecture is running late, how is she supposed to drive? Is the student nurse supposed to speed, breaking her duty to society to uphold the law, or is she supposed to arrive at her lecture late, breaking her duty to arrive early? This scenario of conflicting obligations does not lead to a clear ethically correct resolution, nor does it protect the welfare of others from the nurse's decision.

Kant's theory is in sharp contrast to utilitarianism. The demand to treat all persons as ends, not just as means, will not allow the sacrifice of individuals for the sake of the common good. Kant's theory requires a variety of duties, such as the duty to tell the truth, to keep promises and to be fair and just. Such duties must be followed independent of their consequences. Kant argues that moral reasoning must not proceed from hypothetical imperatives, but from categorical imperatives. The hypothetical imperative is a principle which commands us to do something only if we want to. A categorical imperative is a principle that commands us to do something independently of what we want to do. As implied from this term 'categorical' (without conditions attached) a categorical imperative is one I must act on under any condition.

Pain and the individual's duties

The following examples may serve to illustrate the moral reasoning of nurses. Research evidence suggests that post-operative pain is inadequately managed and a difference exists between what nurses said and actually did in post-operative pain management (Dihle et al., 2006). The most common reasons documented for inappropriate pain management include the failure of nurses systematically to assess and evaluate pain and its management (American Pain Society, 2009), poor communication between nurses and patients and limited use of a valid assessment tool (Manias et al., 2004). If the definition of pain is taken as 'pain is whatever the experiencing person says it is, existing whenever s/he says it does' (McCaffery, 1983, p. 14), the implication is that there must be an appropriate response to relieve that person's pain. However, based on the evidence, is there a case for arguing that the moral reasoning of practitioners often proceeds from a hypothetical, as opposed to a categorical, imperative? In other words, nurses are cognizant of the importance of effective pain management, but may not want to provide the required pain relief due to personal fears about overdosing the patient, or encouraging addictive behaviour and then having to encounter the consequences of their actions. Nevertheless, the relief of pain should be a fundamental objective of any health service (The Royal College of Anaesthetists and The Pain Society, 2003, p. 1). Acute pain is common and occurs most frequently in the post-operative period. The prescription of analgesic drugs and pain-relieving techniques should be reviewed regularly to ensure that analgesia is effective and appropriate to the level of pain experienced by the patient (The Royal College of Anaesthetists and The Pain Society, 2003, p. 4). A nurse is deemed to act in accordance with both ethical and theoretical knowledge to enhance competence in nursing actions related to post-operative pain management. Failure to do so is thus morally and ethically unacceptable.

Kant argues that human beings have value, even if no one cares about them and they are of no use to anyone. Human beings have objective worth and must be treated with special respect. This Kantian view has substantial impact on our moral conduct. Once we recognize that human beings have objective worth, we cannot treat them merely as instruments to promote the common good, or for any other purpose.

Within the practice of caring, pain control is a contemporary ethical issue of great importance because of the devastating and dehumanizing effects pain can have on patients and their families. The deleterious effects of unrelieved acute pain are well recognized as being psychological, physiological and socioeconomic in nature (The Royal College of Anaesthetists and The Pain Society, 2003, p. 4). The NMC Code of Conduct (Nursing and Midwifery Council, 2008) also refers to respecting patients' autonomy by identifying their preferences with regard to care. An example of this respect is illustrated when an ophthalmic nurse assesses a patient undergoing scleral buckling as a treatment modality for retinal detachment. Here, it is advisable to provide the patient with balanced information about the traumatic nature of this operative procedure and the likelihood of experiencing some persistent severe pain post-operatively. This allows the patient to make an informed decision about the type of analgesia to be administered after surgery. It is important, however, that the ophthalmic nurse does not manipulate the situation. This could result in prescribing and the administration of analgesia based on the nurse's personal preferences (hypothetical imperative). This is also ethically linked to the concept of beneficence, which promotes beneficial actions and considers the patient's best interests above the interests of the practitioner (Beauchamp and Childress, 2013).

This discussion raises two important questions as follows:

1. If practitioners agree on the need for a code of ethics, why are they failing to observe its application in daily practice, especially when planning care for those individuals who will experience severe pain following surgery?
2. Do practitioners ever consider that those decisions involving how and when to medicate for pain control fall within the domain of ethics?

These questions are worthy of reflection by practitioners in all areas of nursing practice. The concepts of ethical values and human rights have clearly emerged as an important domain from which to draw knowledge and understanding as a basis for decision-making in nursing practice.

RIGHTS AND FREEDOM OF CHOICE

Kant places great emphasis on the notion of human rights to the extent that basic freedoms are identified that have to be respected. Problems arise, however, when rights conflict. Nevertheless, a Kantian ethic asserts that rights cannot be violated simply for the sake of promoting desirable ends, whether for self or others.

The experience of freedom is an essential condition for moral choice (Thompson, 2008b). However, there are limitations on freedom, and it is these limitations which often give rise to the ethical dilemmas surrounding a patient's rights and freedom of choice. Such limitations include physical, legal and social, personal and psychological, and religious. An individual cannot be morally required to do something of which he or she is physically or mentally incapable. However, for example, if an individual drinks too much alcohol and becomes physically incapable, then that individual is morally responsible for their condition and the resulting consequences. The law and society prevent individuals from doing many things as part of the overall conditioning imposed by such society. The ability to function as a mature adult may be limited by an individual's past personal and psychological experiences. Religion also influences individuals in that they may believe they are not free to oppose God's will.

Conditioning

Individuals are conditioned in various ways. There are influences on individuals' decision-making and on the moral rules that prevail in society.

Conditioning equally applies to the professional community of nursing practice. If practitioners were completely free from all external causes and conditions, they would never stop to consider what they 'ought' to do, because they would never be influenced by anything that might suggest one course of action rather than another. Nurse practitioners are thus conditioned by moral rules implicit within their NMC Code of Conduct (Nursing and Midwifery Council, 2008). Interaction with others is based on the four basic principles of consensus morality: non-maleficence, beneficence, justice and utility (Barker and Baldwin, 1995). These principles imply that people ought to behave in certain ways, out of a desire not to harm others, to be of positive help to others, to treat others fairly and equally, and to ensure the best possible outcome for the majority. These principles also form the basis of the belief in the autonomous person (Barker and Baldwin, 1995). As previously highlighted, respect for an autonomous person, whether self or other, is an overriding ethical principle derived from Kant.

Autonomy

To be autonomous means to be able to choose for oneself. It can be seen to operate through self-determination and self-government. Self-determination involves individuals being able to formulate and carry out their own plans, desires, wishes and policies, thereby determining the course of their own life (Barker and Baldwin, 1995, p. 104). Self-government implies that as part of the notion of autonomy, individuals are able to govern their own lives by rules and values. It is also usually accepted that this involves both the mental and physical capacity to make choices and then carry them out. Most constraints on autonomy are believed to be through non-maleficence, but some may occur through benevolence. Paternalism (acting on behalf of another person in their best interest) is often used to legitimize infringement of a person's autonomy, supported by the principle of beneficence. This is the argument frequently used to impose 'treatment' on patients whether they want it or not.

THINKING POINT

Lucinda is an 83-year-old lady who has been admitted to the care of the elderly mentally ill nursing home with a diagnosis of senile dementia. Her history indicates that she has come from a very well-to-do family, and was previously accustomed to having servants in her household. She now finds herself alone with no living family members.

(Continued)

37

Lucinda has also been diagnosed with a heart condition for which she has been prescribed daily medication. During the drug round when the nursing staff ask her to take her medication, she adamantly refuses on each occasion. She says 'I don't know you; I only take medicine prescribed for me by my doctor'. Unfortunately, no amount of reassurance on the part of the nursing staff that the medication has been prescribed by her doctor will persuade her to take it. The nursing home is also situated a long way from Lucinda's home and because of this, her own GP is not able to attend to provide some assistance in this situation. Because the medication is necessary, the nurses decide to crush the tablet and put it into some jam. They manage to get Lucinda to take it in this way. The nursing staff say that if the medication is not taken, the patient runs the risk of dying from her heart condition.

Do you consider it ethically acceptable to impose treatment on a patient in this way?

In healthcare practice, the duty of care to protect life and health is superseded by the duty to respect autonomy. This means that competent patients have the right to refuse any form of medical intervention. Thus, it is both legally and professionally unacceptable to force treatment on competent patients because the doctor thinks it is in their best interests. The situation differs somewhat in the field of mental health practice where the effects of serious mental illness on levels of competence can sometimes reverse the moral logic of the duties of care. For instance, a mentally ill patient's capacity may become so reduced that the concept of respect for autonomy can no longer supersede protection. For example, a schizophrenic patient with delusions about being poisoned, and who is a danger to himself or to others as a result, may not understand or believe any information that contradicts this belief.

Informed consent

As previously discussed, autonomy refers to one's moral right to make decisions about one's own course of action. Thus, if the ethical principle of autonomy is applied to healthcare practice, it means that clients must be given sufficient information about healthcare prior to surgery, or other clinical interventions, and then permitted to decide for themselves about the proposed treatment. For example, before performing a gastrointestinal endoscopy, a procedure carrying considerable risk of harm, patients must give their informed consent. This involves presenting patients with the factual details, the advantages and the disadvantages of undertaking such a procedure, and the potential complications of this proposed intervention as the basis for making an informed choice. Merely disclosing information to the patient is not good enough. In order for consent to be valid, it also needs to be understood by the patient. However, questions arise about how much information needs to be disclosed to the patient before consent can be truly said to be informed. In *Sidaway v Board of Governors of the Bethlem Royal Hospital and the Maudsley Hospital* [1985], the law lords decided that a doctor's duty to inform a patient is an aspect of the doctor's duty to exercise reasonable care and skill. In this case, the law lords relied upon expert evidence that a body of skilled and experienced neurosurgeons would have regarded it as acceptable to warn not just of the slight but, in fact, well-recognized risk of serious harm that Mrs Sidaway actually suffered following surgery. This case also raises the issue that the patient should have the right to choose whether to accept a slight, but well-recognized, risk of harm (Croft, 2005). Undoubtedly, there will be ongoing tension and litigation over what the reasonably competent medical practitioner regards as being significant to the making of a decision and what the typical patient regards as being important. If a medical practitioner can demonstrate that the patient's best interests were duly considered and justify any decision not to inform the patient of a risk, this is unlikely to be deemed a negligent act by the courts (Croft, 2005, p. 54).

Nevertheless, informed consent should protect patients by providing complete information to make an informed decision. If the healthcare professional in performing a procedure mistakenly believes that the patient's consent has been gained, when, in fact, it has not, the healthcare professional is at risk of litigation, together with those individuals who acted as double-checkers in the situation. In these circumstances, all parties involved are liable to disciplinary proceedings by their employer (Fletcher and Buka, 1999, p. 60). Thus, there exists an interface between the ethical concept and the legal doctrine of informed consent. Both are grounded in the principles of self-determination and autonomy, with disclosure being the main issue. The area of informed consent and the issues raised so far within this discussion will be expanded upon further in Chapter 6, 'Consent to Treatment and Mental Capacity'.

NECESSITY AND THE GREATER GOOD PRINCIPLE

In returning to the issue of autonomy, clearly the way in which consent is obtained from individual clients can raise many ethical dilemmas, in particular when individuals are not mentally competent. This applies equally to young children as well as clients of all ages whose mental state renders them unable to understand the implications of procedures or care. Specific reference has already been made to the scenario involving an elderly mentally ill patient with dementia (see the second thinking point) which was presented for consideration of the ethical principles underpinning the decisions made. However, even where an elderly person is mentally competent to make a decision, the principle of necessity and the greater good can be applied, particularly when the individual's continued presence in a situation poses a threat to himself or herself, or to other people. In these circumstances, the principle of necessity holds good that the practitioner can use the defence that in their professional opinion, and clinical judgement, where consent cannot be obtained, the decision is taken in the best interests of the client. This is especially relevant in circumstances of life and death (see Chapter 9, 'End-of-Life Care'). The following example illustrates a situation where this principle could be applied with effect.

Case study

A frail, elderly lady recently widowed and now living alone in a flat on the third floor of a block of apartments has poor vision and is partially deaf. Her mobility is becoming more limited due to increasing weakness in her legs, which puts her at greater future risk of falling and sustaining injury. She has always been a fiercely independent person and is most unwilling to leave her flat and to move into a nearby nursing home for the elderly.

In this situation, a social worker is empowered by Section 47 of the National Assistance Act 1948 to have such elderly clients removed from unsuitable accommodation to a place of safety for their own sake, or that of others.

ETHICAL FRAMEWORKS AND DECISION-MAKING

There are different sources of ethical standards that can be considered to be the basis for decision-making within ethical frameworks. For the purpose of this section, seven such standards are identified.

The utilitarian approach

The utilitarian approach deals with consequences. An act is morally right if, when compared with alternative acts, it yields the greatest possible balance of good consequences, or the least possible balance of bad consequences. This constitutes the principle of utility (Bloch and Green, 2006). In practical terms, it is a way of identifying the best of several alternative choices and determining whether the selected plan is the best alternative by considering the results and revising the decision accordingly (Phillips, 2006).

The rights approach

The ethical action is the one that best protects and respects the moral rights of those affected. The approach starts from the belief that humans have a dignity based on their nature or on their ability to choose freely what they do with their lives. On the basis of such dignity, they have a right to be treated as ends and not merely as means to other ends.

This approach is underpinned by the ethical concept of 'respecting persons'. This means that actions showing respect for people are morally right and actions that 'use' people are morally wrong. An individual's 'personal autonomy' (right of self-determination) must be respected; otherwise, the individual cannot be allowed the freedom needed to be morally responsible for his or her own actions (Rowson, 1990).

With specific reference to nursing practice, it is thought that basic physical needs, and capacities for emotional and social relationships, are an essential part of being a person. Thus, in order to respect the 'whole person' it must be accepted that an individual has a right to satisfy these needs and capacities. People have basic rights to warmth, food, shelter and sexual, emotional and social life, and such rights should be upheld as part of the general obligation to respect persons. The International Council of Nurses' Code of Ethics for Nurses (2012, p. 1), as an example of an ethical framework, states 'inherent in nursing is respect for human rights, including cultural rights, the right to life and choice, to dignity, and to be treated with respect'. The NMC Code of Conduct (Nursing and Midwifery Council, 2008) also documents the need to respect the beliefs, values and customs of the individual. The code states that the autonomy of the patient should be maintained throughout treatment, restrictions being imposed only when these are demonstrably necessary for the patient's own good.

The fairness or justice approach

Within this approach, ethical actions treat all human beings equally, or, if unequally, then fairly based on some standard that is defensible. For example, access to healthcare and standard medical advice is provided free by the National Health Service (NHS) to every citizen. However, access to an expert consultant's advice and treatment depends upon the citizen's ability to pay. In the context of healthcare practice, all patients are regarded as equally valuable regardless of their age, sex, race, colour, sexual orientation, nationality and religious or political beliefs. Thus, the well-being of each patient is considered equally important.

Plato (c. 428–374 bc) presents the idea that all elements in society need to work together for the general health of the whole, with the physical and assertive aspects (taken to represent the workers and defenders of society) controlled by reason (the philosophers/rulers who alone could judge what was best for society as a whole). Justice is a matter of achieving harmony among the different parts of society, and being determined and imposed by reason (Thompson, 2008a). In a healthcare context, as Fletcher and Buka (1999) indicate, the principle of justice is generally held to go beyond the client as a person and to focus on the wider issues of resource management and the provision of care.

The common good approach

The Greek philosophers contributed the notion that life in a community is a good in itself and individuals' actions should contribute to that life. The approach suggests that the interlocking relationships of society are the basis of ethical reasoning and that respect and compassion for all others, especially the vulnerable, are requirements of such reasoning. It highlights the common conditions, such as the law, police and fire departments, healthcare and the education system, that are important to the welfare of all.

The virtue approach

Virtue ethics is about the virtues that make for the good life (Thompson, 2008a). Examples of virtues are honesty, courage, compassion, tolerance, integrity, fairness, self-control and prudence. Virtue ethics asks of any action 'What kind of person will I become if I do this?', or 'Is this action consistent with my acting at my best?' In other words, virtues are dispositions and habits that enable individuals to act according to the highest potential of their character. Ethical actions ought to be consistent with certain ideal virtues that provide for the complete development of people.

The values approach

Axiological ethics is the term sometimes used for the study of the values that underlie the moral choices people make (Thompson, 2008b). A key question is whether all moral choices are absolute or relative. Moral choices can be related to society, particularly the established values of that society within which they are made. For example, ethical theories based on the legal concept of a contract carry with them the values of those participants who enter into that contract (Thompson, 2008b).

The key question for ethics is whether all moral issues are culturally conditioned and actions judged right or wrong with reference to underlying personal values in society, or whether there is some way of getting beneath the cultural diversity and touching some absolute moral standard. Kant (1724–1804) attempted to do this with the concept of the categorical imperative. This concept focuses on the sense of moral obligation without reference either to the consequences of an action or to the social or cultural matrix of values within which it is experienced. The key issue to be considered in Kant's ethical theory is that of individual integrity. What counts morally is that one should be able to justify what one does rationally and also universalize the maxim on which it is based.

With specific reference to decision-making and the provision of health, patients may sometimes find it difficult to conform to Kant's concept of the categorical imperative (an absolute moral standard) due to the strength of personal values. Indeed, making such a decision based on personal values can often give rise to an ethical dilemma in the patient-nurse relationship. The following case study exemplifies some of the moral difficulties when trying to provide health education to a patient who maintains resolute values and exercises the right not to accept advice and treatment.

Case study

Samuel, a 70-year-old West Indian gentleman, recently widowed, has a son and daughter who are both married and living abroad. Samuel was diagnosed with type 2 diabetes 10 years ago and prescribed oral hypoglycaemic medication. Over the last 18 months he has been suffering from episodes of short-term memory loss resulting in non-compliance with prescribed medication. Over the past few months he has been progressively failing to control his blood glucose levels adequately. He is also beginning to lose sight in both eyes due to the onset of diabetic retinopathy which was diagnosed during an initial retinal screening appointment. Samuel has since been referred to a district nurse who visits him twice weekly to provide information about how to maintain good control of his diabetes and to reinforce the benefits of attending the retinal clinic appointment for laser treatment. However, since attending the first appointment Samuel has been missing successive follow-up appointments for prescribed laser treatment which would help to prevent any further deterioration in his vision.

Whenever Samuel is asked by the nurse why he is failing to attend appointments his justification is that at his age he can expect his health and vision to be getting poor. This is God's will and nothing much can be done. He feels the treatment will not really be able to help him at his time of life.

After reading the above scenario, consider the health education role of the nurse in this situation.

- Is it morally acceptable to impose the principles of health education on this elderly gentleman if his values appear to be contrary to those of the health profession?
- Is the provision of health education as a basis for controlling the diabetes and preventing further sight loss a moral obligation?
- Must Samuel accept and conform to health education as a moral obligation?
- For whose benefit is health education being provided – Samuel's or society's?
- Does Samuel have the right to make a decision about his own health based on his own values?

The existentialist approach

Kierkegaard (1813–55) is generally regarded as the father of existentialism. This is a school of philosophy that is concerned with the nature of human existence and its meaning (Thompson, 2008b). This idea emphasizes an individual's active participation in shaping himself or herself as life is a constant process in which people's decisions are the agents of change. A person should not simply accept the roles that others might allocate, but should allow his or her sense of self to expand outward to take in the things that are experienced (Thompson, 2008b). Human existence is something which is created and shaped by personal choices. However, this approach involves taking responsibility for the consequences of any personal decisions made and actions undertaken.

Ethical implications of an existentialist approach

In undertaking an existentialist approach, individuals will follow their own agenda and their choices will reflect this. Thompson (2008b) points out that the overarching issue here is that existentialism rejects the imposition of moral codes and each individual has to decide for himself or herself. This implies that individuals have to reject all attempts to have masks or images imposed on them and should be free to reject conventions.

The ethical implications for nurses adopting an existentialist approach to practice could have disastrous consequences. Essentially, nursing is a statutorily controlled profession which is governed by a code of practice (Nursing and Midwifery Council, 2008). This code is a well-established professional convention; it is deemed to be the foundation of good nursing and midwifery practice and a key tool in safeguarding the health and well-being of the public. Nurses are obliged to follow the code rigorously and are not in a position to be able to make their own moral choices with reference to their personal behaviour and the duty of care owed to their clients. The implications of any breach of this code could be serious and place nurses at risk of losing their professional registration.

In summary, the above approaches will help healthcare practitioners to determine what standards of behaviour can be considered ethical. However, there may be disagreement about which approaches best serve an ethical decision-making framework due to differing interpretations as to what constitutes 'good' and what constitutes 'harm'. Nevertheless, as approaches, they do provide some basis for determining what is ethical in particular circumstances. In a healthcare context, both the NMC Code of Conduct (Nursing and Midwifery Council, 2008) and the ICN Code of Ethics for Nurses (International Council of Nurses, 2012) embody some aspects of each of these ethical approaches to a greater or lesser extent as part of a composite decision-making framework for practice.

ETHICS AND THE THERAPEUTIC RELATIONSHIP

Currently, the focus is on the value of establishing a therapeutic relationship with patients in healthcare practice. From an ethical standpoint, engaging in a therapeutic relationship involves analysing the ethical aspects of care through competing frameworks, and that engenders the concepts of patient autonomy, patient advocacy and professional autonomy.

Nursing has emphasized patient autonomy as an ethical principle, and has linked this with that of patient advocacy as a prominent aspect of professional practice (Shirley, 2007). The emphasis on the role of the nurse as advocate for the patient, the ideals of patient autonomy as an ethical guideline, and nursing's own pursuit of professional autonomy are concepts that have become part of an increasingly complex inter-relationship (Shirley, 2007). Trying to establish a therapeutic relationship becomes challenging in that agreement needs to be reached with the patient in relation to establishing the balance of power across these three areas.

With specific reference to mental health practice, Hewitt and Edwards (2006) identify the ethics of care, or care-based approach, and the ethics of justice, or principle-based approach, as competing moral frameworks. They present the scenario of a schizophrenic patient found unconscious in his flat by a community psychiatric nurse, having taken an overdose of antipsychotic medication. On admission to hospital the patient states, during an interview with the nurse, that he wants to be allowed to die. However, the patient is prevented from leaving the mental health unit by virtue of his former legal status, and is placed on close observations at all times by a nurse. In trying to establish a therapeutic relationship, the problem identified is whether it is morally justified to detain the patient against his wishes in order to prevent him harming himself.

In this situation, as Hewitt and Edwards (2006) point out, the ethics of care emphasizes the value of involvement with the patient and the promotion of harmonious relationships. Sympathetic understanding is balanced by a need to respond to suicidal ideation with care and support. The care approach accepts that to act in the patient's best interests may sometimes be in conflict with the patient's wishes (Hewitt and Edwards, 2006).

The ethics of justice or principle-based approach (Beauchamp and Childress, 2013) involves four levels of moral thinking. The third level is of most significance in outlining the moral principles of respect for autonomy, non-maleficence, beneficence, and justice. With this approach, obligations generated by the respect for autonomy appear to conflict with those generated by other principles. To promote the patient's well-being, nursing interventions should involve active engagement and help the patient to challenge the validity of his perceptions of hopelessness through specific problem-solving strategies and the development of future-orientated coping mechanisms (Collins and Cutliffe, 2003).

Hewitt and Edwards (2006) conclude that when the client is not capable of autonomous decision-making, the two approaches lead to the same response. When the client is capable of autonomous decision-making, the two approaches lead to different responses. From the scenario it was concluded that from a care-based perspective, intervention to prevent suicide was easier to justify and helped to formulate a nursing response as part of the therapeutic relationship.

CONCLUSION

This chapter has presented and discussed some important ethical concepts in respect of patients' rights. Ethical decision-making is a fundamental part of professional accountability. However, ethical analysis of practice is sometimes rendered very difficult in an increasingly complex moral world of competing ethical standards and frameworks. This is illustrated by the inclusion of thinking points at appropriate stages in the discussion.

It is clear that in the current climate of practice, healthcare practitioners require some knowledge and understanding of the role of ethics and its relationship with patients' rights within healthcare practice.

The focus is on working in partnership with patients, promoting their freedom of choice and maintaining their rights. This can only be achieved by a respectful consideration of the areas of patient autonomy, patient advocacy and professional autonomy and the boundaries that exist across them. Such consideration should form the basis for informed ethical decision-making for maintaining patients' rights and best interests.

REFERENCES

American Pain Society. *Principles of analgesic use in the treatment of acute pain and cancer pain*, 6th ed. Glenview, IL: American Pain Society, 2009.

Barker PJ, Baldwin S. *Ethical issues in mental health*. London: Chapman & Hall, 1995.

Beauchamp T, Childress J. *Principles of biomedical ethics*, 7th ed. New York: Oxford University Press, 2013.

Bloch S, Green S. An ethical framework for psychiatry. *British Journal of Psychiatry* 2006; 188: 7–12.

Collins S, Cutliffe JR. Addressing hopelessness in people with suicidal ideation: building upon the therapeutic relationship utilizing a cognitive behavioural approach. *Journal of Psychiatric and Mental Health Nursing* 2003; 10: 175–85.

Coverston C, Rogers S. Winding roads and faded signs: ethical decision making in a postmodern world. *Journal of Perinatal and Neonatal Nursing* 2000; 14: 1–11.

Croft J. *Health and human rights. A guide to the Human Rights Act 1998*. London: Nuffield Trust, 2005.

Dihle A, Bjolseth G, Helseth S. The gap between saying and doing in postoperative pain management. *Journal of Clinical Nursing* 2006; 15: 469–79.

Fletcher L, Buka P. *A legal framework for caring: an introduction to law and ethics in health care*. Basingstoke: Palgrave, 1999.

Furrow D. *Ethics. Key concepts in philosophy*. London: Continuum, 2005.

Hare RM. *The language of morals*. Oxford: Oxford University Press, 2001.

Hewitt JL, Edwards S. Moral perspectives on the prevention of suicide in mental health settings. *Journal of Psychiatric and Mental Health Nursing* 2006; 13: 665–72.

International Council of Nurses. ICN code of ethics for nurses. Geneva: ICN, 2012.

Keatings M, O'Neil Smith OB. *Ethical and legal issues in Canadian nursing*, 3rd ed. Toronto: W.B. Saunders, 2009.

Manias E, Buckwell T, Botti M. Assessment of patient pain in the postoperative context. *Western Journal of Nursing Research* 2004; 26: 751–69.

McCaffery M. *Nursing the patient in pain*. London: Harper & Row, 1983.

Nursing and Midwifery Council (NMC). *The code: standards of conduct, performance and ethics for nurses and midwives*. London: Nursing and Midwifery Council. 2008. www.nmc-uk.org.

Phillips S. Ethical decision-making when caring for the noncompliant patient. *Journal of Infusion Nursing* 2006; 29: 266–71.

Rowson R. *An introduction to ethics for nurses*. London: Scutari Press, 1990.

The Royal College of Anaesthetists and The Pain Society. *Pain management services – good practice*. London: The Royal College of Anaesthetists and The Pain Society, 2003.

Shirley J. Limits of autonomy in nursing's moral discourse. *Advances in Nursing Science* 2007; 30: 14–25.

Thompson M. *An introduction to philosophy and ethics*, 2nd ed. London: Hodder Education, 2008a.

Thompson M. *Ethical theory*, 3rd ed. London: Hodder Education, 2008b.

Watkinson S. Tacit knowledge and professional judgement. Appraisal. *Journal of Constructive Post-Critical Philosophy and Disciplinary Studies* 1999; 2: 166–69.

3 THE BEGINNING OF LIFE TO ADULTHOOD: HUMAN RIGHTS

Kathleen Chambers and Paul Buka

INTRODUCTION: OVERVIEW

This chapter aims to introduce the legal concepts related to human rights from life at the beginning, through childhood, to adulthood and to explore the fundamental ethics that impact on the care of children. It begins by dealing with the issues surrounding the fetus and the right to life. This is followed by the issues concerning children from conception, birth, to the age of 25 in accordance with the Children Act 2004.

Since around 2000 many changes have taken place regarding law and ethics relating to children; this could result in dilemmas arising where nurses are not up to date or are unfamiliar with providing care for these particular clients. As today's rapidly changing healthcare market continues along its path it is leading to a generation of new issues for doctors, nurses, lawyers, judges and legislators. In this setting the rights of a child are especially challenging in relation to consent to treatment. All the rights stated in the 1989 United Nations Convention on the Rights of the Child are applicable in health care; however, application of the participation rights is perhaps the most challenging. Health and social care professionals for a long time have been of the opinion that they hold power, authority and influence in their roles with children. It is very easy within child health services to substitute the word 'parent' for 'patient'; therefore, the rights of children are often overlooked in favour of the rights of the parents (Brook, 2005). Rights – what are they and who has them? Alderson (2008) describes rights as 'equal entitlements for all members of the human family to respect their worth and dignity'. The United Nations Convention on the Rights of the Child (1989) reflects the philosophy that children too are equal, having the same inherent value as grown-ups. However, in order to have a right the person must be able to understand and comprehend that right as being theirs. Where does this leave the fetus, the preverbal child, the unconscious child, the child with learning difficulties or mental health issues? The relationship between law and ethical principles is always open to debate and examination, but where children are involved these principles present some of the most difficult, intractable and fundamental moral questions. Lee and Morgan (2004), in their book on birthrights, argued that one of the characteristics of the twentieth century was 'more clearly than any preceding century ... we have assumed the power to cause death on a hitherto undreamt of scale'. So where does this statement leave the healthcare worker?

WHEN DOES HUMAN LIFE BEGIN?

Many theories purport that the beginning of human existence as an individual is set by the moral and religious views of society and is not easily defined. Sade (2006) argued that the issues surrounding the beginning of life existing between bioethics and law are not likely to be resolved in the foreseeable future due to the deep disagreement that persists over the question of when life begins. When does life begin and end?

Roe v *Wade* [1973] 410 US 113 highlights the fundamental ethical issue in abortion, arguing at what point and in what circumstances a fetus becomes a person and at what point, if any, that person has rights to an existence. The legal situation in the United Kingdom is that an unborn child has no legal rights, no rights at all, until birth. However, once born alive it can apply retrospective rights for criminal or civil wrongs inflicted during the pregnancy and the delivery process. This uncertainty can produce challenges for midwives, nurses and doctors when providing care and treatment options for pregnant women. This is especially so in today's climate when preterm infants born at 22–23 weeks' gestation are now surviving.

There are three pieces of legislation that affect midwives, nurses and doctors when dealing with pregnant women.

Every woman being with child who with intent to procure her own miscarriage, shall unlawfully administer to herself any poison or other noxious thing … or unlawfully use any instrument of other means…. And whosoever, with intent to procure the miscarriage of any woman whether she be or not be with child shall unlawfully administer to her any poison or other noxious thing…. Or unlawfully use any instrument or other means … shall be guilty of a felony.

Offences against the Person Act 1861, Section 58

Any person who with intent to destroy the life of a child capable of being born alive by any wilful act causes a child to die before it has an existence independent of its mother shall be guilty of a felony … child destruction … no person shall be found guilty of an offence … unless the act which caused the death was not done in good faith for the purpose only of preserving the life of the mother.

Infant Life (Preservation) Act 1929, Section 1(1)

For the purpose of the Act evidence that a woman had at any material time been pregnant for a period of twenty eight weeks or more shall be prima facie proof that she was at that time pregnant of a child capable of being born alive.

Infant Life (Preservation) Act 1929, Section 1(2)

A person shall not be guilty of an offence under the law relating to abortion when a pregnancy is terminated by a registered medical practitioner if two registered medical practitioners are of the opinion formed in good faith.

Abortion Act 1967 (as amended by Section 37 of Human Fertilization and Embryology Act 1990), Section 1(1)

These three pieces of legislation clearly identify termination of pregnancy by a registered medical practitioner with just reason not as a criminal offence, but what about the religious views? Religious-based medical ethics have a clear sense of basic values. In some religious traditions, the belief is that human life is a divine gift, which cannot be disposed of by mortals. 'God gives and God takes away' is a common belief among some religious groups. These values are translated into rules which prohibit abortion or euthanasia, such as those practiced by some worldwide traditions.

This is also linked to the belief that various forms of artificial control of fertility are morally wrong. This religious belief has led to the Abortion Act 1967 but was not recognized in the Republic of Ireland until recently. Northern Ireland is an exception. However, this view is not universally supported even in the event of risk to the life of the mother, but where does this belief leave the midwife who is offering support and advice to mothers-to-be on all aspects of pregnancy, including termination of pregnancy? Moral dilemmas may arise.

How can the abortion/termination issue be resolved? Many believe that it can be resolved but only if the issue of when human life begins can be determined. Marquis (2006) argued that where there is opposition to abortion the thinking is that human life begins at conception. However, those in favour of abortion argue that we will never know when human life begins. Justice Harry Blackmun, writing in *Roe* v *Wade* [1973], claimed that, according to a number of religions and philosophies, 'life does not begin before live birth'. A few religions, however, are opposed to this view, which is based on the concept that a fetus is not considered alive until the 40th day after conception. This objection is equally based on the concept that abortion is murder. Blackmun further defended the view that the law has been reluctant to endorse any theory that life as we recognize it begins before live birth or to accord legal rights to the unborn. He concluded that the court had neither judicial precedent nor philosophical or theological authority for making decisions based on the judgement that life begins before live birth. If that view is true, what is the appropriate way to think of the fetus? Should we now think that the fetus is not alive until after a live delivery? This view still has the potential to create a minefield for practicing midwives, in the advice they give, as the law has a legitimate interest in protecting the potentiality of human life. There are, however, certain basic rights that all humans have in virtue of being human and alive. The right to life is the most basic human right. However, if a fetus is classified as fully human and alive, then it could be argued termination of pregnancy violates a basic fetal right, and is therefore wrong in the eyes of the law (Marquis, 2006).

R v *Bourne* [1938] 3 All ER 615

A 14-year-old girl was raped by five soldiers and became pregnant as a result. An eminent gynaecologist performed an abortion on her and was charged

---

with the offence of conducting an illegal abortion. He was acquitted. Mr Justice Macnaghten opined:

> If the doctor is of the opinion, on reasonable grounds and with adequate knowledge, that the probable consequence of the continuance of the pregnancy will be to make the woman a physical or mental wreck, the jury are entitled to take the view that the doctor is operating for the purpose of preserving the life of the mother.
>
> *http://www.e-lawresources.co.uk/cases/R-v-Bourne.php*

The Abortion Act 1967 was enacted to amend, clarify the law and remove the risk of prosecution relating to termination of pregnancy by registered medical practitioners. The act identified that a person shall not be guilty of an offence under the law when a pregnancy is terminated by a registered medical practitioner if two registered medical practitioners are of the opinion, formed in good faith, that

- The pregnancy has not exceeded its 24th week and that the continuance of the pregnancy would involve risk greater than if the pregnancy were terminated.
- The termination is necessary to prevent grave permanent injury to the physical or mental health of the pregnant woman.
- The continuance of the pregnancy would involve risk to the life of the pregnant woman, greater than if the pregnancy were terminated.
- There is a substantial risk that if the child were born it would suffer from such physical or mental abnormalities as to be seriously handicapped.

The Abortion Act 1967 clearly stipulates the position of the law. The Nursing and Midwifery Council (NMC) Code of Conduct (2008) endorses this and also adopts the ethical aspects stating that you must 'promote the interest of patients and clients'; this includes helping individuals and groups gain access to health and social care, information and support relevant to their needs. Nurses and midwives have a clear responsibility to deliver safe and effective care based on current evidence, best practice and, where applicable, validated research. The NMC provides guidance on conscientious objection for two care areas. The first is the Abortion Act 1967 (Scotland, England and Wales), which gives registrants the right to refuse to have a direct involvement in abortion procedures. This was applied in the following case:

> **Doogan and Anor v NHS Greater Glasgow and Clyde Health Board [2013] ScotCS CSIH 36 (24 April 2013)**
>
> A senior nurse (Band 7) midwife (supervising junior midwives) sought clarification on whether conscientious objection on religious grounds included 'the entitlement to refuse to delegate, supervise and/or support staff in the participation in and provision of care to patients undergoing termination of pregnancy or feticide throughout the termination process'.
>
> Held: This right did not extend to conscientious objection for staff supervising staff who are participating in terminations of pregnancy.

Furthermore, the second guidance, the Human Fertilization and Embryology Act 1990, gives registrants the right to refuse to participate in technological procedures to achieve conception and pregnancy. Registrants who conscientiously object under the above two acts are accountable for whatever decision they make and could be called upon to justify their objection within the law. In Scotland, however, the burden of proof does not rest with the objector if he or she swears an oath before a court of law explaining that he or she has an objection. However, where does this leave the nurse/midwife if her religious beliefs identify abortion/termination of pregnancy as wrong? How can the informed advice be given in an unbiased way?

The NMC Code of Conduct (2008) states 'that you are personally accountable for ensuring that you promote and protect the interests and dignity of patients and clients, irrespective of gender, age, race, ability, sexuality, economic status, lifestyle, culture and religious or political beliefs'. The moral issue here lies with the professional person, as it is their belief that should not be imposed on another. Nurses and midwives need to behave in a professional manner, which means that they must ensure that their beliefs are not imposed upon the client. If this means that they are unable to give the required information in an unbiased way, they are required to pass the care on to another person who will be able to discuss the issue with the client in an unbiased way. Should this request be made at a booking clinic or a general practitioner's clinic it should not be a problem, as there will be others around who are capable of dealing with the situation there and then. The only time that this area of care could be a problem is when a booking appointment is being undertaken in a client's home and the professional is asked for information on terminating the pregnancy.

THINKING POINT

A young woman who appears to be 16 weeks pregnant by dates attends your clinic for the first time. She has not been seen by her general practitioner or any other health service provider and appears to have kept the pregnancy hidden. During the discussion she asks for advice on how to obtain a termination. You have made your views known to the management that you object to being directly involved in abortion procedures.

What advice could you give this client and how could you deal with her inquiry?

CHILDHOOD AND THE LAW

The main acts of Parliament having an effect on children are the Children and Young Persons Act 1933, Children Act 1989, Family Law Act 1996, Education Act 1996, Children and Adoption Act 2006 and Children Act 2004. The Childcare Act 2006 imposes a duty on local authorities to try and reduce child poverty through supporting parents to work, thereby aiming to reduce inequalities among such children.

The impact of these key statutes on children and their carers will be discussed and the factors that affect 'the best interest' principle of the child will be considered in the context of ethics and law.

The social trends in the family have changed and continue to change with more marriages ending in divorce. More couples are living together outside marriage, more children are being born into single-parent families and more couples of the same sex are living openly together (www.statistics. gov.uk, 2006). At the same time, many family members are victims of cruel and destructive behaviour. Physical, sexual and emotional abuse continue to have a significant impact on a number of children and the numbers of victims, including children, continue to rise; therefore, laws need to reflect and respond to these issues.

When the Children Act 1989 was enacted, it was seen as the most influential piece of legislation for children. Since then there have been many changes, amendments and alterations to this act and, in 2004, the new Children Act was enacted. This did not totally replace the 1989 act, as only some parts were changed, which means that now practitioners have to understand both acts, and where changes were made the 2004 act takes precedence. With the implementation of the 2004 act the post of a children's commissioner was established. There has been a commissioner in Wales since 2001, Northern Ireland since 2003 and Scotland since 2004. The first English commissioner was appointed in March 2005 but did not take up the post until July 2005. The general function is to promote the rights and interests of children by 'promoting awareness of the views and interests of children'. Unlike the English commissioner, the commissioners for Wales, Scotland and Ireland are not tied by legislation to any government agenda. The commissioner for England is required to be concerned with the five outcomes set out by the government in Every Child Matters:

- physical and mental health and emotional well-being,
- protection from harm and neglect,
- education, training and recreation,
- the contribution made by children and young people to society,
- social and economical well-being.

Within the enactment of the Adoption and Children Act 2002 a major change, taking effect on 1 December 2003, occurred in relationship to parental responsibility. Parental responsibility is seen as a key principle and a key concept in child law and is defined in Section 3(1) to mean

> *all the rights, duties, powers, responsibility and authority which by law a parent of a child has in relationship to the child and his/her property.*

The law has effectively thrown a ring of care around children by imposing parental responsibility for their upbringing on specific persons until the child reaches adulthood. This is reinforced by the Adoption and Children Act 2002. The description of adulthood, however, has changed within the remit of the Children Act 2004, Section 10(8):

> *A children's services authority in England and each of their relevant partners must in exercising their functions under this section have regard to any guidance given to them for the purpose by the Secretary of State. Arrangements under this section may include arrangements related to*
>
> - *persons aged 18 and 19;*
> - *persons over the age of 19 who are receiving services under Section 23C to 24D of the Children Act 1989 (c41);*
> - *persons over the age of 19 but under the age of 25 who have learning difficulties, within the meaning of Section 13 of the Learning and Skills Act 2000 and are receiving services under the Act.*

PARENTS AND PARENTAL
RESPONSIBILITY: MAJORITY AGE

Grubb and Laing (2010) suggest that parental responsibility is the right of a parent to give consent on behalf of a child. In law a mother always has parental responsibility. The position of fathers is more complicated. Section 2(1) of the Children Act 1989 states:

> *Where a child's father and mother were married to each other at the time of his birth they shall each have parental responsibility for the child.*

This statement is slightly misleading because Section 1 of the Family Law Reform Act 1987 extends this to relationships in which the parties were clearly not married at the time of birth. Parents who are involved in a void marriage are covered by Section 2(1): 'provided that at the time of the child's conception or the time of birth if later, either or both of them reasonably believed that the marriage was valid'. Added to this it is fairly common for parents who were not married at the time of the birth to marry at a later date. This arrangement is treated by the law as if they were married to each other at the time of the child's birth, and the father's status goes from one with no parental responsibility to that of full parental responsibility through the act of marrying. This act also includes the parents of adopted children; if seen as having been married at the time of the birth, adopted children are therefore seen as having been born as a child of the marriage. However, what about unmarried fathers? Section 2(2) of the Children Act 1989 states:

> *Where a child's mother and father were not married to each other at the time of birth –*
>
> *(a) the mother shall have parental responsibility for the child;*
> *(b) the father shall not have parental responsibility for the child, unless he acquires it in accordance with the provisions of this Act.*

This allows mothers to enjoy all the 'rights, duties, powers, responsibilities and authorities' of being a parent with the exclusion of the father. However, the fact that fathers do not have parental responsibility does not affect any obligations they have, for example, the statutory duty to maintain the child. In December 2003, after lengthy discussions which began in 1979, the Law Commission finally changed the law regarding unmarried fathers. Section 111(1) of the Adoption and Children Act 2002 made the following amendment to Section 4 of Children Act 1989:

The father shall acquire parental responsibility for the child if –

(a) he becomes registered as the child's father under any of the enactments specified in subsection (1A);

(b) he and the child's mother make an agreement (a parental responsibility agreement) providing for him to have parental responsibility for the child; or

(c) the court, on his application, orders that he shall have parental responsibility for the child.

Parental responsibility can be challenged and even overridden, and awarded to either grandparents or to social services, when parents and those with responsibility infringe this principle. There is no definitive list that states what are the 'rights, duties, responsibilities and authority' associated with parental responsibility, but they are seen as attributes which parents need to perform their duties properly in the rearing of their children until the children are capable of looking after themselves.

This presents a challenge for professionals in their daily work when dealing with issues involving children. It is usually easier for a healthcare professional to identify who is the mother rather than the father, when it comes to the issue of consent for treatment of a minor. Many professionals prefer the route of asking the mother to sign consent forms rather than having to ask fathers if they are married and to whom or whether they have parental responsibility for their child. This issue can be very problematic in areas such as accident and emergency, paediatrics and neonatal departments, where the child may be accompanied by fathers or carers.

The age of majority (18) is usually defined as a threshold into adulthood as opposed to the age of sexual consent, voting age or marriage.

1 Reduction of age of majority from 21 to 18

(1) As from the date on which this section comes into force a person shall attain full age on attaining the age of eighteen instead of on attaining the age of twenty-one; and a person shall attain full age on that date if he has then already attained the age of eighteen but not the age of twenty-one.

Family Law Reform Act 1969, c. 46, Section 1(1)

For example, there are differences between Scotland and Northern Ireland, where the marriageable age is 16, with parental consent, and

England and Wales, where the minimum age for marriage is 18 (Her Majesty's Government, 2013). Local authorities are required to keep in touch with vulnerable groups until at least the age of 21 (Children (Leaving Care) Act 2000). Arrangements under this section may include arrangements relating to:

(a) *persons aged 18 and 19;*

(b) *persons over the age of 19 who are receiving services under sections 23C to 24D of the Children Act 1989 (c. 41);*

(c) *persons over the age of 19 but under the age of 25 who have a learning difficulty, within the meaning of section 13 of the Learning and Skills Act 2000, and are receiving services under that Act.*

THINKING POINT

You are the admitting nurse on a busy paediatric department and are dealing with a three-year-old child who has been involved in a car accident and requires immediate surgery.

You have discovered that the child is accompanied by her father and a consent form is required to be signed.

1. How would you question his parental responsibility before he signs the consent form?
2. What options are available to you if he is not married to the mother and does not have a court agreement?

CONSENT AND THE CHILD

Consent is seen as a fundamental legal and ethical right for adult patients to determine what happens to their own bodies. Valid consent to treatment is therefore absolutely central in all forms of health care and is seen as a matter of common courtesy between health professionals and their patients. Consent lies at the heart of the relationship between the patient and client and is a fundamental part of good practice and a legal requirement (Department of Health, 2001). Any adult of sound mind who is classed as a subject of the law can refuse to accept treatment irrespective of need or catastrophic outcomes. However, the issue is not simple where children are involved; it is a question of what, if any, consent is required, especially in an emergency. Children in this aspect are classed as objects of the law and therefore do not have the same 'rights' as a subject of the law. The legal framework is governed in the criminal law by the law of assault and in the civil law by the duty to take reasonable care of a patient by the exercise of proper professional competence and to act in the best interests of the patient (see *Appleton v Garrett* BDL 2607950353; [1996] PIQR P1). Hedley (2002) argues that the real difficulties lie in the areas where consent is being refused by a child whom the clinician believes to have the capacity to consent. This is seen by many medical practitioners and nurses as a grave step to overcome, and if the refusal to consent is contrary to the best interest of the child principle, the decision to treat is most likely to be made by the court. (See *Re T (a minor) Wardship: Medical Treatment* BLD 2810960376 [1996] *The Times*, 28 October.)

As we have seen above, in the UK a child's 18th birthday indicates that they have reached the age of majority; this means they have finally become an adult and therefore a subject of UK law. In respect of consent, when children reach the age of 16, provided they are mentally competent, they are considered to be sui juris – capable of consenting to treatment themselves. This applies in healthcare matters, where children of 16 to 17 years old, within a limited extent, can consent to medical treatment independently of their parents.

> *The consent of a minor who has attained the age of sixteen years to any surgical, medical or dental treatment which, in the absence of consent, would constitute a trespass to his person, shall be as effective as it would be if he were of full age; and where a minor has by virtue of this section given an effective consent to any treatment it shall not be necessary to obtain any consent for it from his parent or guardian.*
> **Family Law Reform Act 1969, c. 46, Section 8(1)**

Prior to this age children are seen as 'objects of the law' and unable to make decisions for themselves. The right of younger children to independently consent to treatment is based on their competence, although a child's age is an unreliable predictor of his or her competence to make decisions. The presumed consent may be overruled by a person with parental responsibility or a court of law through a judicial review. In the United Kingdom, the assessment of competence is defined either in terms of *Gillick* competence or by the *Fraser* guidelines. These are often considered to be interchangeable but in fact are quite different. *Gillick* competence refers to a child's capacity irrespective of age to provide valid consent to treatment in specified circumstances but not to refuse treatment. The *Fraser* guidelines are narrower and specifically address the issue of providing contraceptives advice to girls without the knowledge of their parents (Wheeler, 2006).

> ### *Gillick v West Norfolk* and *Wisbech Area Health Authority* [1985] UKHL 7 (17 October 1985)
>
> In 1982, Mrs Victoria Gillick took her local health authority (West Norfolk and Wisbech Area Health Authority) and the Department of Health and Social Security to court in an attempt to stop doctors from giving contraceptive advice or treatment to under 16-year-olds without parental consent.
>
> The case went to the High Court where Mr Justice Woolf dismissed Mrs Gillick's claims. The Court of Appeal reversed this decision, but in 1985 it went to the House of Lords and the law lords (Lord Scarman, Lord Fraser and Lord Bridge) ruled in favour of the original judgement delivered by Mr Justice Woolf:
>
>> Whether or not a child is capable of giving the necessary consent will depend on the child's maturity and understanding and the nature of the consent required. The child must be capable of making a reasonable assessment of the advantages and disadvantages of the treatment proposed, so the consent, if given, can be properly and fairly described as true consent.
>>
>> *http://www.nspcc.org.uk/inform/research/ questions/gillick_wda61289.html*

The Department of Health in November 2001 issued guidelines for professionals in obtaining consent from children, which identifies competence as a child having 'sufficient understanding and intelligence to enable him or her to understand fully what is proposed'. The guidelines have since been updated (Department of Health, 2009). Since 1985 this has been referred to as '*Gillick* competence'. Competence is not a simple attribute that a child possesses or does not possess; much will depend on the relationship and trust between the professional and colleagues, with the child and their family and between family members. Professionals need to work with children to develop competence by involving children from an early age in decision-making and encouraging them to take part in their care. However, where a child is under the age of 16 years it is good practice to involve the family in the decision-making. Even when children are not able to give valid consent for themselves, it is still good practice and important to involve them as much as possible in making decisions about their own health. Age-appropriate methods can be used; for example, a child as young as one or two can consent to an examination of their abdomen. If, when asked if you can look at their tummy, they lift up their clothes to expose their abdomen, this implies consent; however, if they put their arms around their abdomen and refuse to move them, this can be seen as no consent. For a number of years implied consent has been disregarded by the health professional due to fear of being sued for assault.

However, in law it is acceptable if the action by the child is documented in detail in written form; it then becomes a valid consent regarded as the same as a verbal consent. The important issue is clear concise written documentation of the incident, which is clearly signed, timed and dated by the professional.

For consent to be valid the person, child or parent giving the consent (Department of Health, 2001) must be

- capable of taking that particular decision which means competent,
- acting voluntarily not under any pressure or duress from anyone,
- provided with enough information to enable them to make the decision.

When seeking consent from a child it is essential that the information be provided in a form that the child can understand and that you have checked the child understands the format being used. This format could be with the use of age-appropriate language, or use of pictures, toys and play activity. This information giving should be conducted at the child's own pace, allowing time and opportunity for questions concerning fears to be answered. Emergency situations are the exception to this rule. In these circumstances it is lawful to provide immediate necessary treatment and consent is not required, as it is on the basis that it is in the child's best interest.

There may be times when children and those with parental responsibility are going to disagree with a particular investigation or treatment. The legal aspect is complex and the decisions of a competent child to accept treatment cannot be overridden by a person with parental responsibility. However, case law has decreed that when a child refuses treatment, those with parental responsibility may consent on their behalf, and treatment can lawfully be given. The Legal Capacity (Scotland) Act 1991 is broadly similar to that of England and Wales, with one important difference, in that parents cannot override a refusal of consent by a competent child. In Scotland a child under the age of 16 has the legal capacity to consent to his or her treatment where according to the act, 'in the opinion of the qualified medical practitioner attending he/she is capable of understanding the nature and possible consequences of the procedure or treatment'.

ADVOCACY

Advocacy is about speaking up for children and young people and empowering them. Advocacy is seen to safeguard children and young people and protects them from abuse and poor practice. It makes sure that children and young people have their rights respected and their views and wishes are heard at all times. But who are the best advocates for children and young people? It is assumed by many professionals that the parents are the best advocates and that they have the best interests of their child at heart and aim to seek the best health care available for them. However, in agreeing to a course of action involving their child they cannot be assumed to know for certain what their preverbal child would consent to were he or she able to give informed permission for an intervention. The best interest philosophy can be difficult to define with the many social, religious, philosophical and cultural ideas about what constitutes acceptable child rearing and welfare in today's multicultural society. When babies and young children are being cared for it is not always practicable to seek parents' consent on every occasion for every routine intervention such as blood or urine tests or even x-rays. However, in law, obtaining consent is a requirement. When children are admitted it is seen as good practice to discuss with the parents what routine procedures will be necessary and obtain their consent for the interventions in advance.

The Department of Health 2002 guidelines for the provision of children's advocacy services state that one of the core principles should as the client's 'advocates work for children and young people and no one else'. It is often stated and has, in some cases, become a mantra: 'I am acting as the child's advocate'. For health service personnel, it may be difficult to be a true advocate as there may be a potential conflict of interest in working for the child only. Another core principle is 'advocates should help children and young people to raise issues and concerns about things they are unhappy about', including making informal and formal complaints under Section 26 of the Children Act 1989, review of cases and inquiries into representation. If a health service employee continues along these lines and encourages a child to complain about their treatment or suggest that they have a case for suing the health authority, it would have the effect of bringing them into conflict with their employing authority. By not giving true advice to the child they are not working as an advocate for the child but in the best interests of the child. This standard links to Article 12 of the United Nations Convention on the Rights of the Child 1989, which states the right of the child to express an opinion and to have that opinion taken into account, in any matter or procedure affecting the child. The General Assembly of the United Nations (UN) adopted the Convention on the Rights of the Child in November 1989, and this was implemented in English law in January 1992. Linked to this is the Human Rights Act 1998 which came into effect in October 2000. The convention sets out a wide range of measures to safeguard and promote the physical, mental, emotional, social and behavioural development of children. This convention recognizes that children are people who are able to form and express opinions, to participate in the decision-making process and to influence solutions and they are not merely 'adults in training'.

THINKING POINT

1. In your practice area how do you obtain consent from children and young people?
2. What support and guidance would you offer to the child and the parents/carer when a child is refusing treatment?
3. How can you *apply* the principle of the best interest of the child in this situation?

SAFEGUARDING THE VULNERABLE CHILD

Child abuse and neglect are generic terms encompassing all ill treatment of children, including serious physical and sexual assaults as well as cases where the standard of care does not adequately support the child's health or development. Children can be abused or neglected through the infliction of harm or through the failure to act to prevent harm. Abuse can occur in a family or an institutional or community setting, such as a hospital or clinic. Significantly, a child can sustain ocular trauma and other conditions due to certain types of abuse, for example, physical, sexual and neglect.

Her Majesty's Government for *Working Together to Safeguard Children* (2010) requires interagency training, including investigative interviewing. This should also be available to all police working with children.

Children who are defined as being 'in need', under the Children Act 1989, which remains the same under the 2004 act, are those whose vulnerability is such that they are unlikely to reach or maintain a satisfactory level of health development, or their health and development will be significantly impaired without the provision of services (Section 17(10) of Children Act 1989). The critical factors to be taken into account in deciding whether a child is in need under Children Act 1989 are what will happen to a child's health or development without services, and the likely effect the services will have on the child's standard of health and development. Some children may be considered as being in need because they are suffering or are likely to suffer significant harm. This is the threshold that justifies compulsory intervention in family life in the best interests of children (Children Act 1989).

Following the publication of Her Majesty's Government for *Working Together to Safeguard Children* (1999), *The Framework for the Assessment of Children in Need* (2000) and the Laming Report in 2003 on the death of Victoria Climbié, the issue of child protection became part of everyone's role and child protection training in the health service became a priority. Every hospital trust was given a directive that they had to identify a named doctor and nurse with specific responsibility for child protection and put in place a clear child protection policy. The Department of Health in the 1999 document had revised the four categories of child abuse and enhanced the definitions, making them clearer, with the aim of reducing the possibility of ambiguity. This still leaves the practitioner, when faced with a possible child protection case, to decide what constitutes an accident or a non-accidental injury. Even though the definitions have been enhanced it is still not clear-cut as to what constitutes a non-accidental injury. The Department of Health has tried to help in this area by issuing to every nurse on the NMC register a copy of the publication *What to Do if You're Worried a Child Is Being Abused* (Department of Health, 2003). This document gives clear guidance on what to do, who to report to, what will happen following referral and what further contributions may be required.

Her Majesty's Government for *Working Together to Safeguard Children* (1999) sets out definitions and examples of what constitutes abuse in four categories:

1. physical abuse,
2. emotional abuse,
3. sexual abuse,
4. neglect.

Physical abuse may involve hitting, shaking, throwing, poisoning, burning or scalding, drowning, suffocating or otherwise causing physical harm to a child. Physical harm may also be caused when a parent or carer feigns the symptoms of an illness, or deliberately causes ill health to a child whom they are looking after. This situation is now commonly described using terms such as factitious illness by proxy, previously referred to as Munchausen's syndrome by proxy. In order to distinguish between accidental and non-accidental injuries and to make an informed decision, practitioners need to obtain a full and comprehensive history from both the child and parents. It is the history of the coherence and timing of all the accounts of what happened that makes the difference in deciding between an accident and a non-accidental injury. One area in this category causing many problems is a parent 'hitting' a child. English law, unlike that of Scotland and Ireland, has declined to instigate a total ban on this habit. English law has allowed parents to use reasonable chastisement of their own child, without leaving a mark and without the aid of an implement. Should a mark be left this is classed as physical abuse (Children Act 2004). Practitioners need to be aware of this anomaly in the law and be able to act accordingly. Should a parent be observed chastising a child, there is a need to decide if the chastisement being used is 'reasonable' or has an implement been used which would indicate that battery has been committed, and if so, the appropriate action needs to be taken to protect the child from physical abuse. Many practitioners shy away from this aspect and fail to probe and ask the difficult questions, mainly because they are unsure of what to do if the answer suggests non-accidental injury.

Emotional abuse is the persistent, emotional ill treatment of a child so as to cause severe and persistent adverse effects on the child's emotional development. It may involve conveying to children that they are worthless or unloved, inadequate or valued only insofar as they meet the needs of another person. It may feature age or developmentally inappropriate expectations being imposed on children. It may involve causing children frequently to feel frightened or in danger, or the exploitation or corruption of children. Some level of emotional abuse is involved in all types of ill treatment of a child, although it may occur alone. Identification of this type of abuse is difficult and may not be obvious until teenage years or later. This may manifest itself in children being uncooperative and non-compliant, especially when diagnosed with a sight problem and being prescribed 'glasses'. The practitioner may overhear the parent or carer making remarks about the child being 'ugly' with those things on their face. The child may present as being withdrawn, very quiet and have a frightened look. These signs need to be identified and reported as they may not be due to the child's fear of the unknown, such as the hospital setting, but the more sinister aspect of child abuse.

Sexual abuse involves forcing or enticing a child or young person to take part in sexual activities, whether or not the child is aware of what is happening. The activities may involve physical contact, including penetrative or non-penetrative acts. They may include non-contact activities, such as involving children in looking at, or in the production of, pornographic material or watching sexual activities, or encouraging children to behave in sexually inappropriate ways.

Neglect is the persistent failure to meet a child's basic physical and/or psychological needs, likely to result in the serious impairment of the child's health or development. It may involve a parent or carer failing to provide adequate food, shelter and clothing, failing to protect a child from physical harm or danger, or the failure to ensure access to appropriate medical care or treatment. It may also include neglect of, or unresponsiveness to, a child's basic emotional needs. This category is usually identified by observation of the child and parent interaction, but practitioners need to be aware that all neglect is not malicious. If a child is poorly dressed, but appears to be growing and well fed, it may be that the parents have a limited income and are spending the money on feeding the child. Help may be needed as these children could be classed as children in need under Section 17 of the Children Act 1989, but not necessarily suffering significant harm under Section 31 of the Children Act 1989. However, they still need to be referred to social services for help to prevent any further decline in their development. Neglect could also be identified in a case of the parent(s) not complying with the administration of eye drops, or failing to attend follow-up clinics. This type of neglect would be seen as true neglect, and the child in this case could be seen to be in danger of significant harm, without the prescribed treatment being administered correctly. Again, these cases do need to be referred to social services for help and guidance. The protection register was abolished in 2008; the government response was that the register had been abolished on the basis that its effectiveness was not backed by research, regardless of the fact that this had been developed following serious case reviews and that victims of child abuse on the protection register are a relatively small number (Dhanda, 2007; Brandon et al., 2010).

Following several cases of child abuse resulting in death of children, new provisions aim to afford vulnerable children protection.

> *The 2012 Act extends the offence of causing or allowing the death of a child or vulnerable adult in section 5 of the 2004 Act ('the causing or allowing death offence') to cover causing or allowing serious physical harm (equivalent to grievous bodily harm) to a child or vulnerable adult.*
> **Domestic Violence, Crime and Victims (Amendment) Act 2012 (Commencement) Order 2012, SI 2012/1432 (c. 54)**

Section 14 of the Children Act 2004 outlines the main responsibilities of the local safeguarding children boards. The Munro Report (2011) recognized the importance of a local focus of multiagency working to protect the child.

INFORMATION ON CHILD ABUSE – DISCLOSURE

Having considered the four categories of abuse and safeguarding the vulnerable child, the reader is probably asking the question on how to manage a disclosure. Although the information may come from a child, teenager or adult, the guidelines are exactly the same. There is no time limit on a person disclosing child abuse, and the information is treated in the same way regardless of the age of the person.

If a child/young person/adult discloses to you that they have been abused:

- Stay calm and listen to what is being said.
- Take what is being said seriously, regardless of the age of the person.
- Reassure the child/young person/adult, but do not agree to keep the information secret.
- Allow the claimant to talk about the situation but do not pressure them for more information.
- Try to get another person to listen to the disclosure; this is good practice, as the child/young person/adult may deny the conversation if they still feel threatened by the abuser.
- Report the incident if appropriate, remain with the child/young person/ adult, and discuss the situation with a senior manager/member of staff.
- Follow your local policy and procedure; make sure that the conversation is recorded in a written format. The written report needs to identify exactly what has been said to you, not your interpretation of what has been said. Write the report clearly and factually and if appropriate,

get the child/young person/adult to read what you have written and sign it. This provides further evidence and is seen as good practice by the legal profession.

• Report to social services, usually by telephone, and follow this up in writing within 48 hours.

Social services will acknowledge receipt of the referral and decide on the action to be taken, within one working day. The Children Act 1989 and Children Act 2004 provide for children's rights to take part in any decision-making related to their welfare. To be on the safe side, it is always better to report any concerns on child abuse than to do nothing (NMC, 2010). Vulnerable children are also subject to protection under the Safeguarding Vulnerable Groups Act 2006. Under the Protection of Freedoms Act 2012 Disclosure and Barring Service (DBS) merged with Independent Safeguarding Authority (ISA). This allows safer recruitment by organisations looking after vulnerable people aiming to identify individuals who may be unsuitable for caring for vulnerable adults, and children. DBS was formed in 2012 by merging the functions of the Criminal Records Bureau under the protection of Freedoms Act 2012. Munro, however, argued that there was 'no compelling case' for a national reporting system (such as a national protection register) for identifying whether or not a child was subject to a child protection plan and argued on the adequacy of current, 'some kind of system for flagging a child's electronic record to indicate that he or she is the subject of a child protection plan' (Munro, 2011, p. 149).

CONCLUSION

This chapter has identified ethical issues as well as key laws, with relevant changes as they relate to current paediatric practice, that clearly provide major challenges for practitioners in the future. The impact of changes in the law, diagnosis, treatment and delivery of paediatric care is now being seen across all areas, whether it be in health or social care. The expansion of the National Health Service and private provision means that more children are now being identified between the ages of 19 and 25 years, as cited in the Children Act 2004, and this will have a huge impact on the future planning requirements for the provision of facilities for children's services. The implementation of the NHS frameworks and Every Child Matters will impart a fundamental change in thinking about the law, health and social care services, hopefully leading to a cultural shift concerning the delivery of services. This should therefore produce a seamless service which allows transferral from child to adult services, making it as painless as it can be for the child, family and/or carers. In order to support these children through the changes, practitioners in all areas now need a sound professional knowledge and understanding of child development and the law surrounding children. It is hoped that this chapter has increased the reader's understanding and demystified some of the conceptions which surround the law, and will form the basis for a broader outlook on their own practice areas.

REFERENCES

Alderson P. *Young children's rights: exploring beliefs, attitudes, principles and practice*, 2nd ed. London: Jessica Kingsley Publications, 2008.

Brandon M, Bailey S, Belderson P. *Building on the learning from serious case reviews: a two year analysis of child protection database notifications 2007–9*. Research report. London: Department for Education, 2010.

Brook GD. Challenges and outcomes of working from a rights based perspective. *Archives of Diseases in Childhood* 2005; 90: 176–78.

Department of Health. *Assessing children in need and their families: practice guidelines*. London: Stationery Office, 2000.

Department of Health. *Seeking consent working with children*. London: Stationery Office, 2001.

Department of Health. *National standards for the provision of children's advocacy services*. London: Stationery Office, 2002.

Department of Health. *What to do if you're worried a child is being abused*. London: Stationery Office, 2003.

Department of Health. *Reference guide to consent for examination or treatment*, 2nd ed. London: Stationery Office, 2009.

Dhanda P. *Response to parliamentary question by Annette Brooks M.P.* 5 February 2007. London: Hansard, 2007.

Grubb A, Laing J. *Principles of medical law*, 3rd ed. Oxford: Oxford University Press, 2010.

Hedley M. Treating children: whose consent counts? *Current Paediatrics* 2002; 12: 463–64.

Her Majesty's Government. *Working together to safeguard children: a guide to inter-agency working to safeguard and promote the welfare of children*. London: Department for Education, 2013.

Lee R, Morgan D. *Birthrights: law and ethics at the beginning of life*. London: Routledge, 2004.

Marquis D. Abortion and the beginning and end of human life. *Journal of Law, Medicine and Ethics* 2006; 34: 16–25.

Munro E. *The Munro review of child protection: final report*. London: Department for Education, 2011.

NSPCC. Gillick competence and Fraser competence. http://www.nspcc.org.uk/inform/research/questions/gillick_wda61289.html (accessed July 2013).

Nursing and Midwifery Council. *Code of professional conduct standards for conduct, performance and ethics*. London: Stationery Office, 2008.

Nursing and Midwifery Council. *Raising and escalating concerns*. London: Stationery Office, 2010.

Sade RM. Introduction defining the beginning and end of human life: implications for ethics, policy and law. *Journal of Law, Medicine and Ethics* 2006; 34: 6–7.

Wheeler R. Gillick or Fraser? A plea for consistency over competence in children. *BMJ* 2006; 332: 807.

4 WORKING SAFELY WITH SERVICE USERS

INTRODUCTION

This chapter introduces the broad legal concepts applicable to any clinical environment, on working safely with the service user. (The term 'patient' may be preferable.) The quality of the clinical environment as well as the employer-employee relationship may affect the quality of care. Patients' rights are at the centre of health and safety and are affected by the expected conduct of healthcare professionals and others who deliver care. Although it is not always obvious, the professional caring relationship is normally contractual and based on employment conditions of service and terms of service agreed, for example, between the service provider (the employer) and the nurse, healthcare assistants or other health and social care professionals.

Nurses must be guided by the Nursing and Midwifery Council (NMC) standards of care as well as the requirements to comply with health safety legislation.

It is possible, however, to have an informal caring relationship where family and friends are carers involved either exclusively or in partnership with 'employed' health and social care workers. In both types of settings, the users' safety should never be compromised and everything should be done to promote professionals working in corroboration with informal carers to ensure patient safety. Factors which may affect the patient's 'best interests' will be considered in the context of duty of care in ethics as well as health and safety employment law.

The ethical and legal basis of duty of care which is owed to the patient underpins the law of torts or delict (in Scotland), notwithstanding professional regulations by bodies such as the Nursing and Midwifery Council (NMC), General Medical Council (for medical staff) or Health and Care Professions Council (for other health and social care professionals). Based on the assumption that an employee undertakes a role voluntarily, it stands to reason that on appointment, they will be expected to meet the minimum requirements of the role in question as well as the terms, while likewise the employer also honours the contractual terms and the conditions of service (Selwyn, 2011).

In search of a definition of what nursing is, the International Council for Nurses could not have suggested a more fitting outline of this role; there is an expectation that

> *nursing encompasses autonomous and collaborative care of individuals of all ages, families, groups and communities, sick or well and in all settings. Nursing includes the promotion of health, prevention of illness, and the care of ill, disabled and dying people. Advocacy, promotion of a safe environment, research, participation in shaping health policy and in patient and health systems management, and education are also key nursing roles.*
>
> ***International Council of Nurses,***
> ***ICN Code of Ethics for Nurses, www.icn.***
> ***ch/definition.htm (accessed 22 June 2013)***

IN THE COURSE OF EMPLOYMENT

There is a presumption in law that an employer takes credit for the positive actions of their employees; accordingly, it stands to reason therefore that they (employer) should also bear any loss resulting from negligent actions of their employees, based on the principle of 'vicarious liability'. Given that this is the case in a caring environment, the employer should therefore take responsibility for the negative aspects as well. This includes the actions of commission or omissions carried out by employees (in the course of their employment). It stands to reason therefore that the employer should bear the leading and ultimate responsibility for not only safeguarding patients' rights but also owing anyone who comes on their premises, such as patients, staff and family members, a duty of care by providing a safe working environment under Section 2 of the Health and Safety at Work Act 1974, as well as ensuring the welfare of the patients.

Employers have the right to legitimate hiring and legitimate firing of employees, since they set the terms and conditions of service or ground rules and pay the wages, and to provide a safe working environment under Section 2 of the Health and Safety at Work Act 1974. Employees are nevertheless expected to follow reasonable orders and also have a duty of care under Section 7 of the Health and Safety at Work Act 1974.

THINKING POINT

Jane had been working as a district nurse (Band 7) as team leader in the community for the preceding 10 years managing a caseload of mostly elderly patients with long-term conditions. This included Mr Jones (aged 90) and his wife (86 years old). He was a retired engineer who suffered from diabetes type 2 and Parkinson's disease, and had been recently transferred to Jane's caseload following a colleague's retirement about four weeks prior to this. There had been no proper handover as the nurse who had been looking after this patient had gone off sick before retiring on health grounds. Jane assigned one of her nurses, Maria, for direct care. During the first assessment Maria was advised by the patient that he was self-caring apart from weekly home help, mainly cleaning the house and shopping, as well as meals on wheels. The couple managed with mutual support with occasional help from family members.

The district nurse came in every day to give him his insulin injection. One morning the patient was seen by Maria, the staff nurse (who qualified abroad before doing her adaption in the UK). She had many years nursing experience in her country of origin but only 8 months' post-adaptation experience in the UK; nevertheless, she was working well so far, with minimum supervision. On the day in question a second-year nursing student had been temporarily allocated to Maria as the student's mentor was on half-term leave. Under her supervision, the student nurse was instructed to draw up 8 mL (millilitres) of long-acting insulin, instead of 8 IU (international units), and she promptly administered the injection. (She used the wrong syringe as the patient had run out of his own stock.) Soon after they left, the patient went into a hypoglycaemic attack. His wife called for an ambulance which arrived within 20 minutes of the call. Attempts to resuscitate him were unsuccessful. At the inquest, the student nurse said she remembered the patient saying he had a supply of his own syringes and that this was the wrong syringe. She did mention the difference in needles to Maria, who told her that she knew what she was doing.

1. What risk assessments should have been carried out prior to this?
2. Consider your employer's policy on management and administration of medicines.

We have seen (above) that based on the principle of vicarious liability, the law presumes that the employer is liable for any actions or omissions which are incurred by the employee 'in the course of their employment'. Only in a few cases which have gone to law did decisions go against this general principle, when it comes to employee actions 'outside the course of employment'. It is normally the employer's legal responsibility to issue terms and conditions of service to the employee, within two months of employment, as regulated by the Employment Rights Act (ERA) 1996, which was amended by the Employment Relations Act (ERA) 1999 and the Employment Act 2002. If a workforce has good working conditions and nurses are working in a safe environment, they are more likely to deliver better quality care for patients.

The terms of employment are usually in writing, though this is not necessary as custom and practice may be sufficient to establish a contract of employment, in the event of a dispute going to an employment tribunal. This means that where terms of a contract of employment are not written, the court may exercise its prerogative in interpreting implied terms as evidenced by the relationship between an employer and employee (Phillips and Scott, 2008).

There are two of types of employment contracts, i.e. a contract of services and a contract for services:

1. A *contract of services* is the most common type of agreement for most nurses in employment, whether as full-time or part-time. An employee works to an agreed contract or agreement with specific terms for a specified wage or salary, and this is easier to determine liability. In cases where, however, an employee acts illegally or outside the scope of their work (or practice), the question arises whether the employer should be vicariously liable. The point in issue is illustrated by the following case:

> ### *Lister and Others v Hall* [2001] UKHL 22
>
> A warden who was an employee at a boarding school to look after young boys instead abused them.
>
> Held: Although the defendant carried out criminal acts which were not authorized by his employer, this was nevertheless 'in the course of his employment' and therefore the employer was liable under the principle of vicarious liability.

2. A *contract for services*, on the other hand, applies to agency or hired workers who are either self-employed through an agency or working for themselves. To illustrate the problems faced by agency staff (who are self-employed), there may be difficulties in establishing liability. This means that in contract law, a principal for an agency nurse may be sued for the actions of their agency worker, though this is difficult in practice unless it can be proved that they knowingly colluded with

the agency nurse or acted negligently. An example of this principle is illustrated in the following case:

Dacas v Brook Street Bureau (UK) Ltd. [2004] IRLR 358

Mrs Dacas worked on agreed hours and on a set roster as a cleaner exclusively at a mental health hostel for Wandsworth Council for a period of four years. The former supplied the cleaning materials and equipment. Brook Street (the agency) was responsible for discipline, payments to Mrs Dacas, tax deductions of and national insurance contributions to pay, as well as holiday and sick pay. Following allegations of alleged rudeness to a visitor, she was withdrawn from all agency work and she claimed unfair dismissal against both the council and the agency.

Held: The employment tribunal held that as the claimant was not a council employee, there was no contract of employment, and furthermore that there was not contract of employment between her and the agency. This decision was upheld on appeal in respect of employment by Brook Street, the agency (which was the ground for appeal), which was said to be under no obligation to provide work and therefore no control over her and her work.

There is a presumption in law that an employer is in a more financially privileged position in comparison to an employee. This therefore makes the employer the primary target for litigation in seeking substantial compensation for harm in tort or delict (Scots law) for a victim of clinical negligence. It is nevertheless possible for the employee to be jointly cited as co-defendant in a civil action for damages for clinical negligence.

The employer is nevertheless within their right to indemnify their own loss by suing a negligent employee in turn as they seek to make good any losses resulting from the employee's negligent actions (in the event of an employee acting negligently by failing to follow existing policy and procedure). In most cases, nurses may also be indemnified through their union insurance. However, if it can be established that in the course of employment an employee was following established (employer) procedures with resulting injury to a patient, then clearly the responsibility for negligence will lie with the employer. This principle was applied as 'an implied term that the master will indemnify the servant from liability arising out of an unlawful enterprise upon which he has been required to embark without knowing it was unlawful'.

Lister v Romford and Cold Storage Co. Ltd. [1957] AC 555 at 595

In this case, a truck driver while in the course of his employment negligently injured his father who was also an employee of the same firm. The father

---

> successfully sued the employer based on the vicarious liability principle.
> The employer's insurers in turn sued the driver in his capacity as joint
> wrongdoer and for breaching an implied term of the contract of employment
> which requires of him a duty to take reasonable care in the execution of his
> duties.

The Crown Proceedings Act 1947, which came into force in 1948, made the National Health Service, as the largest employer of nurses and provider of care through the healthcare trusts, open to civil litigation. In the event of a patient sustaining injury through negligence of employees of the crown, government ministers or healthcare trusts or health boards as employees of the crown may now be held criminally and civilly liable:

> *(1) Subject to the provisions of this Act, the Crown shall be subject
> to all those liabilities in tort to which, if it were a private person
> of full age and capacity, it would be subject: –*
> *(a) in respect of torts committed by its servants or agents;*
> *(b) in respect of any breach of those duties which a person owes
> to his servants or agents at common law by reason of being
> their employer;*

There are nevertheless a few exceptions; the royal mint and judges who are under qualified privilege are immune from criminal prosecution. Other exceptions are members of Parliament under parliamentary privilege, who are also immune from prosecution.

The National Health Service and Community Care Act 1990 also states on 'crown immunity' that

> *1) the Subject to the following provisions of this section, on and
> after the day appointed for the coming into force of this subsection, no health service body shall be regarded as the servant or
> agent of the Crown or as enjoying any status, immunity or privilege of the Crown ... no health service body shall be regarded
> as the servant or agent of the Crown or as enjoying any status,
> immunity or privilege of the Crown.*
> **Section 60, NHS and Community Care Act 1990 (c. 19)**

Since the enactment of the Health and Safety at Work Act 1974, a new statutory duty of care (of health and safety) on trusts, trust boards and health providers as organizations has been created, making healthcare providers both criminally and civilly liable for the actions or omissions of the organization as a whole. If a healthcare worker fails to follow an employer's policy or procedure, then they may also find themselves jointly or singly liable for any negligent actions. Nurses should have indemnity cover in the event of litigation. This would be provided by membership of a union.

The Health and Safety at Work Act 1974 may now be used for imposing fines and criminal prosecution by the Health and Safety Executive (HSE), as government watchdog. The HSE issues guidelines on health and safety and provides both informal and formal advice on health and safety. They may also issue improvement or enforcement notices with fines. Occasionally they may also serve a prohibition notice, stopping a business from operating. This followed several incidents of food poisoning in National Health Service (NHS) establishments. In 2012, 585 cases were prosecuted by the HSE, securing a conviction of 537 (92 per cent) (HSE, 2013) for all the United Kingdom. Under the Health and Safety (Offences) Act 2008, magistrate courts may impose a maximum fine of £20,000 for breaches of health and safety plus compensation for the victim as well as costs. Because the damages awarded in a criminal health and safety case are relatively small (as low as £5000), the victim may wish to pursue civil litigation for compensation for harm, with potentially more damages.

The government vision had drawn up the white paper *The New NHS: Modern, Dependable* (DoH, 1997), which proposed a statutory duty for chief executives of healthcare organizations to implement systems of clinical governance to ensure good quality care. As a result the consequence of this change has been a rise in litigation in clinical negligence actions:

12H –

(1) it shall be the duty of each Health Board, Special Health Board and NHS trust and of the Agency to put and keep in place arrangements for the purpose of monitoring and improving the quality of health care which it provides to individuals.

(2) The reference in subsection (1) to health care which a body there mentioned provides to individuals includes health care which the body provides jointly with another person to individuals.

(3) In this section 'health care' means services for or in connection with the prevention, diagnosis or treatment of illness.

Section 51 of Health Act 1999

The NHS Redress Act 2006 responding to the government consultation paper *Making Amends – Clinical Negligence Reform* (2003) aimed to give the patient an alternative to litigation for claims of less than £20,000 after deductions of medical care costs. In practice such claims are few and far between. There is no appeal if patients are unhappy with the decision. For a claim in tort, the victim can institute legal proceedings unless they have accepted an out-of-court settlement, which may be preferable due to the practical difficulties in passing through the litigation hurdles of establishing a claim for negligence as well as the length of time this may take (see Chapter 1). Any claims should be within three years of the date of the civil wrong unless this is extended to up to six years at the discretion of the court, under the Limitation Act 1980 or the Prescription and Limitation (Scotland) Act 1973. Under the Employers Liability (Compulsory Insurance) Acts 1969 and 1998 (as amended by the Employers' Liability (Compulsory Insurance) (Amendment) Regulations 2004), employers are required to have insurance cover, in the event of claims. Since 1996, the National Health Service Clinical Negligence Scheme for Trusts (CNST) has been established as the body responsible for an 'insurance policy' for any NHS clinical negligence claims:

> *The Scheme applies to any liability in tort owed by a member to a third party in respect of or consequent upon personal injury or loss arising out of or in connection with any breach of a duty of care owed by that body to any person in connection with the diagnosis of any illness, or the care or treatment of any patient, in consequence of any act or omission to act on the part of a person employed or engaged by a member in connection with any relevant function of that member.*
> **National Health Service (Clinical Negligence Scheme)**
> **Regulations 1996, no. 251**

(On litigation, please see Chapter 1.)

KEEPING THE PATIENT, SELF AND OTHERS SAFE

Health and safety is a broad employment law concept with statutory criminal liability, with its main objective being to safeguard patients, as well as staff and visitors. Most care is provided in designated buildings, but the occupier's duty of care also extends to vehicles such as ambulances where care may be provided. The duty of care in this area comes under what is known as 'strict liability'. The aim is to provide maximum possible protection for a 'visitor'. This includes any person present on the premises who may suffer harm. A victim does not need to prove negligence on the part of the owner of a building. Health and safety also requires the employer to manage substances hazardous to health subject to the Control of Substances Hazardous to Health Regulations (COSHH) 1999. The Ministry of Defence may be exempt under Section 17 of the above statutory instrument. This means that employers are required to reasonably control and protect patients, staff and visitors from exposure to hazardous substances to prevent ill health.

As many as 220 workers were killed, a rate of 0.7 per 100,000 workers, with 361 members of the public, in the workplace including hospitals, while '150 559 other injuries to employees were reported, a rate of 587 per 100,000 employees' (HSE, 2010). It is, however, not clear how many patients died as a direct result of health and safety-related accidents. A hospital looking after patients has the duty to ensure the safe storage of hazardous substances as these may injure a person who comes into contact with them, particularly in a case of a confused patient or children. It is observed nevertheless that the chance of a victim winning a case under health and safety legislation is better than under the normal rules of civil claim in tort (Mandelstam, 2010). The reality is that (as discussed above), damages are much lower.

The Health and Safety at Work Act (HASAWA) 1974 is the key statute in managing risk in the health and safety area. A hazard is the potential to cause harm, while risk is the likelihood of harm to take place depending on certain circumstances. The Safety Representatives and Safety Committees Regulations 1977 and the Health and Safety (Consultation with Employees) Regulations 1996 require employers to

> *inform, and consult with, employees in good time on matters relating to their health and safety. Employee representatives, either appointed by recognised trade unions under (a) or elected under (b) may make representations to their employer on matters affecting the health and safety of those they represent.*
>
> **HSE, http://www.hse.gov.uk/violence/law.htm**
> **(accessed June 2013)**

The issue of safety within the caring environment is important as good risk management aims to enhance patient care. Section 4 of the Health and Safety at Work Act 1974 places a duty on

> *those in control of premises, which are non-domestic and used as a place of work, to ensure they do not endanger those who work within them. This extends to plant and substances, means of access and egress as well as to the premises themselves.*
>
> **Health and Safety at Work Act 1974**

This area is regulated by the Health and Safety Executive (HSE) through its HSE Commission, which is responsible for health and safety regulation in the United Kingdom. Together with local authorities (environmental health) the HSE is the enforcing authority and supports the commission (HSE, 2006). The employer's specific responsibilities in this area include maintaining a safe system of work as well as risk management including a duty to provide appropriate equipment and to ensure appropriate staff training.

HSE case study 1: Hospital trust improves floor cleaning after a slip

A hospital worker opened the door of a meeting room and stepped into the corridor. She slipped and fell, as the vinyl floor had just been cleaned and was still wet. Although she was not seriously injured, this was largely a matter of chance – there was the potential for a serious injury on another occasion.

An HSE inspector happened to witness the incident and immediately made enquiries about how floor cleaning operations were managed by the trust. He was sufficiently concerned to issue an improvement notice. The main concerns were

- wet mopping on vinyl floor – likely to be slippery if left wet,
- no suitable barriers to prevent people stepping onto the wet floor (single cone was in use – insufficient given large area being cleaned),
- direct access from adjoining rooms onto wet area – no warning for people exiting the rooms,
- floor cleaning carried out at unsuitable time (dinner time on main access route to canteen),
- new cleaner – not adequately trained or supervised.

The improvement notice required the setting up of suitable cleaning regimes and safe systems of work to prevent pedestrians stepping onto a wet floor. It also required the trust to set up a system to ensure that the new procedures were working, including appointing someone to be responsible for monitoring them.

The trust responded promptly and positively to comply with the notice. They put in place improved systems and procedures, including the following:

- retraining of staff on use of conventional mopping systems,
- cleaning floors in small sections, followed by dry mopping,
- effective use of cones and barriers,
- better demonstration of the training methods and systems of work used by contract cleaners,
- trust-wide circulation of the lessons learnt from this incident and the remedial actions taken.

From http://www.hse.gov.uk/slips/experience/floorcleaning.htm. By kind permission of the Health and Safety Executive.

The employer is duty bound under health and safety legislation to identify hazards and risks, through risk management and preventative actions (Ridley, 2008), as well as (evaluative) risk assessment. This is covered by Section 2(1) of the HASAWA 1974. (See above.)

THINKING POINT

A new patient is admitted from a residential home to a surgical urology ward. He is an 89-year-old male resident who has a history of dementia, and he gets more confused at nighttime and attempts to get out of bed several times demanding to 'go home to see his mother'. During nighttime, staff were concerned about the possibility of his climbing out of bed and falling since there is only three of them, two qualified nurses and a healthcare assistant. His daughter, who was the next of kin, suggested that nurses should use cot sides as a precaution, as her father was not very steady on his feet and had already had several falls in the home prior to admission.

However, in respect of the nurse as an employee, Section 7 of the HASAWA 1974 requires them to take reasonable measures to ensure their own safety and that of others, primarily the patient, other staff, as well as visitors, in order to ensure that their work environment is safe. They must also avoid risk to health in respect of the patient, themselves, colleagues and visitors. In addition to the requirements of health and safety laws, they must avoid risk by adhering to local safety policy and instructions of their employer as well as report any unsafe practice. In addition, it is impossible to forestall every eventuality in aiming to eliminate potential hazards. There is nevertheless a requirement for a proper risk assessment with the following requirements.

For example, use of bed rails is an important aspect of safety which needs systematic and thorough risk assessment. Nurses should ensure the following (HSE, 2013):

- They (bed rails) are only provided when they are the right solution to prevent falls.
- A risk assessment is carried out by a competent person taking into account the bed occupant, the bed, mattresses, bed rails and all associated equipment.
- The rail is suitable for the bed and mattress.
- The mattress fits snugly between the rails.
- The rail is correctly fitted, secure, regularly inspected and maintained.

- Gaps that could cause entrapment of neck, head and chest are eliminated.
- Staff are trained in the risks and safe use of bed rails.

The courts apply the 'reasonableness' test in determining the best use of available resources in order to minimize rather than eliminate hazards (*Donoghue* v *Stevenson* [1932] UKHL 100). In defence, a healthcare provider, as occupier of premises, will need to demonstrate that they followed a set procedure and did everything reasonable in order to minimize harm through a risk assessment. In the event of a patient suffering harm as a result of negligence, however, exclusion of liability clauses may not limit liability in negligence if there is resulting injury or death, under Section 16 of the Unfair Contract Terms Act 1977. In all other cases strict liability applies.

There is now a legal requirement to report work-related accidents under the HSE Reporting of Injuries, Disease and Dangerous Occurrences (RIDDOR) since the passing of the Reporting of Injuries, Disease and Dangerous Occurrences Regulations 1995. The classification of accidents requiring to be reported falls within the following categories (Croner CCH Group, 2002, pp. 21–22):

- death,
- major injuries to employees such as falls, resulting in sickness of at least three days,
- other significant injury of non-employees requiring hospital treatment,
- specified diseases,
- specified dangerous occurrences including escape of noxious substances.

An estimated 591,000 workers had an accident at work in 2011–12, and 212,000 of these injuries led to over three days' absence from work and 156,000 to over seven days' (Labour Force Survey [LFS]) (HSE, 2013).

Occupier's liability – the patient and others

Subject to land law, an occupier is any person who has possession of premises, and who owns them (in the tenancy sense) and has control of activities in a building or vessel. The term 'premises' should be construed in its broadest sense, to include vehicles; for example, a patient being transported in an ambulance which is not roadworthy should be protected (from injury) by the law. The rationale behind this legislation is easy to understand. Any persons entering premises should be protected from any danger whether this is an obvious or latent defect which may harm them. The common law creates a duty of care to ensure that they are protected. Examples of unsafe premises are slips, trips and falls. There are two categories of persons who can be present on premises, categorized respectively as visitors and trespassers as recognized by the following pieces of legislation that deal in this area:

1. Occupier's Liability Act 1957 (OLA 1957)
2. Occupier's Liability Act 1984 (OLA 1984)

The aim of the first statute is to create a 'common law duty of care' for the occupier to avoid harm toward persons entering premises. The second statute, however, modified this requirement for the purpose of limiting liability where trespassers are concerned.

Occupier's Liability Act 1957

A 'visitor' is anyone who enters any premises for a legitimate purpose. This permission to be on premises is either explicit or implied. The OLA 1957 recognizes the 'common duty of care' to visitors (Section 2(2) of OLA 1957). This duty is to provide reasonable safety (Elliott and Quinn, 2011). As invitees include visitors who are legitimately on premises, such as patients, their visitors, as well as the nurse, these individuals should all be clearly owed a duty of care. The law expects higher standards of care as illustrated in the following case involving children, who are assumed to be less careful than adults.

Glasgow Corporation v Taylor [1922] 1 AC 44, 61

A seven-year-old child died after eating poisonous berries from a bush in a park owned by the corporation. The court considered that tempting to children since they looked like cherries.

Held: The corporation had breached their duty of care.

Subject to this statute, if injury is established, the duty of care arises on a 'strict liability' basis, with no requirement on the part of the victim to prove fault. This means that the law gives a victim additional protection by presuming absolute or strict liability on the part of the occupier of a building.

Occupier's Liability Act 1984

While the 1957 act protects only invited persons or those who are implicitly or explicitly invited by the occupier, in contrast, the Occupier's Liability Act 1984 (OLA) statute may afford protection to those who are uninvited or trespassers, such as children, who may wander onto premises. This statute requires no strict liability unless it can be proved that the occupier (or owner of the premises) knows of or is aware of the danger, in which case the law expects them to afford reasonable protection to the trespasser. This principle is established in the following case:

> **White v St Albans City [1990] CA, reported in *The Times*, 12 March 1990**
>
> The claimant fell down a trench and sustained injury after he had taken a shortcut across council-owned land in order to access a car park. The land was privately owned, and surrounded by a fence, and there was no evidence that the council was aware of its use as a shortcut.
>
> Held: The court of appeal held on evidence that the council had taken reasonable care and was therefore not liable.

As an occupier of premises, a hospital providing health care is entitled in civil law to put forward certain defences to a claim for damages in tort for personal injury, e.g. 'contribution', which means that any damages awarded may be reduced in proportion to a victim's contribution. Another example of a defence is under the volenti non fit injuria principle (Section 2(5) of the 1957 Act), which means that 'the victim knowingly undertook the risk'. If the court finds for the defendant it may in such cases reduce the level of damages awarded. A hospital (as occupier) may put up warning signs pointing out the danger or hazard, but cannot exclude liability under any terms of contract (Section 2(3) of the Unfair Contract Terms Act 1979) in the event of another person being injured or killed.

Manual handling and product liability

This is another important aspect of health and safety legislation safeguarding the patient's welfare for those with mobility needs. Nurses play an important part in this process. As well as the common law duty of care based on the Health and Safety at Work Act 1974, there is a supplementary regulation on the manual handling in the form of Manual Handling Operations Regulations (MHOR) 1992. The aim during any risk assessment should be 'weighing up the risk of injury against the cost or effort required to introduce new measures. Doing nothing can only be justified if the cost of measures greatly outweighs the risk' (Royal College of Nursing (RCN), 2002, p. 4). Supplementary safety legislation must operate within the framework of the HASAWA 1974 (Mandelstam, 2010). Manual Handling Operations Regulations 1992 (as amended) includes regulation of the inspection and use of appropriateness of equipment used for moving and handling patients.

EC Directive 85/374/EEC was intended to apply to all member states in its entirety, in response to the needs of a victim facing the uphill struggle in establishing negligence and product liability. Prior to this Consumer Protection Act 1987 (Product Liability) (Modification) Order 2000 and the Consumer Protection Act 1987 (Product Liability) (Modification) (Scotland) Order 2001, a plaintiff must prove that a manufacturer was negligent before they can claim for damages, now subject to Part I of this statute, on product liability. Injury caused by defective products removes the need to prove negligence, also providing strict liability. The causes for litigation include all defective biomedical equipment and medication which are covered by the Consumer Protection Act 1987. This may be used against a drug manufacturer when a patient has suffered resulting harm.

THINKING POINT

Jane and Jack are second-year student nurses working in a busy nursing home. Both of them were previously experienced healthcare assistants prior to commencing their nurse training and are competent at using the new hoist. They are asked by the staff nurse to transfer a patient back to bed, Mrs X (a stroke victim), who is unable to communicate or stand on her own. Both of them believed they were 'competent' from watching others in moving and handling patients, and had undergone the training, but they had not received any training on use of the new hoist. They said that they jointly carried out all the safety checks for the patient who was confused. While using the new hoist, the resident fell off, sustaining a fractured neck of femur.

1. What risk assessment should have been followed?
2. What actions are required following the accident?
3. What are the actions required by RIDDOR in the event of a patient being harmed?

Universal precautions and infection control

The principle of duty of care to patients is applicable in cases of infection control and safety, as hospitals are required to minimize the risk by taking reasonable measures to prevent harm where possible or to minimize any such risk. There is a reasonable expectation that nurses will follow established procedures in infection control. Negligence arises from a breach of duty of care if the nurse's conduct falls below expected standards, with resulting harm to patients. The employer and/or the nurse may be held liable, although in practice the employer is likely to be sued on the basis of vicarious liability. Consider the following example on hospital-acquired infections (HAI):

> *One in 10 patients who enter a British hospital will contract a nosocomial infection, and of those, 10 percent will die from it. Officially, this amounts to 5,000 deaths from HAIs in the UK every year – almost double that of fatal accidents on British roads. Unofficial records show the figure to be much nearer 30,000 deaths.*
>
> **Hughes and Armitage, 2006**

THINKING POINT

John, a new junior staff nurse on Ward B6, which is an acute medicine for care of the elderly ward, is concerned about the ward which has a poor reputation and a high level of complaints with the following problems:

- There is a chronic staff shortage on the ward and the ward sister says she has raised this with senior nurse managers who have done little about it.
- Recently, he witnessed the sister and another nurse using a method which was not recommended for moving a patient, but he is not sure what to do for fear of reprisals.
- There is a high incidence of methicillin-resistant *Staphylococcus aureus* (MRSA) on the ward and he thinks this may be linked to a generally very poor standard of hygiene on the ward.

1. Consider your employer's guidelines on infection control.
2. Consider the National Institute for Health and Clinical Excellence (NICE) guidelines.

It is clear that in order to contain some infections, patients may need to be nursed in isolation for the purpose of managing and minimizing cross-infection. On the other hand, there may also be a need to balance overall interests of all patients against those of the isolated patients. There are ethical issues here, as the latter may complain on what they perceive to be a limitation of their freedom by being isolated with a possible infringement of their human rights under Articles 4 (related to their freedom) and 14 (in respect of their right not to be discriminated against) of the Human Rights Act 1998, if they feel that they have been provided a lower standard of care. The nurse is required to show that they have provided a reasonable standard of care expected of their peers, following the *Bolam* principle.

Bolam v Friern Hospital Management Committee [1957] 1 WLR 582

The claimant underwent electroconvulsive therapy (ECT) treatment for endogenous depression. The anaesthetist did not administer any relaxant drugs and the claimant suffered convulsions and fractures. There were divided opinions amongst professionals regarding the effectiveness and risk of the practice of giving a muscle relaxant drug. One view suggested a very small risk of death, and another school of thought recognized a small risk of fractures, which is what happened with the claimant. The claimant argued a breach of duty by the doctor in not giving the muscle relaxant drug.

Held: It was held by the House of Lords that the doctor was not in breach of duty.

"A medical professional is not guilty of negligence if he has acted in accordance with a practice accepted as proper by a responsible body of medical men skilled in that particular art…. Putting it the other way round, a man is not negligent, if he is acting in accordance with such a practice, merely because there is a body of opinion who would take a contrary view."

From a health and safety perspective, the hospital as employer has a duty of care to staff and as occupier to patients to ensure that there are adequate resources and staffing levels when delivering care. There has been a suggestion of a correlation between poor nursing staffing levels and mortality levels (Needleman and Buerhaus, 2002) and as a part of unsafe practice (Aiken et al., 2002). The nurse should engage in safe practice on the grounds that they owe a duty of care to the patient, and therefore a breach of that duty may give rise to damages in tort for the harmed patient.

Since 2002, annual figures showed that 70,000 people were estimated to die from infection-related deaths (DoH, 2002), with similar trends as shown by more recent figures, with a total of 2 500 331 of deaths related to MRSA and *Staphylococcus aureus* between 2003 and 2011 (ONS, 2013). It is important for trusts to restore patient confidence by ensuring the cleanliness of ward areas as a way of controlling and minimizing infections. Two comparative surveys between 2002 and 2004 showed that patient ratings on cleanliness had fallen by 3 per cent, from 51 to 48 per cent, for 'very clean' and by 2 per cent, from 41 to 39 per cent, for 'fairly clean', respectively (UNISON, 2004). All organizations should ensure they are complying with legislation that is relevant to managing the risks to employees from exposure to blood-borne viruses. Particular attention should be paid to (HSE, 2013):

- providing written policies and procedures with clear lines of accountability;
- carrying out suitable and sufficient risk assessments, following the COSHH hierarchy, including use of safer devices;
- assessing the contribution and role of competent advisors, i.e. health and safety, risk management, occupational health and infection control;
- ensuring staff are informed of the risks and implementing control measures, including reporting sharps injuries;
- ensuring suitable monitoring and auditing arrangements are in place.

Safe medicines management

Medicine is an important area for safety due to the potential risk. The most frequently reported types of medication incidents involve wrong dose, omitted or delayed medicines or wrong medicine Over 90 per cent of incidents reported are associated with no harm or low harm (National Patient Safety Agency (NPSA), 2013). The NPSA has developed a national framework for serious incidents in the NHS, called National Framework for Reporting and Learning from Serious Incidents Requiring Investigation. The framework is also the first stage in the development of a consolidated Serious Incident Management System replaced the Strategic Executive Information System (STEIS) serious untoward incident system in 2010.

It is therefore important that nurses ensure the safekeeping and administration of medications. In some cases, the fact senior nurses may also prescribe medicines may allow continuity and better monitoring for the patient.

Two examples of legislation in this area include the following:

- Medicines Act 1986, which covers key issues such as the prescription, storage and dispensing and administration of medications;
- Misuse of Drugs Act 1973, which regulates the classification and storage of controlled drugs.

The process of risk assessment in medicine management involves several stages:

- A prescriber should take into account the pharmacokinetics, what effect the medication has on the body, and the pharmacodynamics, how the body reacts to the medication. This may be positive or negative. Adverse reactions may result in a percentage of people. The prescriber must ensure the correct medication dose and the most effective route. They may also need to check the physical condition, age and weight of the patient, as well as other medications. This may cause interaction especially for patients with polypharmacy.
- Prescribing has been traditionally the domain of medical professionals such as the doctor or dentist, though with extended practice, senior nurses and pharmacists who have undergone appropriate training can prescribe.
- The pharmacist's main role is to dispense medication, though some may also be prescribers. The level of safety expected of pharmacists when dispensing medications to hospitals is the same expected of them when supplying and dispensing in the community to individuals.
- The next stage involves preparation of medication, for example, intravenous fluids. It is important on grounds of safety that manufacturers' and prescribers' instructions are followed accurately.
- The nurse administering medication must ensure the accuracy as well as the appropriate route and method. If patients are self-administering medication they should have been risk assessed as competent. If the nurse administers medication, they must ensure the completion of this stage and not rely on others, without checking. An accurate record should be made contemporaneously (NMC, 2010).
- The last import stage is the need to monitor the patient after the medication is given in case of adverse reactions.

Millions of medicines are prescribed in the community and in hospitals across England and Wales each day – the majority of these are delivered correctly and do exactly what they are meant to do. However when an incident does occur, it is vital we learn from this to ensure patients are not harmed.

Fletcher, 2009, chief executive, NPSA, in Tackling Medication Incidents and Increasing Patient Safety, NPSA

The NPSA works with the Medicines Healthcare Regulatory Authority (MHRA) in monitoring standards. The MHRA is authorized by Directive 2001/83/EC relating to medicinal products for human use, amended by Directives 2002/98/EC, 2003/63/EC, 2004/24/EC and 2004/27/EC. They concluded:

> *Safety, quality and efficacy are the only criteria on which legislation to control human medicines is founded. It is the responsibility of the MHRA and the expert advisory bodies set up by the Medicines Act to ensure that the sometimes difficult balance between safety and effectiveness is achieved. MHRA experts assess all applications for new medicines to ensure they meet the required standards. This is followed up by a system of inspection and testing which continues throughout the lifetime of the medicine. Safety monitoring is also continuous and the MHRA also ensures that doctors and patients receive up-to-date and accurate information about their medicines. This is achieved by ensuring that product labels, leaflets, prescribing information and advertising meet the required standards laid down by the Regulations.*
>
> **MHRA, 2013, How We Regulate Medicines, http:// www.mhra.gov.uk/Howweregulate/Medicines/ (accessed July 2013)**

It is important for nurses to always maintain and demonstrate their professionalism to high standards in areas such as record keeping, as these will serve not only as a communication tool but also as proof of the work they have done and a way to safeguard patients in the administration of medicines. Any entries on drug charts which must be factual should be an accurate entry of events and should have clarity and be entered soon after the event. Other relevant requirements include the ability for the reader to identify the prescriber and the person who administers medication, so it is important that records are clearly identifiable and signed with an identifiable designation, in the case of written records (NMC, 2010). Records may also be used by employers and defence lawyers as evidence in a court of law as well as by a litigant patient's counsel. The courts are likely to take the view that if something is not written down, then it did not happen, as verbal accounts of events are unreliable, especially with passage of time due to the failing human memory – events simply become more blurred or individuals may be making them up.

CONCLUSION

Whatever happens in the clinical environment, the courts will look sympathetically toward a respondent or defendant nurse should they be able to demonstrate that they have done reasonable policy and procedures to ensure safety. The starting point for the nurse should be to understand the relevance of employment law relating to the clinical environment, recognizing the importance of the NMC Record Keeping (2010) in setting professional standards. It is also important to be aware of the impact of national policy on health and safety legislation which should underpin decision-making in making clinical judgements. Any breach of professional regulations (misconduct) may also have legal consequences. On the other hand, ethical dilemmas may arise in practice; though this does not necessarily have legal or professional implications, it is almost certainly unethical conduct will likely breach other inextricable aspects of care. In this way, an ethical dilemma therefore presents challenges for the nurse while working in partnership with the patient, family member, carers and multidisciplinary team, as well as collaboration with other agencies. In response to a complaint, a nurse would need to demonstrate that the care they gave was not only in the patient's best interests, but that expected of a reasonable competent clinician who professes to have that skill (the *Bolam principle*). This is what is expected by the law for ensuring safety within the clinical working environment.

REFERENCES

Aiken LH, Clarke SP, Sloane DM, Sochalski J, Silber JH. Hospital nurse staffing and patient, 2002 mortality, nurse burnout, and job dissatisfaction. *JAMA* 2002; 288: 1987–993.

Croner CCH Group. *Health and safety A–Z, essentials.* Kingston- upon-Thames: Croner CH Group, 2002.

DoH. HSC 1998/89, implementing the recommendations of the Caldicott Report. 1998.

DoH. *Getting ahead of the curve: a strategy for combating infectious diseases.* A report by the chief medical officer. London: Crown, 2002.

DoH. *Making amends – clinical negligence reform.* 2003.

DoH. *NHS confidentiality code of practice.* DH, 2003. www.doh.gov.uk. http://www.ico.gov.uk/what_we_cover/data_protection/legislation_in_full.aspx (accessed 5 June 2013).

DoH. *The new NHS: modern, dependable.* 1997.

Elliott C, Quinn F. *Tort law,* 8th ed. Harlow: Person Longman, 2011.

Health and Safety Executive. *Manual handling. Manual handling operations regulations 1992* (as amended). 2004.

Health and Safety Executive. *Moving and handling in health and social care*. 2013. http://www.hse.gov.uk.

Hughes J, Armitage T. The reformation of a national institution; combating the burden of HAIs (healthcare-associated infections); a British perspective. 2006. http://www.infectioncontroltoday.com/archive.html (accessed 1 June 2006).

International Council of Nurses. The ICN code of ethics for nurses. www.icn.ch/definition.htm (accessed on 22 June 2013).

Mandelstam M. *Quick guide to community care practice and the law*. London, Jessica Kingsley, 2010.

MHRA. How we regulate medicines. 2013. http://www.mhra.gov.uk/Howweregulate/Medicines/ (accessed 15 July 2013).

Needleman J, Buehaus P, Mattke S, Stewart M, Zelevinsky K. Nurse staffing levels and the quality of care in hospitals. *The New England Journal of Medicine* 2002; 346 (22): 1715–22.

NMC. Record keeping. Guidance for nurses and midwives. 2010. http://www.nmc-uk.org.

NPSA. http://www.nrls.npsa.nhs.uk/ (accessed July 2013).

Office of National Statistics (ONS). http://www.ons.gov.uk/ons/index.html (accessed 22 July 2013).

Phillips G, Scott K. *Employment law*. Guildford: College of Law Publishing, 2008.

Ridley J. *Health and safety in brief*, 4th ed. Burlington, MA: Butterworth-Heinemann, 2008.

Royal College of Nursing. *RCN code of practice for patient handling*. London: RCN Publication, 2002.

Selwyn N. *Law of employment*, 16th ed. London: Butterworth, 2011.

UNISON. Hospital contract cleaning and infection control. 2004. www.cf.ac.uk/socsi/CREST (accessed 10 July 2013).

5 A TRUSTING RELATIONSHIP

INTRODUCTION

This chapter explores the nature of the professional relationship between the nurse and service users. From a trusting relationship come the expectations of a nurse's accountability and the implications of a breach of trust. A claim to 'professionalism' implies regulation of conduct through standards, set by an empowered body, and to which the individual member subscribes. In the case of the nurse this applies to the Nursing and Midwifery Council (NMC) which is responsible for setting standards of conduct and proficiency as well as the boundaries of the relationship with the patient. The relationship between a nurse and patient is called 'fiduciary', which means that this is based on trust.

The 'professional boundaries' set by the NMC are the basis for professional relationships; for example, it is not acceptable to accept gifts or form intimate relationships with users in our care (NMC, 2008). The NMC was established under the Nursing and Midwifery Order 2001(SI 2002/253) (the order) and came into being on 1 April 2002. If a breach of trust takes place, a user's rights may be compromised and there may be formal (including professional) sanctions to follow.

DUTY OF CARE AND PROFESSIONAL ACCOUNTABILITY

The Nursing and Midwifery Council is responsible for regulation of qualified nurses to whom they are in turn answerable or accountable for their actions. Application of the legal duty of care, and as explained by the 'neighbour principle' (see *Donoghue v Stevenson* case in Chapter 1), renders the nurse accountable for their actions or omissions (which affect the patient), and makes them 'accountable' for the care they deliver.

A very broad definition of accountability is

> *the readiness or preparedness to give an explanation or justification to relevant others (stakeholders, including the patient) for one's judgments, intentions, acts and omissions when appropriately called upon to do so.*
>
> **Hunt, p. 15 at http://www.freedomtocare.org/page15. htm#definition (accessed 9 January 2006)**

There is an expectation that healthcare professionals providing care will be 'accountable for the actions they take as well as the omissions' (Fletcher and Buka, 1999, p. 54).

The Nursing and Midwifery Council (NMC) requires a registered nurse, midwife or health visitor to reinforce this requirement for all registered nurses:

> *You are personally accountable for your practice. This means that you are answerable for your actions and omissions, regardless of advice or directions from another.*
>
> **NMC Code of Conduct, 2008**

Additionally, nurses are expected to give account for their actions to the following persons:

- Patient (those who come under the nurse's care or in the course of employment): This aims to limit reasonable foreseeability and prevent a floodgate of spurious claims against professionals as well as 'volunteers' acting outside the scope of their employment should things go wrong. Where volunteers come forward, outside their work, this is clearly a dangerous area (from a litigation point of view) where there is no (employer) vicarious liability and they are not indemnified by an employer or by insurance. One example is stopping to help someone who collapses in the street.

- The nurses' professional registration body (NMC) and indirectly professional colleagues.
- The employer, under the terms of the contract of employment and employment law.
- Other different branches of the law, for example, health and safety legislation, criminal law.
- Civil litigation for damages for clinical negligence may precede or follow other aspects of law such as criminal law.

Healthcare professionals are required to turn to their own code of professional conduct for guidance, though this may not always provide clear answers, especially when it comes to ethical dilemmas with conscientious objection. The professional may need to reflect on their actions and to consider whether the patient's best interests will have been best served by their actions in any given situation guided by their own morality.

A nurse must comply not only with the requirements of the law, which is something every citizen is required to do, but also with their professional body's code of conduct and professional guidance in addition to national and local policies forming the framework for care. Wider issues on human rights may be identified when complaints are raised. Failure to do so may result in criminal prosecution, civil litigation, as well as disciplinary action from the employer and/or their professional body. Following a complaint, the NMC reserves the right to call to account any registered member whose conduct is alleged to have fallen below professional standards (see the *Bolam* case below). Employers may institute disciplinary procedures and/or seek damages in compensation from the employee who negligently fails to follow established local procedures (e.g. a personal injury case when the employee negligently disregards policies and procedures, inviting damages against the employee for breach of terms of a contract of employment. The NMC Fitness to Practice Committee is responsible for hearing the evidence and deliberates before reaching one of the following outcomes:

1. Suspend for up to a year,
2. Strike off,
3. Conditions of practice,
4. Caution order (one to five years),
5. No action,
6. Restricted practice.

Untrained staff such as healthcare assistants, on the other hand, are currently not answerable to a professional body but to the patient, the employer and the law in general. The primary aim of professional bodies of clinicians such as the NMC is to protect the patient's rights through professional regulation. In other words, an unqualified or disqualified person should be prevented from potential harm to a patient.

THINKING POINT

The night staff in a residential home had been under suspicion of taking 'sleeping night breaks' for some time. Following a complaint from a resident, the manager turned up unannounced at 0200 hours to find that the second staff nurse and healthcare assistant were asleep in the dayroom when she called.

The staff was suspended and dismissed following a disciplinary. The staff nurse was reported to the NMC for a misconduct hearing.

What is the most likely outcome or sanction at the NMC hearing and why would you suggest this?

On a different level, the nurse is also accountable to the patient as well as to professional colleagues and the employer. When considering whether a nurse's standards fell below the expected standard, a court of law should ask of the nurse whether, in conducting themselves in the way they did, they were acting in accordance with a practice which is in accordance with that of competent respected professional opinion (*Bolam* standard) *Bolam* v *Friern Hospital Management Committee* [1957] 1 WLR 582 or supported by evidence-based practice. The *Bolam* standard is applied by the courts thus:

> *The test is the standard of the ordinary competent man [or woman] exercising and professing to have that special skill.*
> ### McNair Justice in Bolam v Friern Hospital Management Committee [1957] 2 All ER 118

The facts of this case were as follows:

Bolam v *Friern* Hospital Management Committee [1957] I WLR 582

A patient suffering from endogenous depression had to undergo electric convulsive therapy. He sustained injury and multiple fractures during shock treatment, having not had a muscle relaxant administered. He sued for personal injury.

Held: The action was entitled to fail if the professionals could show that in exercising reasonable care in carrying out the treatment they had followed a set of procedures (policies), backed by a professional body, even if there was another body of opinion with a contrary view.

The problem with the above approach, however, is that there can be difficulties when dealing with self-regulating professionals, who set their own standards; they are wide open to possible accusations of 'covering each other's backs', while purportedly protecting the patient. A more recent case echoing the standards of professional practice applied *Bolam*.

Bolitho v City and Hackney Health Authority [1997] 3 WLR 582

This is the case where a doctor failed to put a tube down the throat of a child to assist his breathing. Five experts said that the doctor had been negligent and three said she had not. Lord Browne-Wilkinson ruled that only in very rare cases should a judge reject the evidence of a professional expert as being 'unreasonable', but he was entitled to do so. The majority expert evidence was admitted. The principle of this case was that it would be necessary for the court to go beyond the expertise of the alternative practitioner and have regard to the fact that a practitioner was practicing his art alongside what is generally accepted as standard or orthodox medicine.

There may nevertheless be criminal implications for negligence; the case of *R* v *Adamako* [1995] 1 AC 171 is the test for manslaughter in clinical practice.

R v Adamako [1995] 1 AC 171

An anesthetist was assisting in an operation. At some stage during the procedure the ventilator became detached; by the time he became aware, the patient had suffered from irreversible damage and subsequently died as a result of this negligent action. The anesthetist was convicted of manslaughter due to gross negligence as a basis for liability rather than recklessness. The test is objective; i.e. what would a reasonable person think is gross negligence? The jury considered the extent to which the defendant's conduct departed from the proper standard of care incumbent.

In order to establish clinical negligence the victim must show that the doctor, nurse or other medical attendant failed to exercise that degree of skill and care required by law, and that their standard of care 'fell below the expected' (*R v Adamako* [1995]). The test of negligence is whether they were in breach of their duty of care, and this means in addition to any criminal and/or civil liability.

DUTY OF CONFIDENTIALITY AND PATIENT INFORMATION

The nurse is in a privileged position to access confidential and/or sensitive information related to patient care. It stands to reason that they owe the user a duty of confidence arising from the relation of trust and that the nurse may not breach that confidence by passing on this confidential information to a person unless this is on a need-to-know basis only. Access to information should be controlled and limited to those with a need to know.

A health record includes information which is related to a person's health, and this includes both physical and mental aspects. As part of the common law duty of care to the patient (*Donoghue v Stevenson* [1932] AC 562 (HL)), the nurse must ensure that any patient-identifiable information which comes into their hands in the course of their employment is safeguarded and remains confidential. In a therapeutic relationship, legislation also requires a duty of confidentiality stating that 'patient information may not be passed on to others without the patient's consent except as permitted under Schedule 2 and 3 of the Data Protection Act 1998, or where applicable, under the common law where there is an overriding public interest' (DoH, 1996). Healthcare providers have a duty of care in ethics and in law to respect this confidentiality. From an ethical perspective, this is a reasonable expectation within a fiduciary (trust). It is also important that healthcare professionals who have access to patient-identifiable information maintain this trust-based relationship by maintaining confidentiality.

> *You should seek patients' and clients' wishes regarding sharing information with their family and others. When a patient is considered incapable of giving permission you should consult relevant colleagues.*
> **NMC Code of Conduct, 2008**

Furthermore, in employment law, most employers will require a confidentiality clause in the contract of employment. This means that healthcare employees may not divulge confidential information without risking breaching their contract of employment. Litigation for defamation or libel (Scotland) is subject to the United Kingdom Defamation Acts 1996 and 2013, which have limited application to Scotland. If patient records are kept on a computer, the Computer Misuse Act 1990 requires secure storage of such information.

The main statutes regulating this area are the Data Protection Act (DPA) 1988, which regulated the storage of paper (both typed and hand-written) records, and the Data Protection Act (DPA) 1998 (which has largely replaced the 1988 Act), giving patients access to all personal data in general and electronic records specifically. Importantly, this statute also created the role of the Information Commissioner's Office (ICO), with one commissioner for England and Wales and one for Scotland. The ICO has legal powers to enforce tighter controls and to ensure that organizations comply with the requirements of the DPA 1998. It is important to note that these powers are focused on ensuring that organizations meet the obligations of the act.

The data protection powers of the Information Commissioner's Office are to

- *… conduct assessments to check organisations are complying with the Act;*
- *serve information notices requiring organisations to provide the Information Commissioner's Office with specified information within a certain time period;*
- *serve enforcement notices and 'stop now' orders where there has been a breach of the Act, requiring organisations to take (or refrain from taking) specified steps in order to ensure they comply with the law;*
- *prosecute those who commit criminal offences under the (DPA) 1998 Act;*
- *conduct audits to assess whether organisations processing of personal data follows good practice; and*
- *to report to Parliament on data protection issues of concern.*
  **ICO, 2013, http://www.ico.gov.uk/what_we_cover/data_
  protection/legislation_in_full.aspx**

The Access to Health Records Act 1990 (Access to Health Records [Northern Ireland] Order 1993) which used to give a patient access to their records, has now been largely repealed and replaced by the DPA 1998, and covers only release of records in respect of deceased persons (where litigation may follow). Patient's representatives may be charged for access to records. Furthermore, under the DPA 1998, a patient or their representative has free access if they wish to view records only, but has pay much for copies of manual records. Additionally, the Freedom of Information Act 2000 (Scotland, 2002) provides for

(1) any person making a request for information to a public authority is entitled –

(a) to be informed in writing by the public authority whether it holds information of the description specified in the request, and

(b) if that is the case, to have that information communicated to him.

Freedom of Information Act 2000

Section 3 of the Public Records Act 1958 (Public Records (Scotland) Act 1937, Public Records Act (Northern Ireland) 1923 and Government of Wales Act 1998, article 167) allows exceptions to disclosure of records. Records may only be disclosed on three grounds (NMC, 2010):

- if this is in the interest of public health as provided by statute,
- for the protection of persons (including the patient) 'at risk of significant harm'
- when ordered to do so by a court of law.

Furthermore, subject to Section 60 of the Health and Social Care Act 2001, the Secretary of State for Health may authorize use of patient and authorized health service bodies to disclose patient-identifiable information. Section 61 of the same statute established the Patient Information Advisory Group to monitor use of patient information. This includes data which is patient identifiable if this is deemed necessary for supporting essential National Health Service (NHS) activity or if this is in the public interest.

The Caldicott Report (1997) and its principles aimed at setting out the highest practical standards for handling confidential information, and therefore apply equally to all routine and ad hoc flows of patient information, whether clinical or non-clinical, in manual or electronic format. These must also be easily identifiable (HSC 1998/89), implementing the recommendations of the Caldicott Report (1997) which recommended further guidance in the area of record keeping summarized in six principles:

Principle 1: Justify the purpose.

Principle 2: Don't use patient-identifiable information unless it is necessary.

Principle 3: Use the minimum necessary patient-identifiable information.

Principle 4: Access to patient-identifiable information should be on a strict need-to-know basis.

> *Principle 5: Everyone with access to patient-identifiable information should be aware of their responsibilities.*
> *Principle 6: Understand and comply with the law.*
>
> **Data Protection Act 1998**

These principles, combined with national and local guidance, should provide a framework of quality standards. The security and safe storage of healthcare records should be the responsibility of locally appointed Caldicott guardians whose responsibility will be the management of confidentiality as well as access to personal information (DoH, 1997). These guidelines have since been adopted for safeguarding public records. The Freedom of Information Act 2000, giving access to information held by public authorities, may not be used for access to patient-identifiable information.

COMMUNICATION AND RECORD KEEPING

Any team of professionals needs effective communication in order to function effectively and efficiently. Communication may be defined as follows:

> *The word 'communication' embraces a wide range of meanings centering to the concept of sharing. It includes the means as well as the ends of human intercourse.... Communication is one person giving a message to another. Communication is essentially a dialogue: it takes two to communicate.*
>
> **Adair, 1984**

It has been suggested that communication involves both 'a monologue' and 'a dialogue' (Adair, 1984, p. 154). Records become the outward evidence of communication. The generation and maintenance of good quality records can be evidence of the provision of good quality care. Multidisciplinary teams of professionals caring for the same group of patients will benefit from sharing good communication in the form of records, whether verbal or written. The latter nevertheless has the advantage of being more reliable, as it is permanent. Another underlying rationale for ensuring quality record keeping is as evidence of (NMC, 2013):

- high standards of clinical care,
- continuity of care,
- better communication and dissemination of information between members of the interprofessional healthcare team,

- an accurate account of the treatment and care planning and delivery,
- the ability to detect (and monitor) problems, such as changes in the patient's or client's condition, at an early stage.

Due to the importance of the nature of their work, nurses and other healthcare professionals must ensure that the quality of their work is more substantive through documentation of the relevant aspects of communication, rather than reliance on verbal messages, which may become distorted. Any set standards, found in both national and local guidance, must be adhered to. Many systems of work usually have their own relevant formats or templates (with certain criteria required), such as frameworks or tools for ease of information gathering, e.g. for carrying out nursing assessments documentation.

The recording of any professional care activities and related communication must therefore be informative and accurate for it to have any meaningful effect on care.

The RCN (2012) summarizes the key principles of record keeping as follows:

- *All records must be signed, timed and dated if handwritten. If computer held, they must be traceable to the person who provided the care that is being documented.*
- *Records must be clear and accurate, and provide information about the care given and arrangements for future and ongoing care.*
- *Jargon and speculation should be avoided.*
- *When possible, the person in your care should be involved in the record keeping and should be able to understand the language used.*
- *Records should be readable when photocopied or scanned.*
- *In the rare case of needing to alter a record the original entry must remain visible (draw a single line through the record) and the new entry must be signed, timed and dated.*
- *Records must not be destroyed unless you have been authorised to do so.*

RCN, 2012

The importance of effective communication in nursing is underpinned by the need for professionals who are responsible for care to share information with colleagues or other healthcare professionals providing direct or indirect care. This is vital for delivery of care, effectiveness and continuity.

Record keeping is central to communication between the nurse and the patient as well as professional colleagues. It is therefore important that this is done to a high standard.

MISAPPROPRIATION AND PATIENTS' PROPERTY

The topic under discussion is sometimes included under the general heading of 'abuse' when considering vulnerable individuals. It is important for the nurse to recognize and understand the nature of theft. The principle of theft in criminal law is the same, whether the theft is from the employer or from vulnerable patients. At times, this may pose some difficulty in cases of abuse when breach of the patient's human rights may include property rights. As the effect is not always obvious until discovery, this offence may go undetected for some time, especially in the case of vulnerable patients. This chapter also considers the grey areas where gifts may be inappropriate. Theft and fraud are both criminal law offences and are best addressed as separate entities from the general 'abuse' heading.

The standard definition of theft is

> *A person is guilty of theft if he dishonestly appropriates property belonging to another with the intention of permanently depriving the other of it and 'thief' and 'steal' shall be construed accordingly.*
> **Section 1 of Theft Act 1968**

Property is defined as

> *(1) 'Property' includes money and all other property, real or personal, including things in action and other intangible property.*
> **Section 4(1) of Theft Act 1968**

In law, the term 'property' should be taken in the broadest sense (Dennis, 2012). This will also include a person's financial affairs such as money and shares. As a professional, the NMC Code of Conduct expects that the nurse be trustworthy as part of their duty of care (NMC, 2008). Most trusts have a clear policy of safeguarding patients' property. As their capacity may be impaired through illness, a patient may easily lose their valuable property without being aware.

In most people's minds, there exists a very clear concept of the moral obligations and implications of an owner's rights, and of 'theft' and its impact on society at large. Beyond the ordinary meaning of ethics or a consensus of moral connotations of 'theft' in most societies, this word is also associated with fraudulent behaviour, deliberate deception or a lack of probity, dishonesty, cheating and lying. Also, the use of some undue influence in order to gain advantage of another person, especially where there is a breach of trust as in a caring relationship, may amount to the generic term of 'theft'.

The letter of the law may be followed in the court's ability to redress the imbalance by punishing the offender and/or compensating the victim. Punishment of the perpetrator is achieved indirectly in criminal law by paying their (the offender's) debt to society, although not automatically providing the victim of crime with direct redress. The victim may be awarded compensation through the Criminal Injuries Compensation Authority if there is any injury associated with the crime. In addition, they may also seek damages for personal injuries through the civil courts themselves. A victim who feels that justice has not been done may pursue a private criminal prosecution. Unfortunately, this may prove difficult and costly for most people.

A nurse or other carer may resort to theft or fraudulent behaviour, if motivated by corruption, greed or simply a lack of moral consideration, principles or integrity. The use of different terminology, i.e. 'theft' or 'fraud', to describe what could be the same crime may lead to confusion, even for the courts, as is demonstrated by the case of *Ghosh* below.

Theft or fraud

In criminal law, a crime consists of two elements, namely the mens rea, 'a guilty mind', and the actus reus, 'a guilty act'. It is a prerequisite for both elements to be present for any crime to be established (Jefferson, 2007). The main elements of the above offences are similar but not identical. The elements of theft will be discussed more specifically.

The act of theft involves coming into possession of goods belonging to another without the knowledge or permission of the owner. This paints a picture of goods being obtained by stealth or secretively, that is without the overt knowledge of the owner. The mens rea or guilty intention is 'dishonesty' and 'the intention to permanently deprive' the other. The actus reus or guilty act of theft is 'the appropriation of property belonging to another'.

Fraud, on the other hand, is usually more discrete, but achieved through deception, trickery or under 'false pretences'. Goods are handed over to the perpetrator, usually with the knowledge and apparent 'consent' of the victim. The problem is that if the respondent can prove that this consent was given by a person who is deemed by the court to be 'of sound mind', then there is no guilty mind and therefore no crime of fraud or theft. On the other hand, if a nurse has acquired an 'inappropriate gift' or 'loan' from a patient or their representatives, even if this was with the owner's permission, they may be in breach of paragraphs 7.4 and 7.5 of the Code of Conduct (NMC, 2008).

The guilty intention and the guilty act for the fraud offence are very similar to the ones for theft, apart from the way this is achieved. The result is the same. These offences fall under the provisions in Sections 1 and 15 of the Theft Act 1968, respectively. Where a defendant to a charge of theft alleges that in assuming the right to the property, they believed that the owner did consent to the 'appropriation' of goods, they may find themselves facing a charge not of 'theft' but of 'fraud' under Section 3 of the 1968 Act. The principle is illustrated in the following case in Fionda and Bryant (2003, pp. 59–60).

R v Ghosh [1982] 75 CR App R 154

A surgeon who was acting as a locum consultant at a hospital falsely represented that he had carried out surgical operations and claimed payment. Someone else under the NHS had in fact carried out the operations. The defendant was convicted of obtaining property by deception.

The Court of Appeal held that 'in determining whether the defendant was acting dishonestly, the jury had first to consider whether, according to the standards of the ordinary reasonable person, what was done was dishonest. If it was, the jury must then consider whether the defendant himself must have realised that what he was doing was dishonest by the standards of the ordinary reasonable person'.

Within a caring environment, it is possible for a vulnerable patient to be a victim of fraud rather than theft, although theft is also possible. The effect nevertheless is the same – a breach of patients' rights to their property. Fraud is usually carried out through deception or dishonesty, which means that it is possible to establish the owner's consent. The owner is somehow tricked or misled by some action into giving up their property for the benefit of the thief. This aspect of the theft offence is now covered by Section 15A of the Theft Act. This section was inserted by the Theft (Amendment) Act 1996. It provides for a person to be guilty of an offence if 'by deception they dishonestly obtain a money transfer for himself or another and included false accounting'. Obtaining a pecuniary (monetary) advantage, by deception, falls under Section 16 of Theft Act 1968. The obtaining of services by deception and evasion of liability by deception fall under Sections 1 and 2 of Theft Act 1978, respectively. The principle of law that has come to be known as the *Ghosh* test was first applied in *R* v *Ghosh* [1982].

While theft, on conviction, carries a maximum prison sentence of 7 years, fraud can invoke a longer term of 10 years. The heavier sentence is reflected by the fact that fraud often involves higher and substantial sums of money or property, and it may be difficult to detect the crime, especially if the money or assets have been spent by the time the fraud is discovered. the effect on the victim nevertheless is likely to be the same.

A British crime survey (2005–6) showed that 29 per cent of crime was 'other theft'. When broken down as recorded by the police, it was shown that while 'other crime' accounted for 23 per cent of the crime, fraud and forgery amounted to 4 per cent. The Law Revision Committee (1968) acknowledged the difficulty of recognizing theft (Jefferson, 2001).

TRUST AND PATIENTS' PROPERTY RIGHTS

Moral philosophy tries to set the boundaries for merits or demerits of certain human actions such as theft or fraud. Professional ethics follow these and would view any justification of theft or fraud involving disadvantaged patients not only as unacceptable but also as 'unprofessional', in no uncertain terms. Consensus in most societies would agree that theft should never be condoned, and there is no doubt that this is a violation of individual rights. When patients are ill, they may lack the capacity for decision-making or simply lack any will to safeguard their own rights. Incapacity may be temporary, for example, due to the environment or

---

Case study – working while 'off sick'

Staff nurse Mary was off sick from work, but she was not too ill to go to the local supermarket. It was what she did there that was the problem: she walked straight past the aisles of food and drink and into the back office, where she worked with a private GP as a locum nurse for the staff and management. In a year's absence because of a back-related illness, Mary had assisted with fitness tests for the Ministry of Defence, as well as working at a local private hospital. During all this time, she was receiving sick pay from her employer – effectively being paid twice.

The health board not only paid Mary's salary but also had to pay for an agency nurse to cover her post. When Mary was confronted, she claimed not to know that she wasn't allowed to work elsewhere, but the judge didn't agree. Mary lost her job, gained a criminal conviction, had to appear before a professional disciplinary committee and was ordered to pay back the money she had stolen.

(Based on a real case)

What could have prevented this fraud?

Mary's manager had not followed health board's procedures for managing long-term absences. These were based around concern for staff welfare and would also have identified that Mary did not really have a condition which made work impossible. When Mary began working at the health body, the sickness policy was not explained to her at induction – she hadn't been told specifically that she could not work elsewhere, even though it was plain that she could not. In this case, clear rules that were properly explained could have deterred a long-term fraud that squandered NHS resources.

From NHS Business Service Authority, http://www.nhsbsa.nhs.uk/CounterFraud/Documents/CounterFraud/working_while_off_sick.pdf (accessed August 2013).

the medication, or permanent, which may be due to ageing or to disease processes. They should therefore expect nurses to whose care they are entrusted to 'be trustworthy' and 'act to identify and minimise risk to patients and clients' (NMC, 2008, paragraph 7).

Nurses and other healthcare professionals are obliged to consult their professional codes of conduct for direction as well as relevant local policies and guidelines in order to ensure that a patient's property rights are not eroded. In a criminal court, the evidence in the areas of the theft and fraud offences can prove to be difficult to establish, as this may take part in secret. In response, a defendant may allege that he or she honestly

> (a) *believes that they had a legal right to deprive the victim of the property.*
> (b) *believes the victim would have consented to the appropriation of the property if he had known of the circumstances.*
> (c) *finds or otherwise appropriates property when he believes that the owner, possessor or controller cannot be reasonably found.*
>
> **Section 2(1) of Theft Act 1968**

It may be difficult to establish theft due to the relationship of trust. This, however, is open to abuse as the following case illustrates, where a nursing home matron swindled sick and dying patients out of more than £100,000 to fund her extravagant luxury lifestyle. The home matron treated herself to exotic holidays, designer clothes and hundreds of pounds of jewellery as she bled dry the bank accounts of her terminally ill and mentally handicapped patients (*Daily Mail*, 2006).

While a nurse is expected to maintain professional boundaries within a therapeutic relationship, the fact is that this may sometimes be compromised by a close relationship with a patient or their next of kin. It is important therefore that while advocating for the patient, nurses maintain a neutral position and maintain professional boundaries. Should they suspect a colleague of deception, through fraudulently obtaining property from a patient, or by accepting inappropriate gifts from patients, they have a duty to report it.

THINKING POINT

Mrs X, aged 78, was admitted from home following a collapse to the same medical ward where her husband had been a patient for many months previously. The couple was childless and has been married for 54 years. The ambulance paramedics handed in three deposit account bankbooks containing substantial sums and a holdall with £18 655 in cash – they asked the police to check the total of their 'discovery'. Mrs X, who is not normally confused, now says that £3000 of her money is missing. The only people with access to her property are a distant but seemingly caring niece and 'friendly and very helpful' neighbours, a young couple in their thirties. They are both unemployed, and Mrs X's niece, who is the next-of-kin (and who lives abroad), is worried that the neighbours have been spending a lot of time at her auntie's house doing domestic chores. Mrs X also said that over time valuable ornaments had gone missing, but because her neighbours had been so good to her she did not want to cause any trouble.

1. Consider your employer's policy on patients' property.
2. In the above case, consider what action you would take.

CAPACITY AND SAFEGUARDING PATIENTS' PROPERTY RIGHTS

Some patients may be physically or psychologically dependent, and may therefore become a potential victim of theft or fraud from carers. A lack of capacity to consent may also impact on capacity to manage their property. A confused patient is more vulnerable when it comes to safe storage and custody of their property. Hence, the nurse should follow their local policy to ensure that when their (patients') property rights are compromised, they should be prepared to act, insofar as is reasonably practicable and to the best of their knowledge. This threat may come from a patient's family, friends or colleagues. It is the financial aspect where patients are most vulnerable. While there is generally a presumption in law that every individual adult and child should be allowed to make decisions involving their financial assets, it has often been the case that some patients may not be in a position to do so due to their physical or mental incapacity. Such a vulnerable person may therefore be at risk of theft or fraud involving money or other property (Langan, cited in Brayne and Carr, 2010).

As a key healthcare professional, the nurse should be able to identify any signs of financial or property abuse. The patient may choose to confide in them or they may witness in conversation with people close to the patient that something unusual has taken place. The difficulty a nurse has in reporting fraud may be the lack of evidence. Nevertheless, when they have reasonable suspicion of theft or fraud it is best to voice their concerns to senior colleagues or their line manager and document this fact, in case it is required as evidence in future. The nurse has a duty to raise and escalate concerns (NMC, 2010). Other members of the multidisciplinary team should also be involved in any ensuing investigation. Owing to their statutory powers and function, a social worker is usually the key person to lead the process of investigation and reporting. They may resort to informal or formal methods for protection of victims of theft or fraud (Brayne and Carr, 2010). The protections of patients' rights is often triggered by any member of the multidisciplinary team and led by the social worker through application of possible remedies which are open to the team, and these may be formal or informal. Informal protection measures should be implemented with the agreement of the patient, family members and multidisciplinary team members where theft or fraud is suspected. Similarly:

Social workers will

a. *Give priority to maintaining the best interests of service users, with due regard to the interests of others;*

b. *In exceptional circumstances where the priority of the service user's interest is outweighed by the need to protect others or by legal requirements, make service users aware that their interests may be overridden;*

c. *Seek to safeguard and promote the rights and interests of service users whenever possible;*

d. *Endeavour to ensure service users' maximum participation in decisions about their lives when impairment or ill-health require the social worker or another person to act on their behalf;*

e. *Not reject service users or lose concern for their suffering, even when obliged to protect themselves or others against them or to acknowledge their inability to help them.*

British Association of Social Workers, 2012, paragraph 4.1.1

Often this saves time and 'red tape' before going down the formal route; it is best to follow local policies or guidelines (which must take cognizance of the law), in ensuring that the patient's best interests are served. The government introduced the Protection of Vulnerable Adults (POVA) Guidance in July 2004 and the Protection of Vulnerable Groups Act 2006 and the Protection of Vulnerable Groups (Scotland) Act (2007), with the aim of protecting vulnerable people in care settings. This requires social services departments up and down the country to hold an offenders' register, which can disclose any individual's history of abuse to employers. This is in addition to the Criminal Records Bureau, which was run by the Home Office. The Protection of Freedoms Act 2012 Disclosure and Barring Service (DBS) merged with Independent Safeguarding Authority (ISA), and allows safer recruitment by organisations looking after vulnerable people aiming to identify individuals who may be unsuitable for caring for vulnerable adults, and children. DBS was formed in 2012 by merging the functions of the Criminal Records Bureau under the Protection of Freedoms Act 2012 (see Chapter 3). This is also responsible for vetting and barring potential employees before they are engaged. In practice, it may be quite difficult to gather evidence if the victim is unwilling to make a complaint (due to fear of victimization or if they lack the capacity to do so). The protection of children comes under separate legislation, and this is dealt with in Chapter 3, 'The Beginning of Life to Adulthood: Human Rights'. The priority should be to support the victims before and during the prosecution of the perpetrator.

One appropriate response to suspected financial/property abuse is the compulsory removal of an incapacitated victim to a place of safety if

(a) *they are suffering from grave chronic disease or being aged, infirm or physically incapacitated, are living in unsanitary conditions and*
(b) *are unable to devote to themselves … are not receiving from other persons, proper care and attention.*
Section 47 of National Assistance Act 1948

This could then make it more difficult for any fraud to continue. For individuals with mental incapacity, Section 94(2) of the Mental Health Act 1983 defines a 'patient' as 'a person who on medical evidence is incapable, by reason of mental disorder, of managing and administering his property and affairs'. Over a period of time, the courts have seen as one of their roles the protection of rights of those who lack mental capacity. As a result the system of receivership has been developed, which allows the court to appoint an appropriate person who may be a solicitor, spouse or family member who has cared for a patient, a local authority employee or a friend, to manage their affairs

(Rule 7(1) of the Court of Protection Rules 2001). This person is accountable to the courts and is required to submit financial reports periodically.

The Mental Capacity Act 2005 (MCA 2005) came into force from April 2007, thus empowering patients and strengthening current rules. The equivalent Scottish statute is the Adults with Incapacity (Scotland) Act 2000. Under the MCA 2005 the guiding principles for determining capacity are

(1) The following principles apply for the purposes of this Act.

(2) A person must be assumed to have capacity unless it is established that he lacks capacity.

(3) A person is not to be treated as unable to make a decision unless all practicable steps to help him to do so have been taken without success.

(4) A person is not to be treated as unable to make a decision merely because he makes an unwise decision.

(5) An act done or decision made, under this Act for or on behalf of a person who lacks capacity must be done, or made, in his best interests.

(6) Before the act is done, or the decision is made, regard must be had to whether the purpose for which it is needed can be as effectively achieved in a way that is less restrictive of the person's rights and freedom of action.

Section 1 of MCA 2005

THINKING POINT

Mrs X is a 50-year-old widow who has suffered from multiple sclerosis for the last 6 years and has increasingly become dependent on two regular carers for personal care. She is sometimes incontinent and needs helps with washing and dressing, requiring care twice a day. Her son, who lives abroad, suspects that Angela, who is one of her trusted regular carers, has been regularly withdrawing large sums of money without his mother's consent and she does not always provide receipts for shopping. Unbeknown to the son, Angela has a criminal record but has managed to get this job through an agency, which failed to check her credentials on engaging her.

What advice would you give to Mrs X's son?

The Mental Capacity Act (MCA) 2005 is applicable on assessment of a person's capacity, which should be based on a 'decision-specific' test.

- *A presumption of capacity – every adult has the right to make his or her own decisions and must be assumed to have capacity to do so unless it is proved otherwise.*

- *The right for individuals to be supported to make their own decisions – people must be given all appropriate help before anyone concludes that they cannot make their own decisions.*
- *That individuals must retain the right to make what might be seen as eccentric or unwise decisions.*
- *Best interests – anything done for or on behalf of people without capacity must be in their best interests.*
- *Least restrictive intervention – anything done for or on behalf of people without capacity should be the least restrictive of their basic rights and freedoms.*

Section 1 of Mental Capacity Act 2005

There is now no presumption of incapacity based on a patient's medical condition or state of mind (Section 2 of MCA 2005). In any decision-making where the patient lacks capacity their 'best interests' must be considered. The above principles are seen as key to providing new safeguards for people lacking in capacity.

One example of protection of the vulnerable patient (who lacks capacity) based on Scots law is the Mental Health (Care and Treatment) (Scotland) Act 2003. Guardianship is addressed in Chapter 5, Section 7, which states that the guardian, and only the guardian herself or himself, has the power to

- require the person to live at a particular place,
- require the person to go to specific places at specific times for the purpose of medical treatment.

This is nevertheless subject to

2) *The functions of the judge under this Part of this Act shall be exercisable where, after considering medical evidence, he is satisfied that a person is incapable, by reason of mental disorder, of managing and administering his property and affairs; and a person as to whom the judge is so satisfied is referred to in this Part of this Act as a patient.*

Section 94(2) of the Mental Health Act 1983

This section would also allow a judge to administer a decision regarding administering such a patient's property under Section 95 of the same statute.

Section 46 of the MCA 2005 introduces new provisions for the Court of Protection, giving special wider powers to the Court of Protection for deciding on matters related to a patient's incapacity. In Scotland the Adults with Incapacity Act (2008) applies. In the same vein, the Mental Health Act 2007 aims to redefine treatment of those who need treatment while improving the safeguarding of individuals who lack capacity, for example, involuntary commitment, only if 'appropriate treatment' is available. This statute also provides for healthcare advocates or proxies (Scotland) and for supervised community treatment. This provides the power for a supervised discharge with power to return a non-compliant patient to a hospital for compulsory treatment.

For those with mental capacity, they may choose to appoint a financial 'advocate' to manage their affairs when they lack the capacity to choose. There are two main categories: ordinary power of attorney and lasting power of attorney.

Ordinary power of attorney

In this category, a person may choose any person whom they so wish to represent them. When the patient loses their capacity for decision-making, a representative to whom such power is delegated subsequently has the power to make decisions on their behalf. In law, there is a presumption that any decisions they make will be in the best interests of the person they represent. In addition, the person who delegates this power may revoke this power at any time.

Lasting power of attorney

A solicitor is normally required for verifying the wishes of the person drawing up a legal deed and their capacity to do so. A person chosen to manage their financial affairs will have the right to carry out any necessary transactions should the person drawing up the deed lose their mental capacity. The physical or mental incapacity may be due to illness.

Court of Protection (Sections 93–98 of Mental Health Act 1983)

This is required for individuals who lack mental capacity and is the most appropriate route for safeguarding their interests. An application to the court must be supported by consultant medical opinion in the relevant documents of the patient's state of mind. If the court accepts this, it appoints a 'receiver' who is answerable to the court. One way of safeguarding the interests of a vulnerable person is the requirement for accounts to be submitted to the court periodically. The Court of Protection has nevertheless, not without criticism, been seen as 'archaic, bureaucratic, and disempowering' (Lush, 2001, p. 239).

GIFTS, STRINGS ATTACHED AND PROFESSIONAL ETHICS

The issue of accepting gifts is not always clear-cut for some healthcare professionals; for example, research by Levene and Stirling (1980, cited in Lyckholm, 1998) found that 20 per cent of doctors from different specialties admitted receiving gifts from patients. Nurses, however, as healthcare professionals are expected to respect the patient's property and not take any personal rewards.

> 7.4 *You must refuse any gift, favour, or hospitality that might be interpreted, now or in the future, as an attempt to obtain preferential consideration.*
> 7.5 *You must neither ask for nor accept loans from patients, clients or their relatives and friends.*
>
> **NMC, 2008**

The danger in accepting gifts, often given as a sign of appreciation of the care that has been given, is that even if the patient's intention is genuine, it is possible that a healthcare professional who accepts 'gifts' from a patient they have been looking after may subsequently find their position compromised. A conflict of interest may arise, and when clinical judgements are required to be made, they may be expected to return 'favours' or to give the patient preferential treatment. A difficult situation is created when such gifts are given in advance of treatment. It is often difficult to draw the line between the usual festive 'box of chocolates for the nurses' as a blanket donation to all staff and specific gifts aimed at individual nurses (Griffith, 2003). On the other hand, gifts which are given for the benefit of a group of staff are probably easier to reconcile with the standards expected of a registered nurse in this area (NMC, 2008). In addition, there will be trust policies in place, breach of which may result in disciplinary action for the nurse who accepts individual gifts from patients.

The therapeutic relationship between a nurse and a patient is based on trust, and this may put patients in a position that is open to exploitation.

It is important therefore that the nurse's relationship with patients should be seen to have transparency at all times (Dudley, 2002).

CONCLUSION

Theft brings to mind the concept of being perpetrated by strangers through 'stealth', while fraud should more easily be noticed or suspected by clinicians due to 'unusual arrangements'. It is a fact of life nevertheless that fraudulent or dishonest acts of appropriation take place because of the imbalance of power in relation to vulnerable patients. The effect is a breach of the patient's rights. Worse still for the patient may be the long-term effects of the trauma if this breach is in a therapeutic relationship and by someone they trusted. The likelihood of the crime of theft or fraud within a caring relationship is real; the temptation to accept inappropriate gifts is also real. Property-related offences comprise a substantial proportion of crime – hence the need to intervene on behalf of the patient, especially where they are vulnerable. The challenge for the nurse therefore is that 'it is the respectable offender who provides the most interesting illustration of why and how fraudsters frequently care not to be perceived as real criminals' (Ashe and Counsel, 1993, p. 178, cited in Wilson, 2006). The worrying thing is that the real extent of these problems may never be known due to victims' reluctance or inability to report the matter. It is therefore important for health authorities to ensure that robust policies are in place to safeguard the property rights of patients, especially those who are vulnerable.

REFERENCES

Adair J. The skills of leadership. Aldershot; Gower Publishing Company Limited, 1984.

Brayne H, Carr H. *Back to law for social workers*, 8th ed. Oxford: Oxford University Press, 2010.

British Association of Social Workers. Code of ethics. 2012, paragraph 4.1.1(c). www.basw.co.uk (accessed 23 August 2013).

Daily Mail. 2006. www.dailymail.co.uk/pages/live/articles/news/news.html?in_article_id 5 401506&in_page_id51770 (accessed 23 September 2013).

Dennis J. *Textbook of criminal law*, 3rd ed. London: Sweet & Maxwell, 2012.

Department of Health (Caldicott Committee). *The Caldicott Report*. 1997. https://www.gov.uk/government/organisations/department-of-health.

Department of Health. *The protection and use of patient information: guidance from the Department of Health*. HSG (96)18. DoH, 1996.

Dudley N. Dishonest doctors should not continue to practise. *BMJ* 2002; 324: 547.

Fionda J, Bryant M. *Brief case on criminal law*, 3rd ed. London: Cavendish Publishing, 2003.

Fletcher L, Buka P. *A legal framework for caring, law and ethics for nurses*. Basingstoke: Palgrave, 1999.

Griffith R. Generosity or stealing? When accepting a gift can be theft. *British Journal of Community Nursing* 2003; 8: 512–14.

Jefferson M. *Criminal law*, 5th ed. London: Longman, 2007.

Lyckholm L. Should physicians accept gifts from patients? *JAMA* 1998; 280: 1994–96.

Lush D. Partnership in action. In Cull L, Roche J, eds., *The law, social work practice and elder abuse*. Basingstoke: Palgrave, 2001.

NHS Business Service Authority. http://www.nhsbsa.nhs.uk/CounterFraud/Documents/CounterFraud/working_while_off_sick.pdf (accessed 20 September 2013).

NMC. *Record keeping, guidance for nurses and midwives*. 2010. http://www.nmc-uk.org/Documents/NMC-publications/NMC-Record-Keeping-Guidance.pdf.

Nursing and Midwifery Council. Nursing and Midwifery Order 2001 (SI 2002/253) (the order). 2002.

Nursing and Midwifery Council. *Professional code of conduct and ethics*. London: NMC, 2008.

Nursing and Midwifery Council. *Raising and escalating complaints, guidance for nurses and midwives*. 2010. www.nmc-uk.org/publications (accessed 23 September 2013).

Nursing and Midwifery Council. Guidelines for records and record keeping. NMC, 2013.

RCN. Record keeping – the facts. 2012. http://www.rcn.org.uk/__data/assets/pdf_file/0005/476753/Record_keeping_cards_V5.pdf.

Wilson S. Law, morality and regulations: victimization experiences of financial crime. *British Journal of Criminology* 2006; 46: 1073–90.

CONSENT TO TREATMENT
AND MENTAL CAPACITY

INTRODUCTION

This chapter will consider the nature and relevance of consent as well as the exceptions, when a patient is deemed to lack consent. What happens in cases where a patient lacks mental capacity, and can necessity ever be justified as a valid defence for healthcare professionals who may be challenged for breach of human rights (Human Rights Act 1998, Article 3)? What are the requirements for validity of consent? This raises some ethical or moral issues not only about the patient's autonomy, but also about the expected impact of beneficence and non-maleficence of nursing actions, which includes ensuring that consent is properly obtained. The patients should always be presumed to have the competence/mental capacity (related to cognition) to choose – until established otherwise – and consent must always be obtained, or instead provided, in the patient's best interest and within a relevant legal framework. One example is sectioning a client under the Mental Health Act 1983.

NATURE OF CONSENT

The concept of consent goes to the heart of ethics and the issues of human freedom and autonomy to make decisions. This includes the ability to make informed choices about our lives as well as any necessary treatment.

A patient receiving care may be in a vulnerable position if their judgement is impaired in some way. This means that there should be no presumption that blanket consent to all forms of treatment is presumed once the patient is receiving treatment. It is therefore an important aspect of communication that, in normal circumstances, before any treatment, the nurse is very clear that the patient has consented before any treatment is provided. See paragraph 13 of the Nursing and Midwifery Council (NMC, 2008) on expected nursing standards for valid consent. One example is in invasive procedures such as inserting a nasogastric tube or administering an enema to a patient.

Because of fundamental human rights, the client should no longer depend on 'paternalism' for making a choice on treatment decision. Principlism and the ethical basis of treatment means that under the principle of beneficence, any treatment provided should benefit the patient, and the converse is maltreatment with the need to avoid futile treatment, as this could be maleficence (Beauchamp and Childress, 2012). All clients should receive fair treatment, and their right to choose falls under the principle of autonomy (Beauchamp and Childress, 2012).

They should have autonomy, which means that if they have capacity, they are entitled to make an informed choice (Article 8 of the Human Rights Act 1998). The nurse should be guided by a framework of consent, which should be found in the national guidelines as well as local protocol. Some of the key questions they should contemplate are

1. Which category of clients should have the right to consent?
2. How should life-threatening emergency situations be addressed when there may not be an opportunity to obtain consent?
3. What should happen when the client lacks consent?
4. Are there circumstances when consent may be overridden without breaching the client's rights?

Any undue influence is grounds for invalidating that consent (Doyal, 2002). Consent may be classified as

- Expressed – written or oral,
- Implicit – implied or tacit,
- General,
- Specific.

THINKING POINT

A patient is admitted for day stay surgery for a minor gynaecological procedure. This is, however, carried out under a general anaesthetic. Consider the role of the nurse in relation to consent.

What are the ethical and legal considerations for obtaining 'informed' consent?

What tools for determining mental capacity are in use in your workplace?

Expressed (or express) consent

This type of consent involves a clear expression by the patient of their wishes. Expressed or express consent must be explicit or the patient must be given the opportunity to openly express their agreement to the operation or examination and this may be either written or verbal.

> 2. *Consent is often wrongly equated with a patient's signature on a consent form. A signature on a form is evidence that the patient has given consent, but is not proof of valid consent. If a patient is rushed into signing a form, on the basis of too little information, the consent may not be valid, despite the signature. Similarly, if a patient has given valid verbal consent, the fact that they are physically unable to sign the form is no bar to treatment. Patients may, if they wish, withdraw consent after they have signed a form: the signature is evidence of the process of consent-giving, not a binding contract.*
>
> ### Department of Health, 2001a, updated in 2009

Consent may be written or verbal. Both forms are valid, although for evidence it is obviously better for consent to be in writing, as it may be difficult to establish verbal consent with the passage of time since a person may have a different recollection to events, for whatever reason. The use of a witness would be the only way of establishing this, should evidence of past consent need to be proved in a court of law. Problems may arise as a witness may forget the events, their recollection of events may change, they may move away to another job or may have died by the time a case comes to court. There is in fact no legal requirement for express consent to be in writing, as the patient may be unable to write but have the capacity to consent. If a patient is witnessed writing a mark such as an 'x' on the consent form, how easy or difficult is it to ascribe that signature to them at a later date?

For the consent to be valid, the patient must

- *be competent to take the particular decision;*
- *have received sufficient information to take it;*
- *not be acting under duress.*

Department of Health, 2001a, updated in 2009

Implicit or tacit consent

The presence of consent can also be established by inference of the conduct of the patient, although there may be difficulties in establishing this in retrospect. The term 'implicit' is more closely aligned to treatment, while 'tacit' is used in a much wider sense and is applied by moral philosophers such as Locke (Nozick, 1974). This type of consent is sometimes called 'tacit' as the patient does not need to verbally express this, only with action. This may also be open to abuse if treatment is provided on the erroneous assumption that the patient has given permission for treatment or examination; hence, it is important that the nurse should establish the fact that a patient is in agreement for a treatment intervention to go ahead.

Beatty v Cullingworth Q.B. Unreported
[1896] 44 CENT. L.J. 153 (s896)

The patient (who was a nurse) consented to removal of her right ovary, specifically telling the surgeon beforehand that if both ovaries were found to be diseased, neither should be removed. The surgeon said that she should leave that to him, to which she made no reply. At operation, both ovaries were removed as the left as well as the right was found to be diseased. When the case came to trial, the judge said, 'If a medical man undertook an operation, it was a humane thing for him to do everything in his power to remove the mischief.' The jury returned a verdict for the defendant (surgeon) despite the absence of consent.

From http://www.medicalprotection.org/uk/guide-to-consent-in-the-uk/appendix-3-required-reading.

An example of implied consent is where a patient is approached by a nurse with a syringe injection and they offer their hand as a sign that they are in agreement with the procedure being carried out. Compare and contrast the above case with the American case below (which is only persuasive and not binding in the UK courts), which illustrates this point.

> **O'Brien v Cunard SS Co. [1891] 28 NE 266**
>
> In this case an individual (on the defendant's ship) had stood in the queue and offered her arm for vaccination, and then subsequently testified that she did not wish to be vaccinated and had not given her consent. The courts held that there was implied consent – by willingly standing in the queue and offering her arm, and accordingly in a similar instance treatment would be justified.

A similar defence for a clinician may be allowed in court if they acted in the belief that the patient had been able to give consent by actively taking steps in acceptance of any treatment offered. The courts would also accept the use of reasonable intervening actions, which would be supported by the *Bolam* standards of practice (see Chapter 1, 'Concept of Law and Human Rights').

Blanket consent

This section considers the effectiveness of 'blanket' agreements for treatment to go ahead. The danger is that this may be open to challenge should the patient be given treatment without understanding it, or under false pretences. Although this sounds valid from a contractual point of view, there is the possibility of abuse with the patient's rights being overridden under Article 3 of Human Rights Act (HRA) 1998. It is, however, useful in a laparoscopy-type operation where the surgeon has the option to pursue either an alternative course of action or a more extensive operation should the outcome turn out to be different from that expected, as shown in the following case. It is possible that in the course of an exploratory operation a surgeon may find a condition other than the one he expected, which requires a more extensive operation. The patient should be warned of this possibility so that they may give consent prior to surgery. The implication of giving blanket consent is that clinicians cannot give any guarantee that the patient's rights will be ensured. In ordinary circumstances, informed consent must be obtained before any treatment. Exceptions to the rule are clearly laid out in Department of Health (2001b).

Specific consent

Any consent given by a patient must be related to the specific treatment or procedure without the discretion of the nurse to choose a completely different alternative, which may not have been agreed to by the patient.

The following case is authority for the view that a patient should be informed of the nature and extent of the proposed treatment or surgery.

> ### *Williamson* v *East London* and *City Health Authority,* HA [1998], Lloyds Reports, Med 6, [1990] 41, British Medical Law Reports 85
>
> The plaintiff had previously been given silicone gel breast implants at the age of 30 for cosmetic reasons and subsequently developed multiple lumps, which the surgeon associated with a leak from the silicone implant. The plaintiff, having consented to breast surgery silicone replacement and lump excision only, was nevertheless given instead a more radical operation. Having developed multiple lumps, a radical mastectomy operation was performed, without her consent. The court found that there had been no prior explanation by the surgeon and that the patient had not consented to the extensive surgery. She was awarded damages of £20,000 for pain and suffering as a result of the 'negligent' action in failing to obtain consent to the operation performed.

THINKING POINT

A young woman in her late twenties is admitted for a minor gynaecological procedure under a general anaesthetic. How is consent obtained for a range of clinical procedures in your workplace?

CONSENT AND HUMAN RIGHTS

The concept of paternalism has been at the centre of traditional medicine and nursing, with the patient being a small player and not questioning clinical judgements of which he or she is on the receiving end. However, difficulties and ethical issues arise when doctors and nurses start to impose their own values on others who may not share those (Campbell et al., 2001). The general public is now more aware of rights and has access to information from sources such as the media and the Internet. More recently, Article 8(1) of the HRA 1998 asserts that 'everyone has the right to respect for his private and family life, his home and his correspondence'. This article gives individuals some 'moral autonomy' (Hoffman and Rowe, 2013). Thus, for the nurse, safeguarding the patient's autonomy and their entitlement to self-determination through consent to treatment is important. There are, however, exceptions, for example, in infectious disease where maintaining privacy may be putting the public at risk (Public Health (Control of Diseases) Act 1984, as amended by the Health and Social Care Act 2008).

*In a treatment setting 'informed' refers to the choice of useful thera-
pies, usefulness being a professional decision. The informing process
needs a good relationship between patient and doctor. In a research
setting the principles are also generally agreed: The risks must not be
disproportionate; and the patient (or guardian in some psychiatric
settings) has to give informed consent. The first applies also where
consent is not possible but here, determinations of risks and of benefits to self and others have to have the protection of the law.*

WHO, 2003

Within a therapeutic relationship, the patient has a right to informed
consent before treatment. This means that a sufficient degree of information must be given to allow them to make a balanced judgement as to
whether to accept treatment or not. The role of the nurse should be to
facilitate this process for the patient by empowering them to make decisions affecting their treatment. It is possible that a patient may not wish
to receive such information, but nevertheless, the nurse must provide the
patient with that opportunity to seek any clarification for treatment and
the opportunity to give consent or to decline treatment.

The issue of autonomy has been at the heart of the debate for philosophers such as Immanuel Kant (1724–1804), who recognized that
people have a natural right to choose because they have a free will (the
categorical imperative), which every thinking human being is assumed
to have by nature. Others, such as John Stuart Mill (1806–73), have also
suggested that autonomy is a natural human freedom of the expression
of one's opinion as well as to live in a way that expresses 'individuality'
(Mill, 1993). The ethical basis of autonomy is the right to 'respect' a person's right to self-determination (Blackburn, 2001). This principle is applicable to the treatment environment, that is, allowing the patient to choose
treatment, and this was recognized in law in the following landmark case.

**Schloendorff v Society of New York Hospital 211 NY;
105 NE 92, 93 [1914]; 106 NE 93; NY [1914]**

A woman had consented to an abdominal examination under anaesthesia but not to
a surgical operation. Knowing this to be the case the surgeon went ahead to operate
and remove a tumour. The patient sued for battery. Justice Cardozo's opinion
(p. 304) expressed what has now become the foundation for the concept of informed
consent and for an individual patient's right of autonomy and self-determination:
'Every human being of adult years and sound mind has a right to determine what shall
be done with his own body; and a surgeon who performs an operation without his
patient's consent commits an assault for which he is liable in damages.'

Autonomy is a basic human right in ethics and in law, and this is central to consent as human beings have the capacity to weigh the facts before them and make a considered choice (Furrow, 2005). Following the above legal principle, autonomy is also seen as the ability or capacity to weigh the options and then choose moral alternatives (Thompson et al., 2006). The patient has a basic right to autonomy, which is defined in law. When this right is infringed, it is therefore the patient's prerogative to choose to accept or to decline treatment, knowing that the consequences may be detrimental to their health. For the injured party (the patient), infringement of such a right may give rise to an action for damages in tort against another person who is alleged to have violated that right (Fletcher and Buka, 1999). This right is nevertheless not absolute, and it is for the courts to define based on the statutory provisions as interpreted in pre-existing case law. There is also a presumption in law that all adults are competent unless proven otherwise. For individuals who are competent the patient's right to decline treatment regardless of the possible adverse outcome is recognized in common law as illustrated in the *St George's Healthcare National Health Service Trust v S* (no. 2) reported in *The Times* Law Report of 3 August 1998. A patient also has the right to withdraw any previously given and obtained consent.

MENTAL CAPACITY AND INFORMED CONSENT

The right to choose to accept or decline treatment, based on an informed choice, is based on Article 8 of the Human Rights Act 1998, defined as

The rights to respect for private and family life,

1. *Everyone has the right to respect for his private and family life, his home and his correspondence.*

The Mental Capacity Act 2005 defines the nature of consent, and competence is specific to consent, even if the client lacks mental capacity in other aspects or indeed at other times. The relationship between the nurse and their patient is based on trust and a need for purposeful and effective communication by making sure you gain consent prior to treatment and 'uphold people's rights to be fully involved in decisions about their care' and are required to be aware of the law on mental capacity (NMC, 2008). As part of this communication process it is normal that most patients may wish to ask questions related to their treatment. The nurse has a moral and legal duty to ensure that the patient's autonomy is respected. This may, however, not be applicable when a patient lacks capacity. In addition, other ethical principles such as beneficence require the promotion of good, while non-maleficence focuses on avoiding any action which may be detrimental to the patient's health (by denying them their freedom of choice) and within the Beauchamp and Childress framework (2008). The guidelines are clear about the clinician's responsibility for obtaining consent and for empowering the patient. It is now possible for a specially trained member of the multidisciplinary team, who is not carrying out the procedure, to obtain consent from the patient:

1. *The health professional carrying out the procedure is ultimately responsible for ensuring that the patient is genuinely consenting to what is being done: it is they who will be held responsible in law if this is challenged later.*

2. *Where oral or non-verbal consent is being sought at the point the procedure is carried out, this will naturally be done by the health professional responsible. However, teamwork is a crucial part of the way the NHS operates, and where written consent is being sought it may be appropriate for other members of the team to participate in the process of seeking consent.*

Department of Health, 2001c

Where there is lack of consent there is the possibility of litigation for negligence and civil actions for trespass to the person (including assault and battery). Assault is putting another person in a state of fear for their safety, and battery involves unwarranted physical contact. Carrying out procedures without consent may amount to battery or assault. Where a patient is detained in hospital against their wishes this may amount to false imprisonment unless the Mental Health Act 1983 is applied. Assault and battery may be subject to criminal prosecution under the Offences against the Person Act 1861 and other statutes.

To be able to provide adequate information, the clinician should be capable of performing or understanding the nature of the procedure which the patient will undergo. The patient should be given a sufficient degree of information, options and the related benefits and any risks involved. For instance, where a surgical operation is concerned, the law expects a surgeon to inform the patient about the benefits and risks of a procedure.

In order to enable patients to make an informed choice the standard of care is decided by the *Bolam* case, 'standard of a reasonable skilled person who professes to have those skills', and the law will judge a professional by the standard of a 'reasonable' nurse.

It has been acknowledged that the patient has a right to refuse treatment, though updated by the NMC Code of Conduct (2008), and earlier medical guidelines illustrated the patient's right to refuse treatment.

> *You must respect any refusal of treatment given when the patient was competent, provided the decision in the advance statement is clearly applicable to the present circumstances, and there is no reason to believe that the patient has changed his/her mind. Where an advance statement of this kind is not available, the patient's known wishes should be taken into account.*
>
> *GMC, 1999*

A clinician must always look to their own professional code of conduct as well as to local policies and guidelines for guidance. The patient must be given a sufficient degree of information to enable them to make an informed choice about whether to consent to the treatment or procedure. A doctor does not have to disclose all the risks (Giliker and Bethwith, 2011). The *Bolam* principle was applied in the case of *Sidaway v Board of Governors of the Bethlem Royal Hospital and the Maudsley Hospital* [1985] AC 871, where the plaintiff had a chronic neck condition and the surgeon recommended an operation. The surgeon failed to warn the patient of a small risk (1 per cent), as the operation was within less than 3 cm of the spinal cord. The outcome of the operation resulted in severing of the spine, causing paralysis. The patient said that she would not have agreed to the operation had she known the risk. The House of Lords held that as the risk was minimal, autonomy was not absolute and that the patient is not always the best judge on the level of information to be given. On the basis of this case it could be argued that in this instance it was effectively accepted that sometimes paternalism might be justifiable. In contrast, the case of *Hester v Ashfar* [2004] UKHL 41 went the other way, adopting a patient-focused approach, which affirmed the patient's right to be informed of any avoidable risk, no matter how minor.

As a professional, the nurse has a duty to protect their patient's right to autonomy. For patients who are incompetent or lack capacity there is an expectation that nurses will advocate for these patients.

The current framework for consent was set out in the next case.

***Re C* [1994] I All ER 819; [1994] I WLR 290**

A surgeon performing a Caesarean section discovered fibroid tumours. Due to his concern about the risk posed by a second pregnancy he went ahead and sterilized the patient. The patient went to court seeking damages on the grounds that she had not consented to the operation.

Held: The doctor was liable. And furthermore, whilst the first operation was required, the sterilization was convenient at the time as there was no evidence that the fibroids posed an immediate danger to the patient's life or health.

Informed consent and capacity was set out based on Dr Easterman's expert evidence with the decision-making process in three stages, with Thorpe setting out a three-tier test:

- whether the patient comprehended and retained information,
- whether he or she believed it,
- whether he or she could weigh in the balance and arrive at a choice.

THINKING POINT

Mrs X, aged 80, lives on her own and is normally independent, apart from having home help twice weekly. She suffers from mild dementia but has reasonable awareness of what is going on. She has one son, who visits weekly with his own family. She has been admitted to A&E following a fall and the x-rays confirmed a fractured neck of femur requiring surgery. The surgeons are concerned that on admission she is very confused and unable to understand relevant information or give informed consent.

1. What are the current guidelines for managing individuals who lack mental capacity to consent, before surgery can be undertaken?
2. If Mrs X has a 'living will' with advance directives in her medical records, how would this affect her consent to treatment?

CAPACITY TO CONSENT, HUMAN RIGHTS AND BEST INTERESTS

Legal theory writers such as Hart (1968, p. 5) recognize that informed consent is part of human freedom, but nevertheless is not absolute, as 'there may be grounds justifying the legal coercion of the individual other than the prevention of harm to others'. UK law recognizes the clearly defined right of a patient not to be given treatment against his or her will, and not to be treated in the complete absence of consent. However, in interpretation of the law, judges in the UK have not developed a full doctrine of 'informed consent'. Lord Donaldson has subsequently set out the UK position as follows:

> **Re T [1992] 9 BMLR 46**
>
> An adult patient who suffers from no mental incapacity has an absolute right to choose whether to consent to medical treatment, to refuse it, or to choose one rather than another of the treatments being offered. This right of choice is not limited to decisions which others might regard as sensible. It exists notwithstanding that the reasons for making the choice are rational, irrational, unknown or even non-existent.

For patients who lack capacity there are new provisions in the Mental Capacity Act 2005 (Adults with Incapacity (Scotland) Act 2000). The advocate or 'deputy' is a person over the age of 18 who is appointed by the court. Under Section 20 of the Mental Capacity Act 2005, the deputy has limited powers and may not substitute the patient's decisions if they believe that the patient has the power to make that decision. For example, they may only decline treatment but may not demand treatment, as doctors may treat a patient based on their own clinical judgements. Those who lack capacity are defined as follows:

> *(1) For the purposes of this Act, a person lacks capacity in relation to a matter if at the material time he is unable to make a decision for himself in relation to the matter because of an impairment of, or a disturbance in the functioning of, the mind or brain.*

If the lack of capacity is transient, due to an underlying medical condition, an infection, medication or disorientation, the nurse should consider obtaining consent another time, when the patient's capacity is evident (Section 4(2)). This may be difficult in practice if a patient suffers from spells of confusion.

To determine whether a patient has the necessary capacity, the test adopted is that in *Re C Test/Re C Advice: Refusal of Treatment* [1994] 1 WLR 290. At times it is possible that a patient's 'best interests' should be considered due to a patient's lack of capacity only after consideration of the following:

> *(3) He must consider (a) whether it is likely that the person will at some time have capacity in relation to the matter in question, and (b) if it appears likely that he will, when that is likely to be.*

(4) He must, so far as reasonably practicable, permit and encourage the person to participate, or to improve his ability to participate, as fully as possible in any act done for him and any decision affecting him.

Section 4 of Mental Capacity Act 2005

In emergency situations, treatment may be given without seeking the patient's permission. The justification of such intervention is to preserve or save life. A doctor may not be prosecuted for trespass in emergency circumstances provided they can show that in so doing they were acting in the best interests of the patient. In situations dealing with those who lack mental capacity, either temporarily or permanently, decisions may also be made in the patient's best interests, but there is a danger, prompting the need for clear guidelines. When applied, the best interests principle, Section 4 of Mental Capacity Act 2005, should also take into account:

1.14. If you are treating a patient who lacks capacity and who also has a mental disorder, you should be aware of how the mental health legislation across the UK interacts with the law on mental capacity. See the other sources of information at the end of this guidance.

General Medical Council, 2008

There are also exceptions under Article 5(e) of HRA 1998 and public health laws for obtaining consent and for detention for people with an infectious disease, some cases of life-threatening situations and where a patient has previously clearly identified (in living wills) their wishes to decline treatment as illustrated in *Airedale NHS Trust v Bland* [1993] AC 789:

It is established that the principle of self-determination requires that respect must be given to the wishes of the patient, so that if an adult patient of sound mind refuses, however unreasonably, to consent to treatment or care by which his life would or might be prolonged, the doctors responsible for his care must give effect to his wishes, even though they do not consider it to be in his best interests to do so.

Per Lord Goff at p. 864 C

In the event of an action for battery being brought against a clinician, their justification would also be that they acted through necessity. Necessity is a defence in an emergency situation (see below on capacity).

In the case of children, Section 1 of the Children Act 1989, which states (among other issues) the overriding factor which is paramount of the child's welfare, is also applicable to the treatment of children as in 'the ascertainable wishes and feelings of the child (considered in the light of his age and understanding)' and 'any harm the child has suffered or is at risk of suffering'. (For more detailed information see Chapter 3, 'The Beginning of Life to Adulthood: Human Rights').

Gillick v West Norfolk and Wisbech Area Health Authority [1985] 3 All ER 492 is the authority for the principle that in certain circumstances a child under the age of 16 years could give valid consent (in this case contraceptives) without the involvement or knowledge of parents. The test was whether the child had a sufficient degree of understanding of what was proposed (*Fraser*, formerly *Gillick*, competence). This test is about capacity, not merely the ability to make a choice. However, in *Re S* [1994] 2 FLR 1065, a Scottish case, where a girl aged 15 needed regular transfusions due to thalassaemia refused transfusion on religious grounds. It was held that she lacked the Fraser competency. This is based on a young patient's understanding or full appreciation of the nature of the treatment as well as the degree of risks posed by the treatment. For children, however, parental consent cannot override a refusal of consent by a competent child who has the legal capacity to consent to his or her own treatment. The position is also clarified in Scots law: 'In the opinion of the qualified medical practitioner attending to him/her, he/she is capable of understanding the nature and the possible consequences of the procedure or treatment', under Section 2(4) of the Legal Capacity (Scotland) Act 1991.

Parents are normally expected by the law to make decisions on behalf of their children under the age of 18 in England or 16 in Scotland, unless the child has the capacity under 'Fraser competence'. Difficulties may arise to the nurse if there is conflict between the wishes of the parents and those of the child. Parents may not override a competent minor's decision. There is sometimes a need for a judicial review under the inherent parens patriae (Latin), literary 'father of the country' (which is the jurisdiction of the court, which may be exercised by the High Court, Family Division), with the aim of making the child a ward of court. The role of the courts is highlighted in the following case. In *Re A (Children) Conjoined Twins: Surgical Separation* [2001] 2 WLR 480 Jodie and Mary were conjoined twins. Any separation would lead to saving Jodie's life (otherwise she would have died within six months) and the death of Mary (who would not have survived on her own). On religious grounds, the parents objected to an operation, which undoubtedly would have saved Jodie's life but led to the death of Mary. The Court of Appeal held that the operation should go ahead without the parents' consent.

In urgent cases, patients with mental health needs may be detained under Sections 2–5 of the Mental Health Act 1983 and be subject to compulsory treatment for the mental health condition under Section 63 of the Mental Health Act 1983. However, *F v West Berkshire Health Authority and Another (Mental Health Act Commission Intervening)* [1989] 2 All ER at 545 shows that under Section 93(1)b of the same act, managing 'the affairs of patients' (limited to business affairs) did not extend to questions relating to the medical treatment of a patient. The court had therefore no jurisdiction to override such a patient's wishes on medical treatment. Part IV of MHA 1983 (i.e. Sections 56–64) applies only to medical treatment for mental disorder (i.e. psychiatric treatment).

> ### Re R [1991] 4 All ER 177; reported in *The Times*, 31 July
>
> R, a 15-year-old girl, refused antipsychotic treatment for mental illness, which was intermittent, with violent and suicidal symptoms. She seemed lucid and rational at the time of refusal.
>
> Held: The High Court held that R was incompetent and could receive compulsory treatment, though nevertheless only the court may override her refusal. Parents would have no right to make decisions on her behalf.

Section 47 of the National Assistance Act 1948 may be used in conjunction with the mental health compulsory admission powers to remove a person from their usual place of abode to a place of safety, which could be for treatment. In a more recent case:

> *A 41 year old man with learning disability, was deemed capable of consenting to sexual intercourse but could not make a proper decision on use of contraception. His girlfriend, who also had a learning disability and with whom he already had a child and the situation, was causing concern and anxiety for the couple. There was a concern that they would have another child if this was not controlled. The Court of Protection held, applying the issue of capacity under section 2 of the Mental Capacity Act 2005, that it was in the client's best interest to have a vasectomy.*
>
> **Re DE [2013], Court of Protection, http://www. judiciary.gov.uk/Resources/JCO/Documents/Judgments/ de-judgment-16082013.pdf**

Exceptions to the rule where patients may lack competence for consent include the following:

- unconscious patients,
- children below the age of majority – for exceptions see 'Fraser competence' in the *Gillick* case,
- confused patients – this may be due to condition of mental state,
- patients with mental health needs.

When there is uncertainty due to the patient lacking capacity to consent, local guidelines (which are based on national guidelines) must be followed.

Per Lord Goff in Airedale NHS Trust v Bland [1993] AC 789

It is established that the principle of self-determination requires that respect must be given to the wishes of the patient, so that if an adult patient of sound mind refuses, however unreasonably, to consent to treatment or care by which his life would or might be prolonged, the doctors responsible for his care must give effect to his wishes, even … though they do not consider it to be in his best interests to do so.

THINKING POINT

James is a 31-year-old patient who lives on his own, with no known next of kin, and he has been recently diagnosed with bipolar illness and was admitted as an emergency following violent conduct at home. He was detained under the Mental Health Act 1983, following a suicide attempt. On discharge, he claims that he had been 'assaulted' and restrained and given injection medications against his will.

Look at the Mental Health Act 1983 and identify the client's rights in this case.

RESEARCH, CONSENT AND ORGAN DONATION

The Nuremberg Code (1947) emerged as a result of the trial of that name, officially called *United States v Karl Brandt et al*. 'Known as the Doctors' Trial, [it] was prosecuted in 1946–47 against twenty-three doctors and administrators accused of organizing and participating in war crimes and crimes against humanity in the form of medical experiments and medical procedures inflicted on prisoners and civilians' (Harvard University, 2013).

The crimes committed were experiments with people who were subjected to inhuman treatment by the Nazi high command. Examples of the experiments included in the indictments were

1. High-altitude experiments, March–August 1942. Conducted for the German air force to investigate the effect of high-altitude flying; experiments were conducted at the Dachau camp using a low-pressure chamber.
2. Freezing experiments, August 1942–May 1943. Conducted primarily for the German air force to investigate treatments for persons who had been severely chilled, using prisoners at the Dachau camp.
3. Malaria experiments, February 1942–April 1945. Conducted to test immunization for and treatment of malaria; experiments were conducted on more than 1000 prisoners at Dachau.

Subsequently, an international agreement was put in place to regulate medical experiments and clinical trials. The code has 10 requirements, among them:

> 1. *The voluntary consent of the human subject is absolutely essential. This means that the person involved should have legal capacity to give consent: should be so situated as to be able to exercise free power of choice without the intervention of any element of force, fraud, deceit, duress, overreaching, or other ulterior form of constraint or coercion and should have sufficient knowledge and comprehension of the elements of the subject matter involved as to enable him to make an understanding and enlightened decision.*
> **Trials of War Criminals before the Nuremberg Military Tribunals, 1946–49**

Research may involve clinical trials, which not only require consent but may also be regulated by contract law, where a participant is paid money in exchange for participation. Depending on the terms of agreement, the courts may not view favourably where there is an underlying contractual agreement. In the event of adverse reaction the defendant is entitled to a defence of volenti non fit injuria, translated from Latin as 'to a willing person, no injury is done'. This means that potentially, any damages awarded for personal injury may be reduced substantially as a result. Where, however, a contractual exclusion of liability clause is included, the defendant cannot use the above principle or an exclusion or limitation of liability clause where a person is injured seriously or killed as a result of the defendant's negligent actions (Unfair Contract Terms Act 1977). Others, however, see consent in research as a way for the researcher to transfer some of the risk to the informed subject (Alderson and Goodey, 1998).

A sufficient degree of information is vital to enable the participants to make an informed choice. In the following case, had participants known the adverse and dangerous effects and impact of the experiments, they would not have agreed. One leading example is the Tuskegee syphilis study, where clinical research in Alabama between 1932 and 1972 involved a large group of black males, about 600 in total. Of this group, 400 were deliberately infected with syphilis (the rest were in a control group of 200 which was uninfected). The aim was to find out 'whether blacks reacted to syphilis in the same way as whites, and to determine how long a human being can live with untreated syphilis. The men that were used in the research, most of them uneducated sharecroppers were left untreated with syphilis, and suffered tremendously in the hands of doctors from the US Public Health Service' (Ogungbure, 2011, p. 75).

Sections 30–35 of the Mental Capacity Act 2005 now provide for advocacy in research, with additional safeguards (Section 33) for protection of any person lacking in consent who may be involved in research:

> 2) *Nothing may be done to, or in relation to, him in the course of the research*
>   (a) *to which he appears to object (whether by showing signs of resistance or otherwise) except where what is being done is intended to protect him from harm or to reduce or prevent pain or discomfort, or*
>   (b) *which would be contrary to*
>   (i) *an advance decision of his which has effect, or*
>   (ii) *any other form of statement made by him and not subsequently withdrawn, of which R is aware.*
> ### Section 33(2) of Mental Capacity Act 2005

Organs may be donated for research purposes or to save lives; either way, consent should obtained before this. Following the Liverpool and Bristol inquiry reports, the Health Service Circular HSC 2001/023 (Department of Health, 2001d, p. 4) suggests

> *Review of the law on the taking and use of human organs and tissue is currently in progress as part of the follow-up to the*

Liverpool and Bristol inquiry reports. Pending the outcome of this review, the model consent for treatment forms do not yet include a section on consent for the use of tissue removed during medical procedures, but the model policy makes clear that NHS organisations must have clear procedures in place to ensure that patients have the opportunity to refuse permission for such use if they wish.

As nurses are becoming more involved in research, they need to ensure that consent is properly obtained, especially if they are assisting others who may not have properly obtained this (RCN, 2005). Research involving human organs must always be in writing:

5) *Consent in writing for the purposes of subsection (3) is only valid if –*
   (a) *it is signed by the person concerned in the presence of at least one witness who attests the signature,*
   (b) *it is signed at the direction of the person concerned, in his presence and in the presence of at least one witness who attests the signature, or*
   (c) *it is contained in a will of the person concerned made in accordance with the requirements of –*
      (i) *section 9 of the Wills Act 1837 (c. 26)*

Human Tissue Act 2004

One important change introduced by the above statute into this area of law is that any such properly constituted consent may not be overruled by family members.

Another important area is highlighted in the scandals involving illegal organ storage and use for research. The Human Tissue Act (HTA) 2004 took effect on 1 September 2006, outlawing the following practices:

- the removal or storage of human tissue without prior consent, following the Alder Hey scandal;
- the taking and testing of DNA without consent;
- trafficking of organs.

The above offences now attract penalties ranging from a fine to three years' imprisonment or both.

The NHS Plan (Department of Health, 2000) also gives further guidance on good practice and the need to obtain consent in research.

The NHS Constitution (2013) aims to promote patient-centred care and putting the patient at the centre of decision-making.

THINKING POINT

A 21-year-old man (with an organ donor card) who has been in a persistent vegetative state (PVS) since suffering brain damage following a road traffic accident has been on a ventilator and a decision has been made to switch off the ventilator. The family has been approached but is strongly opposed to organ donation.

Consider the legal and ethical implications of organ donation in light of the proposed changes to the law on presumed consent, and in this act in Wales (where there were recent changes on presumed consent).

Human Transportation (Wales) Act 2013

> *The aim of the Act is to increase the number of organs and tissues available for transplant. This will benefit the people of Wales by reducing the number of people dying whilst waiting for a suitable organ to become available and improving the lives of others.*
>
> **Wales government, 2013, http://wales.gov.uk/topics/ health/nhswales/majorhealth/organ/?lang=en**

With respect of consent in organ donation, it is difficult when the decision is not a simple matter of self-determination but a decision which may impact on the views of family members and their rights to object. These objections may be based on cultural or religious grounds. The National Patient Safety Agency (2011) now regulates the NHS research framework through the Health Research Authority.

CONCLUSION

In practice, it is difficult for clinicians to determine whether a patient giving consent does so on the basis of a reasoned judgement, influence from others such as close family members, friends or other clinicians, or purely of their own accord. What is important is that unless it is an emergency, the patient should whenever possible be given a sufficient degree of information to enable them to make a choice on whether to accept treatment or not – the opportunity to deliberate and make an important decision to consent to treatment or likewise, decline it. They should never feel under pressure from nurses, family members or other healthcare professionals. Difficulties may arise when patients do not wish to have this information because of ignorance, fear of coming to terms with any outcome, perhaps in denial, or they may not wish to know (as far as risks of an operation are concerned), or they may believe that the nurse or doctor knows 'what is best for them'. The role of the nurse should be to ensure that where possible, the patient's right to informed consent is safeguarded, unless they lack mental capacity – establishing this is always going to be a challenge for the nurse. No decisions should be made about the patient's treatment without their involvement. With regard to treatment, the ethics of self-determination and autonomy have long been recognized in common law.

REFERENCES

Alderson P, Goodey C. Theories of consent. *BMJ* 1998; 317: 1313–15.

Beauchamp TL, Childress JF. *Principles of biomedical ethics*, 6th ed. New York: Oxford University Press, 2012.

Blackburn S. *Being good: a short introduction to ethics*. Oxford: Oxford University Press, 2001.

Campbell A, Gillett G, Jones G. *Medical ethics*. Oxford: Oxford University Press, 2001.

Department of Health. NHS plan. 2000. www.dh.gov.uk.

Department of Health. *Guidance for clinicians: Model policy for consent to examination or treatment*. 2001a. www.dh.gov.uk/PolicyAndGuidance/HealthAndSocialCareTopics/Consent/ConsentGeneralInformation/fs/en (accessed 21 August 2006).

Department of Health. *Good practice in consent: achieving the NHS plan commitments to patient-centred practice*. HSC 2001/023. 2001b. www.dh.gov.uk (accessed 23 June 2013).

Department of Health. *Good practice in consent implementation guide*. Crown, 2001c.

Department of Health. *Health service circular*. HSC 2001/023. 22 November 2001d, p. 4.

Doyal L. Good clinical practice and informed consent are inseparable. *Heart* 2002; 87: 103–5. heart.bmj.com/cgi/content/abstract/87/2/103.

Fletcher L, Buka P. *A legal framework for caring: an introduction to law and ethics for healthcare professionals*. Basingstoke: Palgrave, 1999.

Furrow D. *Ethics: key concepts in philosophy*. London: Continuum, 2005.

General Medical Council. *Seeking patients' consent: the ethical considerations*. London: GMC, 1999.

General Medical Council. Consent guidance: patients and doctors making decisions together. 2008. http://www.gmc-uk.org/guidance/ethical_guidance/consent_guidance_index.asp. (accessed on 3 January 2013).

Giliker P, Bethwith S. *Tort*, 2nd ed. London: Sweet and Maxwell, 2011.

Hart HLA. *Punishment and responsibility.* Oxford: Oxford University Press, 1968.

Harvard University. Indictment in trials of war criminals, 16–18. http://nuremberg.law.harvard.edu/NurTranscript/TranscriptSearches/tran_about.php (accessed 10 July 2013).

Hoffman D, Rowe J. *Human rights in the UK: an introduction to the Human Rights Act 1998,* 4th ed. London: Pearson Longman, 2013.

Mental Health Act 1983. www.doh.gov.uk/mentalhealth/ (accessed 6 July 2013).

Mill JS. *On liberty,* Everyman edition. London: JM Dent, 1993.

National Patient Safety Agency (Amendment no. 3). Directions 2011 published on 1 December 2011. http://webarchive.nationalarchives.gov.uk/20111202162649/http://dh.gov.uk/health/2011/12/creation-hra (accessed on 12 September 2013).

Ogungbure AA. The Tuskegee syphilis study: some ethical reflections, thought and practice. *Journal of the Philosophical Association of Kenya (PAK)* 2011; 3(2): 75-92.

NHS Constitution. http://www.nhs.uk/choiceintheNHS/Rightsandpledges/NHSConstitution/Documents/2013/handbook-to-the-nhs-constitution.pdf (accessed 4 August 2013).

Nozick R. *Anarchy, state, and utopia.* New York: Basic Books, 1974.

Nursing and Midwifery Council. *Professional code of conduct and ethics: standards for conduct, performance and ethics.* London: NMC, 2008.

Royal College of Nursing Research Society. *Informed consent in health and social care research.* RCN Guidance for Nurses. 2005.

Thompson I, Melia K, Boyd K. *Nursing ethics,* 6th ed. London: Churchill Livingstone, 2006.

Trials of War Criminals before the Nuremberg Military Tribunals under Control Council Law No. 10. Nuremberg, October 1946–April 1949. Washington: U.S. Government Printing Office (n.d.), vol. 2, pp. 181–82. www.cirp.org/library/ethics/nuremberg/.

WHO. *Ethics of the health systems: report of the Third Futures Forum for High-Level Decision-Makers.* Stockholm, Sweden, 27–28 June 2002. WHO, 2003. www.euro.who.int/document/e77651.pdf (accessed on 14 September 2013).

7 VULNERABLE ADULTS, OLDER PEOPLE AND ABUSE

INTRODUCTION

The main focus for this chapter is on elder abuse involving vulnerable clients, but it has to be acknowledged that there are also other groups of vulnerable adults who many fall victim of abuse. The principles herein are applicable as vulnerability is linked to most people with health and social care needs. In contrast, in child abuse the Children Acts 1989 and 2004 have put in place effective measures to protect the child, although cases like that of Victoria Climbié (from children's perspective) have shown how ineffective the system can be if healthcare professionals fail to intervene and safeguard victims. In that area, the Children Act 1989 and the Children (Scotland) Act 1995 regulations and guidance, and the Children Act 2004 were an appropriate response in providing clear safeguarding of the child's best interests, and in the latter statute establishing a national children's champion who focuses on national issues related to child abuse. There is, however, no such specific provision for the protection of older people who may fall victim to abuse. What is the official definition of who is a vulnerable adult?

A person aged 18 years or over

who is or may be in need of community care services by reason of mental or other disability, age or illness; and
who is or may be unable to take care of him or herself, or unable to protect him or herself against significant harm or exploitation.
Lord Chancellor's Department, Who Decides, 1997

Furthermore, this includes a broad group of vulnerable clients – anyone who has also been associated with a person who

is receiving any form of health care;
is detained in a prison, remand centre, young offender institution, secure training centre or attendance centre or under the powers of the Immigration and Asylum Act 1999;
is in contact with probation services.
Department of Health, No Secrets, 2000

BACKGROUND

The National Service Framework for Older People (2001) classified people over the age of 65 as older people. While it is not the case that all older people are vulnerable, they represent the largest proportion of clientele receiving care in the NHS and from private healthcare providers. With age, the likelihood of vulnerability increases as we become more dependent physically and psychologically. In different types of abusive situations, there is a common element – a breach of trust (see Chapter 5). The general principles are applicable to any type of abuse in respect of all client groups receiving health and/or social care. This chapter focuses on the older patient, although the principles are equally applicable to other groups of victims of abuse such as children and all other groups of vulnerable adults. Depending on the given situation, interventions to deal with the problem will be different. It is always difficult to establish the extent of abuse, due to possible underreporting as well as lack of evidence in support of any complaints as abuse may be perpetrated behind closed doors.

THINKING POINT

1. What are the 'tell-tell' signs of abuse?
2. Based on your experience, what interventions could be applied in order to redress actual and to prevent any potential further abuse?

When abuse involves a vulnerable person, it could prove to be more difficult to manage if the abuser is a carer or a close family member, currently caring for the victim. Available responses are through piecemeal legislation without specific safeguards as in child law. This may cause confusion and frustration not only in the minds of the victims and their advocates but also in that of the perpetrator, who may not be aware that their action may be tantamount to abuse. An established definition of elder abuse is:

> *A single or repeated act or appropriate action occurring within a relationship where there is an expectation of trust which causes harm or distress to an older (dependent) person.*
>
> ### Action on Elder Abuse, 1995

For the purposes of this chapter, the terms 'abuse' and 'elder abuse' are used interchangeably. The term 'elder abuse' has been in use for some time in the United States but is relatively new in the UK (Bennett and Kingston (1995) are accredited with adopting its use). Others may prefer the term 'maltreatment' or 'mistreatment' to include both 'abuse' and 'neglect'. The latter is just as bad despite the passive element of 'doing nothing'. The effect may still be abuse. It has been suggested that up to 2.6 per cent of people aged 66 and over living in private households admitted having experienced mistreatment by a carer, including family members, close friend or care worker (O'Keefe et al., 2007).

The debate on elder abuse has rekindled issues on the welfare and rights of people over the age of 65, especially those who may be dependent for their care and are therefore vulnerable and open to abuse. Abuse may take place either in the victim's own home or in an institution providing care such as a residential care home or hospital. It is possible that some abuse may remain unreported due to the secretive nature of abuse – behind closed doors.

Abuse involves violation of an individual's human and civil rights by any other person or persons covering a broad range of situations. This breach may be covered by law – the European Convention on the Protection of Human Rights and Fundamental Freedoms 1950 under Articles 3 and 17, Schedule 1 HRA 1998, although the number of cases which have gone to law in this area are limited.

Given the definition of abuse in the government paper *Protection of Vulnerable Adults (POVA)*, it is possible to conceive of victims of elder abuse as only those who are dependent on another for their care (POVA, 2000). In fact, any older person may be subject to abuse without the 'dependency' requirement. The emphasis should therefore be on 'vulnerability' instead. Studies have shown that 40 per cent of members who are practicing district nurses have either witnessed or been aware of elder abuse, with half of them having knowledge of a patient who had been a victim of abuse (Community and District Nursing Association (CDNA), 2004).

KEY THEORIES OF ABUSE

Criminological theories attempt to offer some explanations on why some perpetrators become violent and abusive and why some victims accept abuse as part and parcel of life. There is a link between the term 'abuse' and its generic term 'violence'. The difference is that violence may take place between strangers, while abuse occurs within a trusting relationship between the abuser and the victim. In the latter situation there is a breach of trust and there may be fear and dependency from the victim's perspective. Often, deception is involved, but it is unlikely that there is collusion on the part of the victim. Usually there is no choice in the outcome from the view of the victim as they may have been let down by those they trusted. A further element is the imbalance of power between the abuser and the victim. This is the position in which older people that are vulnerable find themselves. Only the main theories are included here in the attempt to explain why violence is perpetrated, with vulnerable people in general as well as the elderly in particular at the receiving end.

Biological and psychological theories

These two terms are related and have been put forward to explain how biological or psychological makeup may affect the behaviour of a potential abuser. The main theories aim to link behaviour with genetic traits, which are thought to cause a predisposition toward violent behaviour. It has been suggested that some violent men possess an extra male Y chromosome (Herrnstein and Murray, 1994). For some individuals this may include paranoia, which is supposedly determined by abnormalities in the chromosomes relating to the XXY and XYY factors (Williams, 2012). This condition is treatable through hormonal therapy. From the above, there has been a suggestion of a link to criminality for the XYY factor, which is the syndrome where the extra male chromosome is present, and another view is 'that chromosome abnormality and criminality are not closely related, and more significantly, if general explanations are wanted, the incidence of XXY and XYY males is so rare as to be of little practical significance' (Williams, 2012, p. 147).

The so-called 'naturalistic studies' have suggested that the children of criminals are more likely to become criminals themselves in later life, as a 'natural tendency' (Fitzgerald et al., 1981, p. 371). Eysenck (1977), however, has explained this behaviour as merely conditioned responses, which are achieved through operant conditioning, in the Pavlovian sense.

Cultural and social learning theories

These theories attribute the apparently higher level of domestic violence and abuse of wives and children in some cultures than in others to a learned process of the adoption of certain norms of behaviour from an early age. Some authorities suggest that society sets norms which become accepted and standard for that individual society. These norms may be enacted into law (Williams, 2012). The values of a society in how it relates to the treatment of women seem to be based on the acceptance of certain norms of behaviour. The cultural basis of the prevalence of violence only serves to explain the existence of accepted standards of behaviour in any given situation. This does not necessarily lend support to the myth that some ethnic groups are more violent than others toward their female partners. Some studies have shown that cultural behaviour is passed on from generation to generation. On people in relationships, Hertzberger (1996, p. 109) concluded that the 'majority of abusive spouses and their victims are more likely to have a history of abuse by their parents'. These norms are supposed to reinforce the concept of a male-dominated society, with women, children and the elderly as victims, and this is unfortunate as it may give the impression that most abusers are male. It is not possible to prove conclusively that culture, whether racial, geographical or social class related, is per se responsible for domestic violence and the abuse of vulnerable people such as the elderly. It is possible that partner abuse may be used as a tool to exercise control and subjugate the weaker person. Other attempts to explain violence in the family context have been based on social learning. Some base domestic violence and cultural abuse on the 'subculture of violence', by attributing it to men's 'susceptibility', which Curtis (1975) put down to racism and economic oppression. Walker (2003) suggests that abusive relationships may result in a cycle of violence. She puts forward her theory of 'learned helplessness' on the part of the victim.

The social learning theory of Albert Bandura (1977) is one of the most fascinating contributions from behaviourists who have made an important contribution to the debate on learned criminal behaviour which is said to result in abuse of elderly persons by their own children, if the latter have been brought up previously experiencing a culture of abuse. The basis of this theory is that behaviour is learnt through observation of violent behaviour. This could be explained by a negative effect not only from the family, but also from society as a whole (which may be seen as uncaring toward its older persons) as well as media sources such as television and press; 'children and adults acquire attitudes, emotional responses and new styles of conduct through filmed television modelling' (Bandura, 1977, p. 39). This process is called 'modelling'. This would explain the future presence of criminal or violence behaviour in individuals who have been exposed to violence as children. As to the question why there are more men abusers and more female victims, Bandura (1977) suggests that 'boys more readily imitate the aggression they observe in others ... girls in contrast refrain from imitating, unless explicitly informed that aggressive behaviour is acceptable' (cited in Hertzberger, 1996, p. 118).

Other factors, for example, alcohol and drug abuse, can be contributory to violence and elder abuse, and may sometimes be used as an excuse. Studies have shown a correlation between alcohol and substances and criminal behaviour in the home by someone who already has a criminal propensity (Williams, 2012). Alcohol not only is a depressant but also may remove inhibitions, thus making it easier for a carer of an elderly person who has experienced pent-up feelings of stress to be more aggressive and abusive. It is possible that alcohol will be used as an excuse for violence. There may very well be other related causes, such as 'paying back' old scores to a previously abusive parent or spouse for whose care they may be responsible.

The feminist perspective – learned helplessness

Feminist theories generally attribute the trend toward violence as evidence of the inequality between men and women. This view is consistent with other factors such as economic dependence and the lower earning power of women, as well as a conflict of interests between spouses. These principles could apply to any relationships or equally to men who are subjected to abuse in their own homes by women. Some attribute the 'imbalance' between men and women to men's 'economic strength' and support in the home (Williams, 2012). The issue of dependence can limit the victim in the options available to them.

> *I remember the first time he hit me, he was quite sorry and I forgave him because I was madly in love with him and I thought, oh hell it was just one of those things and it wouldn't happen again, so I suppose the first time he did it he got away with it, but it just got worse and worse.*
> **National Children's Home (NCH), 1994, p. 22**

TYPES OF ABUSE

A survey of older people (Bennett, 2002) suggested that the only three broad areas they (as potential and actual victims) considered to amount to abuse were as follows:

- neglect – this may be caused by the victim themselves or may be a result of omissions of others;
- violation of human rights which may have legal as well as medical implications;
- deprivation of some privilege, which may include substitution of choices and decisions.

The above categories demonstrate that there are aspects of abuse that elderly people themselves may not consider to be abuse. Therefore, they may not feel it necessary to report the abuse and may consider it as their 'lot', an acceptable phenomenon (Bennett, 2002). Understanding classifications of abuse is important for healthcare professionals, so that they may appreciate the range of issues they may have to deal with. It is generally accepted that there are at least five types of abuse.

There is a consensus of other common classifications, which includes the following:

- Physical: This involves contact or battery, which may include inflicting physical harm such as restraining as well as the inappropriate administration of medications.
- Psychological: This would include swearing, threats of violence, insults, mental torture, humiliation, belittling someone and social isolation.
- Financial/property: This covers misappropriation of all forms of possessions belonging to an elderly person (see Chapter 8, 'Equality and Diversity'). This would also include unauthorized and unexplained changes in wills and suspect bank or benefit transactions, often with the alleged abuser as beneficiary.
- Sexual: This involves rape, indecent assault, as well as any form of unwarranted touch and sexual innuendo (which is strictly speaking 'psychological'). Any sexual activity must be between consenting adults with mental capacity.
- Neglect: This may be carried out by others such as family members or carers, or self-inflicted. In some cases, the victim may not be aware of the resulting harm. It is nevertheless possible that self-neglect can take place, hence the need for a thorough investigation before accusing carers

or family members. Should a person choose to take their own life, it is no longer a criminal offence for individuals to take their own life, under Section 2 of the Suicide Act 1961. It is nevertheless a crime to assist a suicide (see Chapter 9). As well as a breach of duty of care, professionals may be found to be in breach of their duty of care when they fail to act to prevent abuse.

These categories are based on the British Geriatrics Society classification (1998). The Department of Health (2000) in the government White Paper *No Secrets* added another category, 'discriminatory abuse', to this (sometimes described as 'institutional'). This includes inadequate provisions for the elderly – it is questionable whether this should be a separate class (of ageism) from other grounds of discrimination such as religion, race, gender and sexual orientation (which may be recognized by the law). This may be related to a provision against age discrimination in employment law under the Employment Equality (Age) Regulations 2006. This is now covered by the Equality Act 2012.

An abuser could potentially be 'from a wide range of people including relatives and family members, as well as professional staff, paid care workers, volunteers, other service users, neighbours, friends and associates, people who deliberately exploit vulnerable people and strangers' (paragraph 2.10 of *No Secrets* (Department of Health, 2000)).

It is important to consider the effectiveness of current responses in light of any staff training as well as clear guidelines, which should be proactive to minimize the risk of and counter abuse. However, these do not always offer sufficient protection to a victim. Abuse involving violent acts may amount to a criminal offence provided the elements of a crime, a guilty intention (mens rea) and a guilty act (actus reus), are proven. The Crown Prosecution Service under criminal law may prosecute the perpetrator. The difficulty is that the generic category of domestic abuse ranges from seemingly minor and harmless actions such as psychological abuse or harassment to those with more serious consequences like rape, serious assault or murder. It is possible that there may be 'window dressing' of the criminal act by using the term 'abuse' instead of more serious terminology. The difference between violence in general and elder abuse is the context within which it generally takes place. Research based on the British Crime Survey (1995) suggests that the highest number of assaults took place in the home, with '8 out of 10' victims of abuse being women (Donnellan, 2001, p. 2). Following several hospital episodes, signs of suspected abuse may be 'discovered' by a healthcare professional on admission assessments in accident and emergency departments, often unrelated to the apparent reason for admission:

> *The signs of abuse are not always very obvious and may be uncovered secondary to other issues, perhaps when a client is admitted to care following alleged 'falls', clinical findings may not be consistent with the pre-admission history and the client's health status.*
> **Fletcher and Buka, 1999, p. 155**

The central problem facing the healthcare professional in dealing with vulnerable adult abuse is that it is difficult to prove abuse and a victim may not wish to report it if this involves a close family member. Nevertheless, if they suspect abuse healthcare professionals are duty-bound to report it to other members of the multidisciplinary team. They must follow their own local guidelines on the process for reporting abuse. Nurses may find themselves in a dilemma between the need for confidentiality and the necessity to breach this if their patient's safety is under threat (if a crime has been or is about to be committed), if disclosure is in the public interest, as required by statute or if ordered to disclose by a court of law (NMC Code of Conduct, 2008).

The Caldicott principles provide further clarification in this area (Department of Health, 1997). Any disclosure of confidential information is subject to the Data Protection Act 1998.

INTERVENTIONS

Before responding vigorously to allegations or apparent elder abuse, it may not in the first instance be necessary to warrant legal or other formal interventions, as things may not be what they seem (Buka and Sookhoo, 2006). There may also be a possibility of intervening informally (with limited evidence of abuse available) or reporting the matter to authorities in that a victim may through their own choice be considered responsible for their own self-neglect. It is important for clear guidelines in the clinical environment to minimize the risk to vulnerable older people. Doing nothing in the hope that things will resolve themselves is not an option as it is not hard to imagine the outcome of doing nothing. The problem is that without the active cooperation of a victim in any complaint investigation where there is suspected abuse, it may be difficult if not impossible to prosecute (Potter, 2004). Interventions should always be through interdisciplinary settings so as to encourage a balanced and fairer outcome for both the patient and the alleged abuser, especially if this turns out to be unsubstantiated. Those involved should include multidisciplinary healthcare professionals, as well as other interagency groups such as social services, the police and any local advocacy agencies (for example, Victim Support and Citizens Advice Bureau) to provide support. Cases of suspected abuse, in which there is evidence of a criminal act involving serious injury or death, must always be reported to the police in addition to following local procedure. Thereafter, the Crown Prosecution Service may decide to prosecute on the basis of the evidence, or may not prosecute if it is not in the public interest to do so. Healthcare professionals may be reluctant to report the matter if there is any doubt, as they may be concerned about making the situation worse for the victim should their suspicions turn out to be ill founded. Abuse may amount to a criminal offence if the guilty intention is proven. Unintentional abuse also has adverse effects on an elderly victim, and depending on the degree of recklessness, if proven, could also be criminal negligence. The government responded to cases of abuse with 'No Secrets, the Protection of Vulnerable Adults' (POVA). Current legislation is regulated by the Protection of Freedoms Act 2012.

Case study

Fitzgerald (the director of Action on Elder Abuse) pointed out that many people would be familiar with the case of Victoria Climbié, but few knew about Margaret Panting, a 78-year-old woman from Sheffield who died after suffering 'unbelievable cruelty' while living with relatives. After her death in 2001, a postmortem found 49 injuries on her body including cuts probably made by a razor blade and cigarette burns. She had moved from sheltered accommodation to her son-in-law's home – five weeks later she was dead, but as the cause of Margaret Panting's death could not be established, no one was ever charged. An inquest in 2002 recorded an open verdict (House of Commons, 2004).

The link between crime rates and elder abuse is not always easy to establish. An overview of related crime rates demonstrates that certain abuse-type crimes may also be on the increase (Home Office, 2003). Victim gender differences may also be indicative of the extent of the vulnerability of older people. Up to 20 per cent of persons over 85 years old attending A&E presented with trauma conditions, which could be linked to abuse (British Geriatrics Society, 1998). These figures should, however, be treated with caution as they do not distinguish between other violent crimes and abuse (Home Office, 2003). For the 2010–11 British Crime Survey (2011), 18.8 percent of victims were aged over 65.

THINKING POINT

M and S are the married daughters of Jim X, who was now unable to cope on his own and required to be placed in a local authority nursing home three months following his wife's death (he had been the main carer for several years). Over the last two months they have noticed that he appears to be losing a lot of weight and he has bruises on his upper arms. He is very sleepy whenever they visit; the staff nurse in charge says that he has been given (as required) zopiclone tablets as he keeps other residents awake. This makes him rather groggy and unsteady during the day. They also noticed that he often smells of urine, has not been bathed for several days and they often have to ask the staff to change him, as it seems to take a long time before he is changed, during the duration of their visits. They (staff) say that the reason he is not attended to is that he refuses to get changed. He also appears to be frightened of one particular male agency carer. He begs his daughters to take him home. They suspect abuse. Consider the case in the light of your local guidelines for managing elder abuse.

CRIMINAL LAW RESPONSES

Where there is evidence of a criminal act having taken place, the matter should be reported to the police. Based on the investigation and evidence, the Crown Prosecution Service may subsequently prosecute the abuser. It is necessary to prove the mens rea (a guilty mind) and actus reus (a guilty act). The burden of proof depends on the 'preponderance' or persuasiveness of evidence or how convincing the evidence may be, and this should go beyond reasonable doubt. An example is when there is a history of unexplained falls as well as suspicious behaviour. Some of the areas of law concerned with abuse are

- Trespass to the person offences are covered by the Offences against the Person Act 1861, involving ranges of physical contact resulting in harm. In England, assault consists of verbal abuse only, while battery is contact ranging from unwanted physical touch to inflicting actual harm; in Scotland assault covers both aspects. Unwanted treatment, for instance, giving a patient an unwanted enema while purportedly acting 'in their best interests', is one example of the offence of battery. The patient's right to privacy under Article 8 of the Human Rights Act (HRA) 1998 is applicable here.
- Property offences are subject to Sections 1 and 15 of the Theft Act 1968, the Theft Act 1978 and the Theft (Amendment) Act 1996. This may involve a criminal offence of openly stealing goods (Section 1) or

the more subtle aspect of obtaining goods by deception (Section 15). For theft offences, please see Chapter 5.

- Sexual offences are mainly covered by the Sexual Offences Act 1984 and the Sexual Offences (Amendment) Act 2003. The courts will take the view that in cases where consent is given by a patient who lacks capacity, that is not valid, and hence is an absolute offence where children are involved.

- Exclusion orders were introduced into Section 40A of the Powers of Criminal Courts (Sentencing) Act 2000, by Section 46 of the Criminal Justice and Courts Services Act 2000. This enables the courts to ban a perpetrator from entering the premises (where the elder abuse victim is currently living) for a period of up to two years.

- Antisocial behaviour orders (ASBOs) came into being under the Crime and Disorder Act 1998. Subject to Section 1(a), an offender whose behaviour harasses or causes 'alarm or distress' may be excluded (under a court order) from the alleged victim's place of residence. The landlord, the police or local authority may apply for this for protection of the victim.

CIVIL REMEDIES

In addition, a victim can also seek remedies in the civil courts for personal injury, in conjunction with the above (criminal) measures. The victim may apply for an injunction (which is a court order preventing conduct such as contact with the victim). Breach of such a court order will result in penalties. The following category demonstrates the nature and levels of current legal responses.

Personal injury claims

It is a long-established principle in negligence under tort law that if an individual, who is owed a duty of care, suffers harm as a result of another's negligence, they are entitled to damages for personal injury. The basic duty of care principle originated in *Donoghue v Stevenson* [1932], and this law is further developed in *Caparo Industries* v *Dickman* [1990] below. Care providers owe a duty of care not only to do good (benevolence), but also to avoid harm (non-malevolence) to the persons for whom they provide care (through their actions or omissions). If the nurse as a carer has been in breach of a duty of care and the victim suffers harm (personal injury) as a result, the victim may be entitled to recover damages in compensation under tort law (or law of delict in Scotland).

In his famous judgement, in the same case, Lord Atkins established the duty of care principle:

> *You must take reasonable care to avoid acts or omissions which you can reasonably foresee would be likely to injure your neighbour. Who, then, in law is my neighbour? The answer seems to be – persons who are so closely and directly affected by my act that I ought reasonably to have them in contemplation as being so affected when I am directing my mind to the acts or omissions which are called in question.*

Lord Atkins, at p. 562, Donoghue v Stevenson
[1932] AC 562

A three-stage test for determining 'duty of care' has subsequently been applied by the courts in establishing the duty of care in the following case.

Caparo Industries v Dickman [1990] 2 AC 605

This was a landmark case where an auditor working for the defendants had compiled a report for Caparo, which showed that Fidelity Co. was in profit. Relying on this information Caparo bought shares. As it turned out, this was not the case and the plaintiff's shareholders lost money. The shareholders for Caparo sued the auditors who had compiled the report for negligence. It was held that there was no sufficient proximity of relationship between auditors and shareholders, thus setting out the three-stage test for duty of care:

1. whether there was foreseeability of harm,
2. whether there was a sufficient proximity of relationship between the parties,
3. whether it was just, fair and equitable for the court to impose a duty of care.

Section 46 of the Domestic Violence, Crime and Victims Act 2004 introduced a provision for the court to issue non-molestation orders for the protection of victims of abuse, provided the victim is living in the same household as the perpetrator of the abuse. There is law for protecting occupancy rights in Scotland in the form of the Matrimonial Homes (Family Protection) (Scotland) Act 1981. Such legislation may nevertheless still be breached, thus putting the victim of abuse at an even greater risk of retribution. Home Office (2011) sought to broaden the definition of domestic violence to include a broader group of clients, not simply adults in a relationship. Similarly, the duty of care is applied by the NMC Code of Conduct (2008) by the requirement for the nurse to

> *work with others to protect and promote the health and wellbeing of those in your care, their families and carers, and the wider community.*
>
> **Nursing and Midwifery Council, Code of Conduct, 2008**

Following several cases of domestic violence resulting in abuse and death of children, a new statute is in place which

> *extends the offence of causing or allowing the death of a child or vulnerable adult in section 5 of the 2004 Act ('the causing or allowing death offence') to cover causing or allowing serious physical harm (equivalent to grievous bodily harm) to a child or vulnerable adult ('the causing or allowing serious physical harm offence').*
>
> **Domestic Violence, Crime and Victims (Amendment) Act 2012 (Commencement) Order 2012, SI 2012/1432 (c. 54)**

PUBLIC AUTHORITIES AND HUMAN RIGHTS

The European Convention on Human Rights 1950 became part of UK human rights law after the passing of the HRA 1998 (implemented in 2000). Under articles in Schedule 1, for example, Articles 3 and 17, a victim of abuse may take a public body such as a local authority or a healthcare trust to court. In dealing with them, the issue of abuse may not be resolved in the UK courts, and then an appeal is lodged to the European Court of Human Rights in Strasbourg. It also means that a victim may rely on the human rights legislation (in UK courts) without seeking redress from the European Court of Human Rights (Leach, 2011).

Although this was intended to enhance the rights of victims, the statute does not go far enough as it is limited to abuse in a caring environment which is provided by a public body only. A victim of abuse who is in care provided by a private home may not rely on this legislation but instead pursue criminal and civil law.

VICTIMS WITH MENTAL HEALTH NEEDS

It may be necessary to protect an elderly patient with mental health needs. In this case, compulsory orders are available for compulsory admission to a healthcare facility for either a victim of abuse or the perpetrator (who has mental health needs) (Sections 2–5 of Mental Health Act 1983 or corresponding aspects of the Mental Health (Scotland) Act 1984). The mental health provisions may be used to protect the needs of individuals with mental health needs or those of their carers. For example, under Section 37 of the Mental Heath Act 1983, the courts have powers to order hospital admission or guardianship. Alternatively, Section 43 of the same act defines the power of magistrates' courts to commit for a restriction order. Section 35 of the Mental Capacity Act 2005 provides additional protection for a vulnerable person to have appointed another person (an independent mental capacity advocate) to look after their interests regarding consent to treatment, as they may be open to abuse. Mental capacity for the purposes of this statute includes both those who may have a temporary or permanent need. This power includes treatment as well as financial interests.

INTERAGENCY WORKING AND ABUSE

For nurses paragraph 3 of the Nursing and Midwifery Council (NMC, 2008) code of professional conduct requires the client's informed consent to treatment (treatment here is used in its widest context). Without obtaining (informed) consent, there may be abuse of the client's rights, and the NMC (2008) Code of Professional Conduct requires the nurse to 'identify' and minimize any risk to patients and clients. It is important for interagency communication to ensure that these rights are safeguarded and that preventative interventions are in place where there may be suspicion but insufficient evidence of abuse. The essential elements of establishing abuse should include evaluation and assessment.

It is important to recognize that abuse may come from the healthcare or care professionals who are supposed to protect the client. This is due to the dependency and the imbalance of power within the client-carer relationship. The nurse should be aware of the ethical values underpinning respect for their patient's values and ensure their right to autonomy or informed choice. Failure to consider this right may result in breach of human rights (Article 3 of the Human Rights Act 1998).

The government's response to several cases of abuse in the press was to produce some guidance in *Modernizing Social Services – No Secrets*, reinventing the definition of a vulnerable adult as someone 'who may be in need of community care services by reason of mental or other disability, age, or illness; and who is or may be unable to take care of him or herself against significant harm or exploitation' (Department of Health, 2000, paragraph 2.3), but as discussed above, this was not sufficient. The White Paper may be seriously flawed as it does not include those who may be victims of abuse but who do not receive community services (Parliamentary Select Committee on Health, February 2004). The aim of the above guidance is to bring together the various agencies responsible for the provision of care in the development of policies and procedures for the protection of vulnerable adults (including the elderly) from abuse. Health and social care providers benefit from working with all other agencies that may be involved in the care of the client.

THINKING POINT

Mrs X is an 84-year-old lady who has been widowed for 10 years, having had no children from her marriage. She has a niece who lives in Australia who is not able to visit and she last saw her at her husband's funeral. Apart from that time, they never keep in touch. Mrs X has become increasingly dependent on private carers as well as on her neighbours, Peter and his wife. He happens to be a qualified practicing adult nurse and his wife is a district healthcare assistant. They pop in every day and help with the shopping. Over the years Peter and his wife have become very close to Mrs X, who often treats them like family. She buys them and the children gifts for Christmas and birthdays. Peter also pays her bills and is an authorized signatory to Mrs X's bank accounts. She has three accounts but does not keep track of the large amounts in the bank since her husband died. She trusts Peter with her debit cards, and the district nurse who visits regularly suspects he might be withdrawing unauthorized large sums of money without Mrs X's knowledge. Peter has just bought himself a car paid for with Mrs X's (fraudulently obtained) money, but when confronted by the district nurse he says he bought the car (with Mrs X's permission) for taking Mrs X to the hospital for her appointments and a drive at the weekend, even though he also uses the car for personal use.

I. Look at the NMC Code and consider what actions you would need to take in order to protect the patient.

The problem is that it is difficult to monitor what happens in individual private homes where most abuse is alleged to take place (CDNA, 2004). In cases which may be drawn to their attention, social workers have at their disposal the powerful protective powers of Section 47 of the National Assistance Act 1948, to help them remove a victim of abuse to a place of safety if it is felt that they may be a danger to themselves or to others. In practice, this is difficult to enforce unless the victim has mental health needs. The Mental Capacity Act 2005 introduced additional guarantees of healthcare advocacy from April 2007, bringing English law into line with Scottish law, Mental Health (Care and Treatment) (Scotland) Act 2003.

Informal arrangements alone may occasionally be adequate when the patient, family members or friends all agree that the multidisciplinary team can pre-empt the situation by putting in place measures to minimize harm or remove a victim from the abusive environment. The following statute provides a welcome relief for a carer who may require respite and thus provide some relief.

> *The carer may request the local authority, before they make their decision as to whether the needs of the relevant person call for the provision of any services, to carry out an assessment of his ability to provide and to continue to provide care for the relevant person.*
>
> ### Section 1(b) of Carers (Recognition and Services) Act 1995

> *Safeguarding relates to the need to protect certain people who may be in vulnerable circumstances. These are people who may be at risk of abuse or neglect, due to the actions (or lack of action) of another person. In these cases, it is critical that services work together to identify people at risk, and put in place interventions to help prevent abuse or neglect, and to protect people.*
>
> ### Office of Public Guardian, Safeguarding Policy, 2013, http://www.justice.gov.uk/downloads/protecting-the-vulnerable/mca/safeguarding-policy.pdf (accessed 20 August 2013)

As part of the nurses' role in providing the best care in fulfilling their duty of care, they must ensure that especially where the client lacks capacity, they always act in the patient's best interests (Mental Capacity Act 2005). The NMC (2010) also requires the nurse to 'raise and escalate concerns'.

> *If you witness or suspect there is a risk to the safety of people in your care and you consider that there is an immediate risk of harm, you should report your concerns without delay to the appropriate person or authority.*
>
> ### NMC, Raising and Escalating Concerns, Guidance for Nurses and Midwives, 2010, paragraph 6

A fairly recent trend showed an increase in abuse with '108,000 cases of alleged abuse or neglect against vulnerable adults in 2011–12 – a rise of 11%' (HM Government, 2013). More therefore needs to be done to raise awareness about and disclose instances of abuse (Public Interest Disclosure Act 1998).

Scotland pioneered the free provision of personal care by local authorities, something which may be important in lessening the chances of abuse in the home (Community Care and Health (Scotland) Act 2002). Addressing assessments and safeguarding against elder abuse should be inclusive, and we must consider the informal carers who may themselves be vulnerable elders, and some concerns and frustration about the limitation of the care framework in the UK (Bradley, 1996).

The Disclosure and Barring System, as provided by the Protection of Freedoms Act 2012, now aims to improve the vetting of abusers, actual or potential. It also merges the functions of the Criminal Records Bureau (CRB) and Independent Safeguarding Authority (ISA) (Home Office, 2013a).

CONCLUSION

The Public Interest Disclosure Act 1998 should make it easier for healthcare workers who 'blow the whistle' on suspected abuse to be protected against victimization. In practice, victims may still be reluctant to go through the difficult procedures of having to give evidence against a loved one or losing them through imprisonment or enforced separation for their own protection. This has been recognized by the House of Commons (2004, paragraph 2) in the government's response to the recommendations and conclusions of the Health Select Committee's Inquiry into Elder Abuse. It is clear that as long as the causes for violent crimes exist, it is possible that vulnerable patients may be victims. Elder abuse, as any other type of abuse, tends to be subtle and secretive, and vulnerable older people may continue to suffer in secret, partly for fear of further victimization or because they feel disempowered. The importance of the healthcare professional's intervention is in being able to recognize the signs, being proactive and in being able to prevent abuse from occurring.

As an integral part of a trusting relationship between nurse and patient, the patient (or client) should feel confident that the nurse (together with other carers and family members) is able to safeguard and afford them the protection and dignity they deserve and not victimize them.

REFERENCES

Action on Elder Abuse (AEA). Bulletin, May–June 1995.
Bandura A. *Social learning theory*. New York: General Learning Press, 1977.
Bennett G. Age and ageing. British Geriatric Society, 2002. www.bgs.org. uk/Publications/age_ageing.htm (accessed 20 July 2013).

Bennett G, Kingston P. *Concepts, theories and interventions*. London: Chapman & Hall, 1995.

Bradley M. Caring for older people: elder abuse. *BMJ* 1996; 313: 548–50.

British Geriatrics Society (BGS). The abuse of older people. 1998. www.bgs.org.uk/ (accessed 29 August 2013).

Buka P, Sookhoo D. Current legal responses to elder abuse. *International Journal of Older People Nursing* 2006; 1(4): 194–200.

Community and District Nursing Association (CDNA). 2004. http://www.thecampaigncompany.co.uk/cdna/ (accessed 7 July 2013).

Curtis L. *Violence, race and culture*. Lexington, MA: Lexington Books, 1975.

Department of Health. *Caldicott guardians*. HSC 1999/012. 1997.

Department of Health. *No secrets, guidance on developing and implementing multi-agency policies and procedures to protect vulnerable adults from abuse*. HSC 2001/007: LAC (2001)12. London: Crown, 2000.

Donnellan C. *Alcohol abuse issues*. Cambridge: Independence Educational Publishers, 2001.

Eysenck H. *Crime and personality*, 3rd ed. London: Routledge and Kegan Paul, 1977.

Fitzgerald M, McLennan G, Pawson J. *Crime and society: readings in history and theory*. London: Open University Press, 1981.

Fletcher L, Buka P. *A legal framework for caring*. Basingstoke: Palgrave Macmillan, 1999.

Herrnstein RJ, Murray C. *The bell curve: the reshaping of American life by differences in intelligence*. Free Press: New York, 1994.

Hertzberger S. *Violence within the family. Sociology perspectives*. Oxford Social Psychology Series. Boulder, CO: Westview Press, 1996.

HM Government. *Abuse of vulnerable adults in England, 2011–12: provisional report, experimental statistics*. www.data.gov.uk (accessed 22 August 2013).

Home Office. Crime in England and Wales, London: Home Office statistical bulletin. Crown, 2003. http://www.helptheaged.org.uk/CampaignsNews/News/_items/elderabusecasestudies.htm (accessed 2 July 2013).

Home Office. *Cross-government definition of domestic violence: a consultation*. London: Home Office, 2011.

Home Office. National Archives, Barring and Disclosure Service. 2013a. http://webarchive.nationalarchives.gov.uk/20130107105354/http://homeoffice.gov.uk/agencies-public-bodies/dbs/ (accessed 30 August 2013).

House of Commons. The government's response to the recommendations and conclusions of the Health Select Committee. Crown, 2004.

Leach P. *Taking a case to the European Court of Human Rights*, 3rd ed. Oxford: Oxford University Press, 2011.

NCH. *The hidden victims: children and domestic violence*. London: NCH for Children, 1994. http://www.nch.org.uk/information/index (accessed 12 May 2013).

Nursing and Midwifery Council. *Professional code of conduct and ethics.* London: NMC, 2008.

Nursing and Midwifery Council. *Raising concerns: Guidance for nurses and midwives.* 2013.

Office of the Public Guardian. *Protection of vulnerable adults.* 2000. https://www.justice.gov.uk/downloads/protecting-the-vulnerable/mca/safeguarding-policy.pdf.

O'Keefe M, Hills A, Doyle M, McCreadie C, Scholes S, Constantine R, Tinker A, Manthorpe J, Biggs S, Erens B. *UK study of abuse and neglect of older people.* Prevalence survey report. National Centre for Social Research, King's College London, 2007. https://www.warwickshire.gov.uk/Web/corporate/wccweb.nsf/Links/6EA919F805F3B54180257885002E4C6B/$file/Full+Report_UK+Study+of+Abuse+and+Neglect+of+Older+People+v2.pdf (accessed August 2013).

Potter J. Behind closed doors: abuse of the elderly patient. *Nursing in Practice* 2004; 14: 21–23.

Walker L. The cycle of violence: Lenore Walker's model. 2002. http://mesa6.mesastate.edu (accessed 1 June 2013).

Williams K. *The Oxford handbook of criminology,* 7th ed. Oxford: Oxford University Press, 2012.

8 EQUALITY AND DIVERSITY

INTRODUCTION: BACKGROUND

This chapter considers the importance of ethical and legal principles in the need to provide care for diverse patients, with inclusivity and fairness and without preferential treatment. Owing to the complexity of this area, which affects patient's rights, the chapter aims to give an overview of aspects of discrimination and why it is important to treat different patients with diverse needs equally. Fairness is sometimes defined as 'justice', which is an established principle in ethics. This requires equal and non-discriminatory treatment for all. *Diversity* is defined as

> 1. *the condition of having or being composed of differing elements: variety; especially: the inclusion of different types of people (as people of different races or cultures) in a group or organization <programs intended to promote diversity in schools>.*
> 2. *an instance of being composed of differing elements or qualities: an instance of being diverse <a diversity of opinion>.*
> ***Merriam Dictionary, http://www.search.ask.com/ web?o=100000027cr&l=dis&tpr=4&gct=bar&q=merriam+ webster+dictionary+online (accessed 20 August 2013)***

The concept of 'discrimination' is never easy to define, especially as it is widely used with a variety of slightly differing contexts. This is based on a subjective element as the victim needs to demonstrate that they were treated differently. The onus lies with the defendant to prove that they did treated the complainant fairly.

Prejudice has long been defined as

> *hostile or negative attitudes based on ignorance and faulty or incomplete knowledge. It is characterized by a tendency to assign identical characteristics to whole groups regardless of individual variations.*
> ### Twitchin and Demuth, 1985, p. 170

It is possible for individual prejudices to influence treatment decisions; however, nurses should rise above this in order to demonstrate their respect for ethical principle of fairness as well as refraining from discriminatory treatment based on any deeply rooted, stereotyped attitudes which may be prejudicial toward individuals or a certain group of people.

At the end of the Second World War, it was recognized internationally that something needed to be done to ensure fair treatment of all individuals and this extends to healthcare provision. Under the auspices of the United Nations, the Universal Declaration of Human Rights 1948 emerged, recognizing, inter alia:

> *Article 2: Everyone is entitled to all the rights and freedoms set forth in this Declaration, without distinction of any kind, such as race, colour, sex, language, religion, political or other opinion, national or social origin, property, birth or other status.*
> ### United Nations, 1948

This is applicable to health care, and if ethical principles are followed, this means that the nurse must balance patients' interests according to their needs as well as subject to available resources.

This is not always clear-cut, as any patient's treatment will be dependent on their needs and on the basis of defining what those needs are. To those receiving care, certain practices may be interpreted as discriminatory. Any patient's needs are those which contribute to good health, as stated in the WHO Constitution:

> *The enjoyment of the highest attainable standard of health is one of the fundamental rights of every human being without distinction of race, religion, political belief, economic or social condition.*
> ### WHO Constitution, 1946

Most of the antidiscrimination case law is found in employment law, with a limited number of cases in healthcare provision; nevertheless, the principles therein are also applicable to healthcare law where a patient feels discriminated against. Antidiscriminatory practice is required by law, for example, the Race Relations Act 1976 or the Disability Discrimination Act 1995 (now repealed except in Northern Ireland). Another example in healthcare provision is discrimination against older people. It is also clear that while some patients are aware of and are able to assert their right not to be discriminated against, many may not be prepared to complain or may simply lack the knowledge and ability to do so. Where discrimination is established there may not only be breach of an ethical principle but also legal consequences and/or implications for professional registration.

Discrimination goes to the heart of patients' fundamental human rights, which must be respected as 'all men *and women* [emphasis added] are created equal and independent … they derive rights inherent and inalienable, among which are the preservation of life and liberty and the pursuit of happiness' (Thomas Jefferson, cited in Boyd, 1950, p. 423).

All types of discrimination involve a breach of fundamental rights through mistreatment or treatment of one person less favourably in comparison to another, as well as the positive aspect where the favoured individual is given privileged or preferential treatment, again, in comparison to others. Both aspects are equally unacceptable in nursing as they result in unfair and unequal provision of care, hence the reason why discrimination should be tackled as an infringement of patients' rights as much as that of any other ordinary citizens.

The converse or negative aspect, that one or more patients are given preferential treatment, should also be considered, even if this means that this may be difficult to prove. The effect on the disadvantaged person(s) is the same, being left out in the cold. The victim(s) may therefore have grounds for discrimination under the law. This is clearly in breach of ethical principles (which are embraced by the Beauchamp and Childress's principlism framework (2012)). This means that patients in their care should be treated neither as 'favourites' nor as 'outcasts'. This is also reflected in the NMC Code of Conduct (NMC, 2008).

DISCRIMINATION IN HEALTHCARE PROVISION

Discrimination can be defined as either direct or indirect:

> *Direct discrimination is when one person receives less favourable treatment than another person because of a protected characteristic. For example, if a clinic refuses to offer fertility services to a lesbian*

couple because they are not heterosexual, this constitutes direct discrimination on grounds of sexual orientation.

**NHS Choices, http://www.nhs.uk/NHSEngland/thenhs/
equality-and-diversity/Pages/equality-and-diversity-in-
the-NHS.aspx (accessed on 18 October 2013)**

Furthermore, this should be distinguished from indirect discrimination:

*Indirect discrimination is when there is a condition, rule, policy
or practice that applies to everyone, but which particularly disadvantages people who share a protected characteristic. For example,
a social care provider that runs a day centre decides to apply a
'no hats or other headgear' rule to its service users. If this rule
is applied to every service user, then Sikhs, Jews, Muslims and
Rastafarians, who may cover their heads as part of their religion,
will not be allowed to use the drop-in centre. Unless the social
care provider can objectively justify using the rule, this is indirect
discrimination.*

**NHS Choices, http://www.nhs.uk/NHSEngland/thenhs/
equality-and-diversity/Pages/equality-and-diversity-in-
the-NHS.aspx (accessed on 18 October 2013)**

It can nevertheless be argued that the Code of Conduct (NMC, 2008)
requires of nurses the provision of non-discriminatory care for all users.

*Everyone counts. We maximise our resources for the benefit of the
whole community, and make sure nobody is excluded, discriminated against or left behind. We accept that some people need more
help, that difficult decisions have to be taken.*

**NHS Constitution, 2013, http://www.nhs.uk/
choiceintheNHS/Rightsandpledges/NHSConstitution/
Documents/2013/the-nhs-constitution-for-england-2013.pdf**

THINKING POINT

Ms C is a 60 year-old a retired schoolteacher who is well known to the staff
for multiple emergency admissions via accidents and emergencies. She has been
known to complain and threaten nurses with litigation if she does not get her
own way. This time she is admitted in accidents and emergency for investigations
for abdominal pain and nausea. As a result, she appears to be given preferential
treatment in comparison to other patients. On this occasion, she is not happy that

(Continued)

the on-call surgeons are in theatre carrying out an emergency operation. She has settled since coming in but now demands immediate attention. You also have other patients with their own needs.

1. How do you prioritize care for a number of users with different needs?
2. What does the Nursing and Midwifery Council (NMC) require of you in prioritizing needs for this vis-à-vis those of other patients?

RECENT DEVELOPMENTS OF THE LAW ON DISCRIMINATION

The Equality Act (EA) 2006 (now obsolete) can be seen as an effective modern-day piece of legislation targeting discrimination and as the first step to bring together existing legislation by updating legislation in most of the six areas of discrimination legislation. It also aimed to be some kind of legal 'umbrella', which attempted to bring together all types of discrimination. Most of the existing antidiscrimination legislation remains intact, and this statute aims to coordinate the fight against discrimination by having one central body, the commission. The importance of this area of legislation is that victims should feel that they have access to justice and are not put off by any red tape. The effectiveness of antidiscriminatory legislation depends on the willingness of victims to complain. The difficulty is that while some persons on the receiving end may wish to complain about discrimination, others who lack the competence, such as incapacitated patients or those who lack knowledge about their rights, may do nothing. Some patients may feel that they do not wish to 'rock the boat' and indeed choose to put up with discrimination in the case of victimization.

Disability discrimination

Owing to their physical and possible mental incapacity, a large number of patients may fall into this category, often being impaired (from a physical or mental incapacity) or having limited ability to function. This is an important area of law which the nurse needs to understand as they provide care for this group of (disabled) patients. It is the impairment of any part or parts of the body on which disability focuses (WHO, 2002). It is this impairment and the absence of or limitation of 'bodily mechanism' (Oliver, in Helman, 2007) that is seen by some as the basis for determining the presence of disability. For the purposes of government agencies, such as social services and the department of employment, any persons who are disabled were covered by the Disabled Persons (Employment) Act 1944, Section 1 classification of those with the following:

> *(1) These include injury, disease or congenital deformity is substantially handicapped in obtaining or keeping employment, or in undertaking work on his own account, of a kind which would be suited to his age, experience and qualifications.*

The Disability Discrimination Act (DDA) 1995, Section 20(1), suggested that discrimination exists when there is 'less favourable treatment' of a person with disability. The Equality Act 2010 is a consolidation of and repealed the DDA 1995 (except for Northern Ireland), and focuses on areas such as public transport and housing provision by regulating public authorities to ensure they treat all users fairly. Disability also includes mental illness under the Mental Health Act 1983, Section 1, which includes the following four categories:

1. mental illness,
2. mental impairment,
3. severe mental impairment,
4. psychopathic disorder.

The Human Rights Act 1998 came into force in 2000. It was felt, however, that the issue of discrimination was fragmented, and this culminated in a major change with the enactment of the Equality Act 2010. The catalyst for change was the House of Commons itself in a body which would police the implementation on human rights and related antidiscriminatory legislation; 'an independent commission would be the most effective way of achieving the shared aim of bringing about a culture of respect for human rights' (Joint Committee on Human Rights, 2002–03).

Furthermore, it is important to note the differences between the two statutes, the Disability Discrimination Act (DDA) 1995 and the Equality Act (EA) 2010. The EA generally carries forward the protection provided for disabled people by the DDA. However, there are key differences:

> *• The DDA provided protection for disabled people from direct discrimination only in employment and related areas. The EA protects disabled people against direct discrimination in areas beyond the employment field (such as the supply of goods, facilities and services).*

- *The EA introduced improved protection from discrimination that occurs because of something connected with a person's disability. This form of discrimination can be justified if it can be shown to be a proportionate means of achieving a legitimate aim.*
- *The EA introduced the principle of indirect discrimination for disability. Indirect discrimination occurs when something applies in the same way to everybody but has an effect which particularly disadvantages, for example, disabled people. Indirect discrimination may be justified if it can be shown to be a proportionate means of achieving a legitimate aim.*
- *The EA applies one trigger point ... a duty to make reasonable adjustments for disabled people. This trigger point is where a disabled person would be at a substantial disadvantage compared to non-disabled people if the adjustment was not made.*

Office for Disability Issues (ODI), 2013, http://odi.dwp. gov.uk/disabled-people-and-legislation/equality-act-2010- and-dda-1995.php (accessed 20 August 2013)

In addition, there are further differences which make it easier for clients with disability to raise a complaint, where discrimination may be subtle, difficult to prove or result from making a complaint, as follows:

- *The EA extends protection from harassment that is related to disability. Previously, explicit protection only applied in relation to work. The EA applies this protection to areas beyond work.*
- *The EA provides protection from direct disability discrimination and harassment where this is based on a person's association with a disabled person, or on a false perception that the person is disabled.*
- *The EA contains a provision which limits the type of enquiries that a recruiting employer can make about disability and health when recruiting new staff. This provision will help prevent disabled candidates from being unfairly screened out at an early stage of the recruitment process.*

Office for Disability Issues (ODI), 2013, http://odi.dwp. gov.uk/disabled-people-and-legislation/equality-act-2010- and-dda-1995.php (accessed 20 August 2013)

Age discrimination

The National Service Framework (NSF) for Older People recognizes that elderly people may be discriminated against and sets a benchmark for healthcare professionals to aspire toward when delivering care for elderly people. This is a requirement for Standard 1 (rooting out age discrimination) of the NSF for the elderly (Department of Health, 2001).

> *NHS services will be provided, regardless of age, on the basis of clinical needs alone. Social care services will not use age in their eligibility criteria or policies, to restrict access to available services.*

The aim of NSFs such as the above is to improve national standards and hence the quality of care for patients. Breach of such standards does not mean an automatic breach of statutory provisions. However, where a trust fails to meet these standards, this may be evidence of liability in law, as when they fail in their duty of care to the patient in areas such as tort law. An example of an important aspect of discrimination which may affect the elderly in the provision of care is the provision of care packages. It is possible that this may be seen as a soft target in the need to save money, and effectively discriminates against the elderly. Discrimination takes place as a result of providers having stigma and prejudice. Prejudice has been defined above.

The nurse responsible for the care of an older person should never make assumptions, based on physical appearance and impairments alone, that the patient lacks mental capacity and will therefore be unaware of discrimination (DoH, 2012).

Racial discrimination

In most instances the concept of 'discrimination' takes many forms, with a range of definitions. The difficulty of racial discrimination is that it depends on a subjective perception or interpretation of concerning the victim of the alleged racist act.

> *A person discriminates against another in any circumstances relevant for the purposes of any provision of this Act if*
>
> - *on racial grounds he treats that other less favourably than he treats or would treat other persons; or*
> - *he applies to that other a requirement or condition which he applies or would apply equally to persons not of the same racial group as that other.*
>
> **Section 1 of Race Relations Act 1976 (repealed by the Equality Act 2010)**

Again, the onus or burden of proof is on the defendant to show that there was no unfair treatment on grounds of race. When patients lack either mental or physical capacity, it may be very difficult to establish discrimination on the grounds of race. Discrimination on the grounds of race may also result from indirect discrimination by way of victimization.

A study by Shah and Priestley (2001) showed that subjects who came from black and ethnic minority backgrounds had experienced discriminatory practices while receiving care. They perceived this to be based on their race when they compared their treatment with that of others.

OTHER TYPES OF DISCRIMINATION

It is difficult to establish how widespread other types of discrimination are in health care. This is because vulnerable people may be unwilling or unable to make a complaint under legislation such as the articles in Schedule 1 of the HRA 1998. This included discrimination on grounds such as gender, sexual orientation and religious beliefs. Discrimination on grounds of gender is now forbidden in the Equality Act 2010, while discrimination on the grounds of sexual orientation is outlawed; the passing of the Civil Partnership Act 2004 afforded same sex couples the right to civil unions with the latest legislation, the Marriage (Same Sex Couples) Act 2013 (c. 30), now affording same sex couples the same rights as heterosexual couples. Furthermore, discrimination on religion or on religious belief is now also outlawed under the Employment Equality (Religion or Belief) Regulations 2003.

The law (under the Equality Act 2010) now recognizes all the above aspects and contexts of discrimination. It is hoped that nurses can now turn to their own ethics, their professional code of conduct, national benchmarks such as the NSF for Older People and their local policies and guidelines which should all enshrine equal rights to fair treatment and care for all patients.

THINKING POINT

Jane is a junior qualified staff nurse who has worked on an acute care of the elderly ward for six months post-qualifying. One patient, Mrs S (a widow, aged 80), happens to live on the same street as Jane. She considers her 'a neighbour' as they have met in the supermarket and Jane has helped her carry her shopping. Jane decides not to

(Continued)

tell other staff members. However, it has also become clear that there is an issue of boundaries between Jane and this patient, including exchanging phone numbers. Other patients have noticed and made comments to the effect that Jane spends more time talking to Mrs S. She had been bringing in feature magazines for Mrs S but not for the other patients. Sara, who is one of her colleagues working on the ward, has also noticed this.

1. Find out about your organization's antidiscrimination policies.
2. Based on this information, what advice would you give to Sara and Jane?

GROUNDS FOR DISCRIMINATION AND THE LAW TODAY

The Act has two main purposes –

1. *to harmonise discrimination law, and to strengthen the law to support progress on equality.*
11. *The Act brings together and re-states all the enactments listed in paragraph 4 above and a number of other related provisions. It will harmonise existing provisions to give a single approach where appropriate. Most of the existing legislation will be repealed. The Equality Act 2006 will remain in force (as amended by the Act) so far as it relates to the constitution and operation of the Equality and Human Rights Commission; as will the Disability Discrimination Act 1995, so far as it relates to Northern Ireland.*

Equality Act 2010

The aim of the Equality Act 2010 is to provide protection from discrimination for any members of the society-at-large. Prior to this antidiscrimination was piecemeal and the Equality Act brought together antidiscrimination legislation which included:

- Sex Discrimination Act 1975
- Race Relations Act 1976
- Disability Discrimination Act 1995

This brings all pieces of discrimination legislation under the same umbrella. The statute redefines the grounds for discrimination.

Owing to the difficulty in amassing such evidence, it is only possible for the purposes of this chapter to have focused on three areas, which are those likely to have been experienced by patients within a caring environment. However reprehensible the concept of discrimination per se may sound, there is in fact no automatic recognition of it by the law; the law recognizes discrimination only within certain defined parameters. It could be argued that ethical or moral principles would dictate otherwise. Through legislation, Parliament has redefined grounds for discrimination recognizing a diverse society (Monaghan, 2013).

Grounds for discrimination – the protected characteristics

Under the Equality Act 2010, the following characteristics are grounds for complaint or 'protected characteristics':

- age,
- disability,
- gender reassignment,
- marriage and civil partnership,
- pregnancy and maternity,
- race,
- religion or belief,
- sex,
- sexual orientation.

The Equality Act 2010 now applies to England, Wales and Scotland but not to Northern Ireland. This is an attempt to consider all forms of discrimination under the same umbrella. In reality, it is more probably based on anecdotal evidence only that some types of discrimination will be more common than others. The Equality Commission main aim is one of promoting and 'encouraging', with limited powers of enforcement, and is perhaps one of the weaknesses of the law in the area of discrimination. The overall aim is to create 'fairness' (Government Equalities Office, 2013).

Since October 2013, it has been unlawful to victimize anyone who has made a complaint on discrimination.

THINKING POINT

A, aged 40, used to work as a barman after emigrating with his boyfriend and living in the UK for 10 years. He was admitted to a busy orthopaedic ward for leg surgery

(Continued)

following a road traffic accident. His operation went well though his rehabilitation was limited.

- He is partially sighted and registered blind, which makes him increasingly dependent on others for activities of living. As he is in a side room, he tends to be left until last for washing and dressing. He had overheard private conversation between the physiotherapist and the occupational therapist that (in an apparent reference to his ethnicity) 'they should go back to their own country'.
- A is now suffering from depression after splitting with his partner of 10 years (an older man, 20 years his senior) who had recently left him for another man. One morning, a male staff nurse refused to give him personal care claiming cultural religious grounds, as he believed it forbidden to have same sex relationships.

1. Consider the issues which you think may amount to discrimination.
2. How would you ensure that your patient does not feel discriminated against?

The NMC (2011) has shown its commitment to equality and diversity:

We will value and embrace differences and individuality in our stakeholders – that is, our staff, our Council members, our partners who work on our behalf, nurses and midwives, and the public we serve. Our aim is to ensure that all of our stakeholders receive a high level of service from us, and that everyone is treated fairly.

NMC, Nursing and Midwifery Council Equality and Diversity Strategy, 2011

Disability is now defined as below to include clients with long-term conditions:

6. *Disability*
   (1) A person (P) has a disability if –
       (a) P has a physical or mental impairment, and
       (b) the impairment has a substantial and long-term adverse effect on P's ability to carry out normal day-to-day activities.

Equality Act 2010

CONCLUSION

Unfair or unequal treatment of patients may be discriminatory. The Equalities Commission has as its main objective the promotion of equality and diversity in all aspects of life (EA 2006, Section 8). The problem with discrimination is that under present UK law, the alleged victim has to make a claim about what they may perceive as discrimination. This may not pose any difficulty for patients who have the mental capacity. For those who lack capacity, however, they may be unaware of any discriminatory acts affecting their care, hence the importance of the Mental Capacity Act 2005 to safeguard their interests.

On the issue of diversity and equality, nurses as professionals should recognize that there are differences among the people who are their patients. Their patients are entitled to non-discriminatory treatment under human rights legislation and in ethics. While some differences may be visible, others may not be visible or obvious. This means that making assumptions about a patient's capacity (physical or mental) or their needs can never be justified, as this may result in discrimination. The standard of care nurses deliver should be influenced not purely by the law and by their own ethical beliefs but also by a professional culture, which recognizes and values patients as individuals. They should always respect the patient's human rights. Together, the EA 2006, the Race Relations (Amendment) Act 2000, the DDA 2005 and related statutes should make it easier for healthcare providers and others such as social services to have an integrated approach to the fair treatment of users in the elimination of discrimination.

Antidiscriminatory practice is a key requirement for 'fairness' in ethics (Beauchamp and Childress, 2012) and in nursing. A nurse responsible for providing care must respond to the needs of patients from 'diverse' backgrounds. They need to avoid favouritism or disadvantaging any individual patients, and care for all their patients without fear and favour. Providing preferential treatment for one patient happens to detract from other patients' rights while also compromising the treatment of other 'less advantaged' patients. This may mean that the care given to all patients falls below the expected standards of a person possessing their skills under the *Bolam* principle (see in Chapter 1). All professional codes of conduct for healthcare personnel require of their members fair treatment as well as non-discrimination of patients or clients.

We have seen some improvement in the focus of the aim of legislation in improving equality and diversity, under the Equality Act 2010, which attempts to bring grounds for discrimination under an 'umbrella'. In practice, it may not be as easy for an alleged victim to prove this or to be courageous to bring a complaint forward without fear of victimization. There may still be grounds of discrimination which may still not be directly recognized by and enforceable under existing law. One example is discrimination on the grounds of social status or class. The fact is that discrimination may often be subtle and difficult to prove.

REFERENCES

Beauchamp T, Childress J. *Bioethics*, 7th ed. Oxford: Oxford University Press, 2012.

Department of Health. National service framework for older people. 2001. www.dh.gov.uk/en/Policyandguidance (accessed 18 July 2013).

Department of Health. Implementing a ban on age discrimination in the NHS – making effective, appropriate decisions. 2012. www.dh.gov.uk/publications (accessed 12 August 2013).

Equality Commission. http://www.equalityhumanrights.com/advice-and-guidance/new-equality-act-guidance/equality-act-starter-kit/video-understanding-the-equality-act-2010/ (accessed 22 August 2013).

Government Equalities Office. Creating a fairer and more equal society. 2013. https://www.gov.uk/government/policies/creating-a-fairer-and-more-equal-society.

Jefferson T. Rough draft of the American Declaration of Independence. In Boyd J, ed., *Papers of Thomas Jefferson.* Princeton, NJ: Princeton University Press, 1950, p. 423.

Joint Committee on Human Rights. *The case for a human rights commission.* Sixth Report, Session 2002–03, HL Paper 67-I and II, HC 489-I.

Monaghan K. *Monaghan on equality law*, 2nd ed. Oxford: Oxford University Press, 2013.

NHS Constitution. NHS choices. 2013. http://www.nhs.uk/NHSEngland/thenhs/equality-and-diversity/Pages/equality-and-diversity-in-the-NHS.aspx (accessed 18 October 2013).

NMC *Equality and Diversity Strategy*. 2011. http://www.nmc-uk.org/Documents/Consultations/Equality-and-Diversity/NCM_Equality-and-diversity-strategy-2012.pdf.

Nursing and Midwifery Council. *Code of professional conduct and ethics.* London: NMC, 2008.

Office for Disability Issues (ODI). 2013. http://odi.dwp.gov.uk/disabled-people-and-legislation/equality-act-2010-and-dda-1995.php (accessed 20 August 2013).

Oliver M. In Helman C, ed., *Culture, health and illness*, 5th ed. London: Hodder Arnold, 2007.

Shah S, Priestley M. Better services, better health: the healthcare experiences of black and minority ethnic disabled people. 2001. www.leeds.ac.uk/disability-studies (accessed 20 June 2013).

Twitchin J, Demuth C. *Multi-cultural education: views from the classroom*, 2nd ed. London: BBC, 1985.

United Nations. The universal declaration of human rights. 1948. www. un.org/Overview/rights. html (accessed 20 July 2007).

World Health Organization. Towards a common language for functioning, disability and health international classification of functioning (ICF). 2002. www.who.int/medicines_technologies/human_rights/en/ (accessed 16 August 2013).

9 END-OF-LIFE CARE

INTRODUCTION

This chapter explores an important aspect of care for people in the final continuum of life. Based on everyday experience, human mortality is a certain and an indisputable fact. Dying has been described as 'a human process in the same way that being born is a normal and all-human process' (Kubler-Ross, 1991, p. 10). Nowadays, it is much more difficult to determine when death occurs due to advanced medical science interventions (Campbell et al., 2005). The core ethical question on the end of life issue is how and when the end of life may be allowed.

There are views at both ends of the spectrum – on the one hand, absolute preservation of life (and delaying the inevitable), and on the other hand, allowing death or 'letting go', if not assisting or hastening the end. In either case, there is a potential conflict of interests, between the patient's best interests and those of other stakeholders and possibly those of society as a whole, in consideration of the ethical and legal implications. Society's motives may be driven by caring and altruistic concerns to prolong life, or (cynically) economic reasons may play a part, by considering the costs of maintaining what seems to be a futile life.

The court's role is usually a balancing act and may find that there is no absolute obligation on doctors to prolong life regardless if treatment outcomes are poor.

Under certain provisions, states assume their right through legislation to determine when a life can be ended, actively or passively. This may be in the case of retributive justice, when a capital sentence is allowed for murder, on the basis of the 'life for life' principle. Sometimes it could be argued in ethics and law that justifiable homicide (one person killing another) will be accepted, but this is only in clearly defined circumstances, such as in self defence or as an act of war.

CLINICAL DECISION-MAKING

Death is difficult to determine; 'as a result of developments in modern medical technology, doctors no longer associate death exclusively with breathing and heart beat, and it has come to be accepted that death occurs when the brain, and in particular the brain stem, has been destroyed' (Lord Goff in the following case).

The definitions of 'life' and 'death' are the subject of debate throughout healthcare professional frameworks. Consider the following definition of end of life below:

Airedale NHS Trust v Bland [1993] I All ER 821

Anthony David Bland, a Liverpool Football Club fan, then aged 17, attended the Hillsborough ground for a match. During the disastrous course of events of that day, he was crushed and subsequently suffered brain damage from a lack of oxygen supply to his brain, with resulting irreversible brain damage. By the time the case went to court, he had been in a persistent vegetative state (PVS) for some time. The question for the court was whether his artificial feeding should be discontinued, and with the agreement of the consultant and the family, this was allowed.

> People are 'approaching the end of life' when they are likely to die within the next 12 months. This includes people whose death is imminent (expected within a few hours or days) and those with
>
> - advanced, progressive, incurable conditions
> - general frailty and co-existing conditions that mean they are expected to die within 12 months

- *existing conditions if they are at risk of dying from a sudden acute crisis in their condition*
- *life-threatening acute conditions caused by sudden catastrophic events.*

General Medical Council, 2010, in RCGP, 2012

When applied to the clinical setting, it is a reasonable expectation in civil law and in ethics that healthcare professionals owe a duty of care to provide a reasonable standard of care to maintain the welfare of patients under their care (*Donoghue* v *Stevenson* [1932], AC 532). Their primary goal should be to promote health as well as to save lives. A dilemma may arise when healthcare professionals must engage in end of life decisions. Healthcare professionals may experience contrasting roles, from fighting to save a life to accepting the fact that treatment may be futile with death being inevitable. It has been suggested that 'nurses have to implement ethical decisions to withdraw treatment when they have not been party to the decision making process' (Viney, 1996, p. 182) in the first place. The most important ethical question is to determine whether in their role they can foresee circumstances in which it is justifiable to either actively or passively terminate that life by withdrawing treatment.

EUTHANASIA

Some Ancient Greek moral philosophers believed that there might be situations in which euthanasia would be acceptable provided that it was 'easy and gentle'. The word 'euthanasia' had a somewhat wider connotation then, having no specific reference to so-called 'mercy killing' (Teichman, 1996, p. 65). In consideration of patient care by physicians, the Hippocratic Oath (500 bc) required physicians to sustain and enhance the quality of life of their patients. These are related to a general consensus evident in professional codes of conduct across disciplines of healthcare professionals including nursing. This means that most ethical philosophies and religions view life as a gift from a supernatural 'being', some form of deity or from 'Mother Nature'. This entity is seen as having the ultimate right to give or to take life. There, however, appears to be no consensus on the stage at which life begins and equally no agreement as to when life should end. Medical science can now sustain life at a basic level to a greater extent than in the time of the Ancient Greeks. Incidentally, the legal definition of death is much broader, to include biological life, while the clinical-medical one is limited to brain stem dysfunction as the basis for determining death, a persistent vegetative state (PVS). The law on human rights takes into account the fact that every patient is entitled to a right to life (Article 2 of Human Rights Act 1998); hence, this has been used as a basis for litigation to assert that right.

> *Everyone's right to life shall be protected by the law. No one shall be deprived of his life intentionally save in the execution of a sentence of a court following his conviction of a crime for which this penalty is provided by the law.*
>
> **Article 2 of Human Rights Act 1998**

This nevertheless should be qualified. There are many definitions of euthanasia, and the preferred one serves as a starting point for defining euthanasia as

> *An easy and painless death, mercy killing.*
>
> **Dorland Medical Dictionary**

Another definition is

> *The literary origin of the word 'Eu-thanasia' is the Greek translation for, a 'good-death'. It has been argued by some that the concept of euthanasia should include a positive 'enabling' aspect which includes the patient's autonomy and the right to choice.*
>
> **Davies, 1998, p. 344**

Healthcare professionals, in general, and doctors, in particular, face a dilemma when trying to establish a patient's capacity to choose treatment which, in their professional judgement, they may consider to be futile. This task is difficult considering that a patient's judgement may be influenced by poor physical and/or psychological impairment resulting from disease. The ability to establish the patient's best interests is even more difficult when they (the patient) are totally mentally incapacitated or have intermittent spells of consciousness and rationality. The question posed here is whether there are any circumstances where substitution of that judgement by another person's judgement would be justifiable. There follows a definition of 'best interests' with an explanation for determining them.

> *(1) In determining for the purposes of this Act what is in a person's best interests, the person's best interests, the person making the determination must consider all the circumstances appearing to him to be relevant.*
>
> *(2) In particular, he must take the following steps.*

(3) He must consider (a) whether it is likely that the person will at some time have capacity in relation to the matter in question and, (b) if it appears likely that he will, when that is likely to be.
Mental Capacity Bill 2004, paragraph 4

Active euthanasia

A person may legally take active measures to end their life by consuming a concoction of drugs or by any other means, knowing that that action will end their life, which is suicide. A similar effect may be achieved through the assistance of another person, in which case this becomes 'assisted suicide' as well as the crime of aiding and abetting (Section 2(1) of Suicide Act 1961). These are offences subject to criminal law scrutiny and possible prosecution. Physician-assisted suicide is an alternative to withdrawal of treatment, when a patient requests a doctor to provide them with drugs that will shorten or end life. Euthanasia is murder in the UK. This is on the basis of the following case.

Regina v Cox [1992] 12 BMLR 38

A 70-year-old woman suffered from severe arthritis with severe pain. It could not be established how much longer she would have lived (but for the administration of a potent substance resulting in her death). She had suffered from severe arthritic pain for several years, which was not controlled by analgesia. She had requested her consultant, Cox, to put her out of her misery. Dr Cox then knowingly injected her with a lethal dose of potassium chloride resulting in her death. He was initially charged with murder but subsequently found guilty of attempted murder. The judge directing the jury said that 'if it is proved that Dr Cox injected Lillian Boyes with potassium chloride in circumstances which make sure that by that act he intended to kill her, then he is guilty of attempted murder'. The case resulted in a suspended sentence. As the body had been cremated before the case was brought to the attention of the police, it was not proven that the injected potassium was the cause of death.

Physician-assisted suicide may be either voluntary, in the case where a patient is mentally competent and gives permission, or this may be involuntary, where the patient lacks the capacity to make a choice, in the case of an unconscious patient. Incompetent patients have no legal rights to refuse consent to treatment. There are now new provisions under the Mental Capacity Act 2005, while the Mental Health Act 1983 is replaced by the Mental Health Act 2007, with Adults with Incapacity (Scotland) Act 2000 and Mental Health (Care and Treatment) (Scotland)

Act 2003 applicable, respectively. Unless it can be proven otherwise, there is now a presumption in law that every adult patient has the capacity to make an informed decision. The difference between 'suicide' and 'physician-assisted suicide' is that the latter is carried out within a clinical setting and protected by the law in only a handful of countries. Physician-assisted euthanasia is illegal under current UK legislation.

Passive euthanasia

This involves those situations in which a patient's treatment is either withdrawn by stopping current treatment or by making a decision that no new interventions will be instituted. One example is where antibiotics may be indicated for treatment of a chest infection and a conscious decision is made not to administer antibiotics because any further treatment would not have any meaningful benefit to the patient. Since *Airedale NHS Trust* v *Bland* [1993] 1 All ER 821 HL (above), where there is a lack of clarity, the court's permission must be sought before making a decision to withdraw treatment.

Voluntary euthanasia

Voluntary euthanasia involves a patient who possesses the mental capacity to make an informed choice. Such a patient may choose to accept a form of treatment or refuse it even with the awareness that the consequence will be detrimental to their health. A patient's right to exercise autonomy in accepting or refusing treatment should be respected in ethics, since the passing of the Suicide Act 1961 (Section 1). In some countries, for example, the Netherlands, voluntary physician-assisted suicide would be granted if the conditions for the relevant framework were satisfied. This is different in the UK, although the Mental Capacity Act 2005 of England and Wales which implements the Convention on the International Protection of Adults (signed at The Hague on 13 January 2000 (cm. 5881)) changes the balance in favour of the patient. On the other hand, doctors and nurses may not be forced to carry out any clinical actions they consider contrary to their professional judgement or which they find morally reprehensible unless this is within the confines of the law. Establishing the 'voluntariness' based on informed consent is at the centre of decision-making.

Involuntary euthanasia

Involuntary euthanasia applies to situations where a patient lacks the capacity to make a rational choice and this raises questions on the extent to which, in reality, a patient's autonomy can influence outcomes related to treatment. There has been long-standing provision for a formal proxy to make decisions on behalf of the patient in financial matters (the proxy having been granted a power of attorney), but not decisions on treatment. The power of the 'healthcare proxy' was different under Scottish law, where the former may, in certain circumstances, make a choice on behalf of the patient. Since the passing of the Mental Capacity Act 2005, however, a deputy in England and Wales and Northern Ireland now has similar powers. This introduces a new dimension and a presumption in law that every adult has the capacity to make an informed decision. An advocate or healthcare proxy may not override a clinical decision.

Adoption of an ethical framework for decision-making (which is considered as universal in its application) is necessary for healthcare professionals in order to reach the correct decisions related to the end of life. Principlism (or bioethical principles) aims to define basic human rights starting with autonomy, beneficence, non-maleficence and fairness in the decision-making framework, making the four ethical principles an essential part of the medical/nursing ethical framework for decision-making. Beauchamp and Childress (2008) first termed them 'universal'. Euthanasia may be subject to a person's own choice or through 'assistance', whether at the hands of a professional or another person, someone's own actions or the actions of others. An example of own actions is refusal of treatment, which may result in termination of life. The general principle of a patient's right to autonomy was nevertheless altered in the following case.

Re T (Adult: Refusal of Medical Treatment) [1992] 4 All ER 649, CA

A pregnant woman aged 20 had suffered serious injuries in a road traffic accident. The injuries included a haemorrhage, which resulted in the birth of a stillborn baby. She had been 34 weeks pregnant and, on admission, had consented to a Caesarean section. Her mother, who was a strict Jehovah's Witness, had then influenced her daughter (Ms T), who subsequently told doctors that she objected to a blood transfusion. Her boyfriend and his father, on the other hand, objected and sought a judicial review authorizing a blood transfusion as a life-saving measure.

Held: It was held by the Court of Appeal (Lord Donaldson's judgement) that

1. Her mental capacity to choose whether to accept a blood transfusion or not had been impaired by her injuries.
2. She had lacked sufficient information to make an informed (rational) decision to accept or refuse treatment.
3. Undue pressure from her mother may have influenced her subsequent decision to appear to reject a blood transfusion.

> The courts therefore could not apply the ethical principle of autonomy under these circumstances and ordered a transfusion to be given to Ms T without her consent.

SUICIDE – HUMAN RIGHT OR A CRIMINAL ACT

In consideration of the concept of 'human rights' there is a presumption that every person may make a choice about how and where they lead their lives and therefore arguably, this right should include how and when to terminate their own lives. This may be acceptable to some while others may find this morally reprehensible.

Under Section 1, Suicide Act 1961 suicide is no longer a crime, meaning that prosecution will not follow but this provision does not necessarily mean that the UK sanctions the act of suicide.

> *Suicide to cease to be a crime.*
> *The rule of law whereby it is a crime for a person to commit suicide is hereby abrogated.*
>
> ### *Section 1 of Suicide Act 1961*

However, Section 2(1) of the Suicide Act 1961 states that physician-assisted or 'other person-assisted' suicide is illegal. Other competing interests in society may limit individual rights and choices. A patient's expressed wish to commit suicide may be motivated by unbearable pain and/or depressive illness as well as by social pressures. Assisted suicide takes place when another person is involved, be it a doctor or a layperson.

A person who assists another person to take their life may be charged with murder under Section 1 of the Homicide Act 1957. Furthermore:

> *A person who aids, abets, counsels or procures the suicide of another or an attempt by another to commit suicide shall be liable on conviction on indictment to imprisonment for a term not exceeding 14 years.*
>
> ### *Section 2(1) of Suicide Act 1961*

As amended by the Coroners and Justice Act 2009, which provides a definition:

> 2   *Criminal liability for complicity in another's suicide*
> *(1) A person ('D') commits an offence if –*
> *(a) D does an act capable of encouraging or assisting the suicide or attempted suicide of another person, and*

>   *(b) D's act was intended to encourage or assist suicide or an attempt at suicide.*
>
> **Coroners and Justice Act 2009**

Subject to Section 4 of the Suicide Act 1981, however, where evidence of a suicide pact is present, the charge may be reduced from murder to manslaughter. Section 2(1) of Suicide Act 1961 (above) sets a maximum sentence of 14 years' imprisonment. This section was unsuccessfully challenged in the case below.

Pretty v the United Kingdom (European Court of Human Rights), application no. 2346/02, Strasbourg, April 29; [2002]

In this case, a woman with motor neuron disease invoked her right to choose refusal of treatment, under Articles 2, 3 and 8 of the European Convention on the Protection of Human Rights and Fundamental Freedoms 1950. She sought immunity from prosecution for her husband on assisting her to die with dignity. This was unanimously rejected by the House of Lords and on appeal, that decision was upheld by the European Court of Human Rights.

Mainstream religions such as Christianity, Islam and Judaism do not accept an individual right to commit suicide on the basis of what is regarded as the 'sanctity of life'. Buddhism also rejects the notion of suicide or self-harm as morally reprehensible and wrong. Some Hindu writers would argue, however, that 'there is a right time (natural) "kala" for death' and also hold that there should be 'the acceptability of willed death, where a man may control his death by refusing to take food or drink' (Morgan and Lawton, 1996, p. 3). They nevertheless believe that only the supernatural or 'Divine Being' has the right to give and take life. Some moral philosophers, such as Kant (1724–1804), propose that under no circumstance should suicide be justifiable. His 'categorical imperative' concept includes a moral duty to do what is right, and cannot include suicide, as this would be absurd. It is not a question of choice. On the other hand, utilitarianism would argue that whatever course of action produces the greatest benefit or happiness for the greatest number of people should be followed, and hence could justify suicide in some circumstances. From a pragmatic point of view, it could be argued that, at least for those with loved ones and dependants, suicide is an inconsiderate option. The views of other interested parties (for example, loved ones) are often not considered. Attitudes toward life and death matters and how to deal with end of life decisions through euthanasia vary internationally and across Europe, as shown by one view on euthanasia.

> *Wherever a sick person in perfect clarity of mind demands strongly that an end be put to an existence which has lost all meaning for him and wherever a committee of doctors convoked for the purpose recognises the unavailability of any other treatment, euthanasia should be granted.*
>
> ***EC Human Rights Commission, 1991***

A more recent case had the following ruling by the High Court, which redefined the meaning of withdrawal of treatment in the following case.

Burke v General Medical Council [2005] EWCA Civ 1003

A patient suffering from a degenerative brain disease effectively challenged the GMC guidelines for deciding on withdrawal of treatment for a patient diagnosed as being in a persistent vegetative state. According to *The Times*, 'the ruling reflects a shift from the medical profession and into the hands of patients. It also however, forms part of a less welcome shift in power out of the hands of practitioners and into the hands of the courts' (*The Times*, 31 July 2004). The effect was to oblige the medical staff to continue with active (probably relatively expensive) treatment which some may see as futile, even though Mr Burke was considered to be in the terminal stages of life.

On appeal, the House of Lords and further the European Court of Human Rights held that doctors should not be expected to continue treatment of a patient (who suffered from muscle ataxia in this case) if in their judgement this was considered futile.

DO NOT ATTEMPT RESUSCITATION ORDERS

Here, examples of the terms commonly used are 'do not resuscitate', 'do not attempt resuscitation', 'not for resuscitation', 'not for the call', 'not for e.g. 2222' or any other number assigned for cardiopulmonary arrest emergency calls. The Resuscitation Council outlines situations when resuscitation is considered futile (BMA, 2007).

The first recorded attempt to administer resuscitation was around 800 BC in Elijah's attempt to give a child 'mouth to mouth' (King James' Version Bible, 2 Kings 4:34–35). Mouth-to-mouth resuscitation was first attempted as early as 1950. Cardiopulmonary resuscitation was not then used in hospitals except to 'prevent premature death in previously "fit" patients, who sustained a sudden cardiac or respiratory arrest' (Levack, 2002, p. 2). There are times when questions may be asked about the appropriateness of the use of cardiopulmonary resuscitation, especially when this is deemed futile due to a poor outcomes prognosis – a quality of life issue.

Healthcare professionals need a theoretical moral framework, such as 'principlism', to guide them in making ethical decisions when issues on end of life decisions may be related to a resuscitation status. There is debate as to whether a patient should be involved in decision-making related to their resuscitation status, and whether every patient's permission should be sought for doctors to initiate a 'non-resuscitation' status in a patient's notes. This could be interpreted as withdrawing treatment.

Case study

A 67-year-old cancer patient found she had had a 'DNAR' order written on her medical notes without her consent. The patient saw that her notes had a 'do not resuscitate' entry from a previous admission. She complained she had not been consulted about this decision or options on whether she would like to be resuscitated. As it happened, the patient in question had a wish to be resuscitated in the event of a cardiac arrest: 'she was understandably distressed by this as no discussion had taken place with her or her next of kin', said a doctor (BBC News, 27 June 2000).

An inappropriate 'do not resuscitate' order may result in conflict and breach of trust between the patient, family members and healthcare professionals (Beigler, 2003). Owing to threats of litigation, modern healthcare practice may develop a culture of defensive medicine, assuming that prior to every death, cardiopulmonary resuscitation should be pursued. Professional bodies have issued the guidelines *Decisions Relating to Cardiopulmonary Resuscitation*, as an example of joint work by the British Medical Association (BMA), the Resuscitation Council (UK) and the Royal College of Nursing (RCN). The BMA as well as related medical royal colleges and the RCN have all agreed on a code of practice (BMA, 1995) (see also the GMC's (2006) *Guidance to Good Medical Practice*).

There are recent changes to the guidelines:

> *The overall clinical responsibility for decisions about cardiopulmonary resuscitation including DNAR decisions rests with the most senior clinician as defined by local policy. This could be a consultant, GP or suitably experienced nurse.*

> *BMA, 2007*

THINKING POINT: A FRAMEWORK FOR DECISION-MAKING

Decision-making framework

Is cardiac or respiratory arrest a clear possibility in the circumstances of the patient? **NO**	If there is no reason to believe that the patient is likely to have a cardiac or respiratory arrest it is not necessary to initiate discussion with the patient (or those close to patients who lack capacity) about CPR. If, however, the patient wishes to discuss CPR this should be respected.

YES

When a decision not to attempt CPR is made on these clear clinical grounds, it is not appropriate to ask the patient's wishes about CPR, but careful consideration should be given as to whether to inform the patient of the DNAR decision (see section 6).

Where the patient lacks capacity and has a welfare attorney or court-appointed deputy or guardian, this person should be informed of the decision not to attempt CPR and the reasons for it as part of the ongoing discussion about the patient's care (see section 6).

Is there a realistic chance that CPR could be successful? **NO**	

If a second opinion is requested, this request should be respected, whenever possible.

YES

Does the patient lack capacity and have an advance decision refusing CPR or a welfare attorney with relevant authority? **YES**	If a patient has made an advance decision refusing CPR, and the criteria for applicability and validity are met, this must be respected. If an attorney, deputy or guardian has been appointed they should be consulted (see sections 8 and 9).

NO

Are the potential risks and burdens of CPR considered to be greater than the likely benefits of CPR? **YES**	When there is only a very small chance of success, and there are questions about whether the burdens outweigh the benefits of attempting CPR, the involvement of the patient (or, if the patient lacks mental capacity, those close to the patient) in making the decision is crucial. When the patient is a child or young person, those with parental responsibility should be involved in the decision where appropriate. When adult patients have mental capacity their own view should guide decision-making (see section 7).

NO

CPR should be attempted unless the patient has capacity and states that they would not want CPR attempted.

- Decisions about CPR are sensitive and complex and should be undertaken by experienced members of the healthcare team and documented carefully.
- Decisions should be reviewed regularly and when circumstances change.
- Advice should be sought if there is uncertainty.

Source: From the British Medical Association (BMA), Withholding Life-Prolonging Medical Treatment, 2007. Reproduced with kind permission of the British Medical Association.

The Department of Health requires clinical areas to have in place resuscitation policies 'which respect patients' rights in place, understood by all staff and accessible to those who need them, and that such policies are subject to appropriate audit and monitoring arrangements' (NHS Executive, 2000, p. 1). Such a policy should be published locally for all interested parties.

It is important to involve family members in the decision-making (where possible to ascertain the patient's wishes); however, only the court may have the final decision on withdrawal of treatment. In cases where there is a diagnosis of persistent vegetative state (PVS) the state 'results from severe damage to the cerebral cortex, resulting in destruction of tissue in the thinking, feeling part of the brain. Patients appear awake but show no psychologically meaningful responses to stimuli and it is common for cerebral atrophy to occur. The condition is distinguished from a state of low awareness and the minimally conscious state (MCS) where patients show minimal but definite evidence of consciousness despite profound cognitive impairment' (BMA, 2006). The patient is required to have been in such a state for more than six months. It is the responsibility of the healthcare professionals to keep the family informed of any changes. The effect of any perceived or real shortcomings in the care of their loved ones may adversely affect them. Many would argue that the role of the healthcare professional is one of promoting rather than terminating life (Keown, 2002).

Where a user lacks competence or capacity, healthcare professionals and the next of kin can agree to withdraw treatment or not to initiate new active treatment, provided this is in the patient's best interest (Section 2 of Mental Capacity Act 2005). Competence may be specific to informed consent, which means that the user may be confused in some respects though demonstrate an understanding of the benefits and risks related to the treatment. On withdrawal of treatment please see the decision in the Tony Bland case. When there is disagreement between healthcare professionals and family members, the matter should be referred to the courts for a judicial review. By carrying out inappropriate treatment there is a danger of raising the hopes of family members close to the patient without achieving much. The most difficult moment for both healthcare professionals and the family members is likely to be when a decision to withdraw treatment must be made. This has to be done when it is obvious that despite acute interventions, the patient is going to die, and the treatment is said to be futile. Winter and Cohen (1999) observe that there are difficulties in justifying the use of the term 'relatively futile' in respect of such treatment. It may be dangerous, as it introduces an unknown and potentially variable factor – namely the doctor's judgement (Winter and Cohen, 1999, p. 3). A clinical judgement may turn out to be wrong, as in the following case.

Glass v United Kingdom [2004] (application no. 61827/00)

The case followed the admission of a patient, a child who suffered from learning disabilities, who was in a poorly state suffering from a chest infection. He was represented by his mother as guardian, who sued the trust because doctors had made the decision not to treat the patient and place a 'do not attempt resuscitation order' above his bed and started a diamorphine pump. This was all done without consulting his mother. A physical fight ensued during which several police officers and two doctors were injured. His mother nevertheless wanted his treatment continued. The court held unanimously in favour of the patient on the basis that the trust had been in breach of Article 8 (right to respect for private life) of the European Convention on Human Rights 1998.

The point on the validity of DNAR orders is also highlighted in the following case:

Re R (Adults: Medical Treatment) [1996] 31 BMLR 127

A 23-year-old man who was born with brain damage had multiple medical problems which included having developed epilepsy as a child. Unable to communicate, he appeared to be constantly in considerable acute pain. He was, however, conscious, having required constant care in a nursing home for the previous four years with weekend respite care, and he had been in and out of hospital with various ailments. There had been an agreement between the family and doctors that he should not be a candidate for active resuscitation. The trust, however, sought a declaration on withdrawal of treatment. It was held by Sir Stephen Brown that the 'do not resuscitate' order was lawful, on the basis that in cases where cardiopulmonary resuscitation was unlikely to succeed, this could be justified.

Leading case law in Scots law (*Law Hospital NHS Trust* v *Lord Advocate* [1996] 2 FLR 407) inclines toward a different approach in favour of withdrawal of treatment. However, the GMC's guidelines on withholding and withdrawing life-prolonging treatments (GMC, 2002, paragraph 16) require that, in the first place, 'doctors must take account of patients' preferences when providing treatment. However where a patient wishes to have a treatment that in the doctor's considered view is not clinically indicated, there is no ethical or legal obligation on the part of the doctor to provide it'. This was updated in 2007 and is due for further update in 2014. Difficulties may arise when family members disagree with the decision to continue treatment, as illustrated in the following case.

W Healthcare NHS Trust v H [2005] I WLR 834

A nasogastric feeding tube for a 59-year-old MS patient fell out. The patient was conscious but had lacked mental capacity for decision-making, having been on tube feeding for five years prior to this. The family objected to the tube being reinserted. It was held by the court that in the absence of a valid advance directive, it was in the patient's best interest for the tube to be reinserted.

PERSISTENT VEGETATIVE STATE (PVS)

One definition for PVS is

A person who has lost cognitive neurological function, meaning that the upper part of the brain that controls the more sophisticated functions, such as speech, movement and thought, has died. People in PVS are able to breathe unaided as the lower part of the brain (the brain stem) is still functioning.

NHS Direct Online Health Encyclopaedia, 2002

It is important to attempt to distinguish between PVS and a comatose state. In the case of the former, the condition is scientifically irrecoverable once the harm is done. If a patient is in a coma there is a chance of recovery. The Royal College of Physicians acknowledged that 'any diagnosis of PVS is not absolute but based on probability' (Royal College of Physicians, 1996, pp. 119–21). In the case of a patient in a PVS who may be on a ventilator, the withdrawal of treatment must be more formal and guidelines set out by the BMA and the GMC should always be followed (see *Bolam* v *Friern Hospital Management Committee* [1957] 1 WLR 582). There may be difficulties in establishing the criteria as PVS stems from the distinction between a 'brain stem' death where there is loss of neurological functions and evidence of basic life and a biological death (Campbell et al., 2005).

A patient who is being fed by artificial means may be considered alive only in the most basic of the biological or vegetative sense if they are deprived of brain function. It is believed that the true sense of death means that when this occurs, it is irrevocable and the functioning is irreversible (Campbell et al., 2005). The brain damage must be so severe that the condition cannot be reversed. Ongoing expensive treatment raises questions about how far medical science should go to sustain life for a 'brain dead' patient.

> *Some view sustaining these patients' lives as unethical because of its expense. Still others centre the debate on whether or not PVS patients are persons. If not, they see no obligation to continue providing food and fluids. Others propose resolving this dilemma by creating new criteria for determining when death occurs. If PVS patients are actually dead, there should be little argument over withholding or withdrawing their food and fluids.*
>
> **O'Mathuna, www.venos.org/ministries**

A patient is regarded as having been in PVS or a condition closely resembling PVS if this has persisted for at least six months. In England and Wales a court order to withdraw treatment should be sought for a review (BMA, 2003).

> *Artificial nutrition and hydration from a patient in PVS … the judgment made it clear that it was not necessary to apply to the courts in every case where withdrawal of artificial nutrition and hydration is proposed from a patient with PVS.*
>
> **BMA, 2000, p. 2**

THINKING POINT

John, a 25-year-old single young man who was a successful professional footballer, suffered head and multiple injuries in a car crash, requiring an emergency admission to hospital. He was the only child of a middle-aged couple. He had undergone two surgical procedures to remove a blood clot following a sub-dural haemorrhage and returned to the Intensive care unit. He had not made any significant improvement since the last operation and had in fact suffered from a stroke and resulting brain stem damage. Over the following week post-operatively, his general condition steadily deteriorated, the prognosis is poor and his family was obviously devastated by the news.

A week later, the consultant physician responsible for John's care advised the parents that their son was not making any progress, and that he was now in a PVS, having been an inpatient for the last six and a half months in the high dependency unit. The consultant discusses discontinuing treatment with the family, who disagree.

Consider the ethical and legal issues in the above scenario.

LIVING WILLS/ADVANCE DIRECTIVES AND THE RIGHT TO CHOOSE

Advance directives are a patient's formal instructions on their wishes to refuse certain specified treatment should their condition deteriorate. They may only be used as an indication of treatment a patient may choose to decline, not as a basis for demanding certain forms of treatment. An advance refusal of treatment is defined as

> *a refusal made by a person aged eighteen or over with the necessary capacity of any medical, surgical or dental treatment or other procedure and intended to have effect at any subsequent time when he or she may be without capacity to refuse consent.*
>
> ### *Law Commission, 1995*

Living wills are the physical evidence of a patient's wishes should their condition deteriorate and they are too incapacitated to indicate their wishes. Similar arrangements are now in place in England and Wales (Sections 24–26 of Mental Capacity Act 2005) following Scotland (Adults with Incapacity (Scotland) Act 2000), where a healthcare proxy document is used to describe either a living will or the full power granted to a proxy to make decisions on the patient's behalf. In the case of *Airedale NHS Trust* v *Bland* [1993] 1 All ER 821 HL, Lord Goff, at 872, in particular said that the courts would reject the 'substituted judgment test', which means the court will not recognize any decision on the basis of informal arrangements for proxy decision-making.

The Law Commission report on mental incapacity (Law Commission, 1995) recommended acceptance of any advance 'refusals' of consent to treatment as well as the principle of patient autonomy. This recognizes human rights for patients and includes the right to accept or refuse treatment.

Since the ruling in *Airedale NHS Trust* v *Bland* [1993] 1 All ER 821 HL, living wills have been recognized as evidence of 'the patient's wish' to limit or refuse treatment. Any will drawn up prior to a patient's deterioration must satisfy the above prerequisites, and for the will to have legal validity must originate from a person who is of competent mind.

The essential elements of a living will are similar to those of an ordinary will in trust law. They are based on the BMA 1995 code of practice on advance directives (Dimond, 2002):

- full name,
- address,
- name and address of next of kin,

- whether advice was sought from health professionals,
- signature,
- date drafted and reviewed,
- witness signature,
- a clear statement of patient's wishes,
- name, address and telephone of nominated person.

Since October 2007, living wills have been recognized in law related to treatment decisions following the passing of the Mental Capacity Act 2005, with Sections 24–26 dealing with advance directives:

> *Advance decisions to refuse treatment: general*
>
> 24. (1) *'Advance decision' means a decision made by a person ('P'), after he has reached 18 and when he has capacity to do so, that if*
>   (a) *at a later time and in such circumstances as he may specify, a specified treatment is proposed to be carried out or continued by a person providing healthcare for him, and*
>   (b) *at that time he lacks capacity to consent to the carrying out or continuation of the treatment.*
>
> **Mental Capacity Act 2005**

Assessment of a patient's mental incapacity should be based on what is called the 'functional approach', based on the common law. This depends on whether at the time of decision the patient is

> (1) *Unable by reason of mental disability to make a decision on the matter in question or,*
> (2) *Unable to communicate a decision on that matter because he or she is unconscious or for any other reason.*
>
> **Law Commission, 1999, paragraph 3, 14**

In the absence of a living will, healthcare professionals are obliged to act in the patient's best interests in light of any evidence of the patient's previously expressed wishes (Section 4 of the Mental Capacity Act 2005). The case of *Burke* (discussed above) illustrates this point.

Incapacity may be temporary or permanent. Caring for an unconscious or PVS patient can be a stressful experience and a dilemma for the healthcare professional under whose care the patient is entrusted (Brazier, 2011). The American lawyer Louis Kutner is credited with the concept of 'living wills' in 1969, arguing that 'the legal trust established over property should be equally permissible and applicable to one's body' and emphasizing 'the importance of consent or withholding consent to treatment, whatever the prospect of recovery' (Kendrick and Robinson, 2002, p. 39). We have considered above how the law in the landmark Tony Bland case *Airedale NHS Trust* v *Bland* [1993] 1 All ER 821 HL [1993] paves the way for advance directives, and echoes the Natural Death Act 1979 in Washington, which puts the emphasis on 'the dignity and privacy which patients have a right to expect, the legislature hereby declares … the right of an adult person to make a written directive instructing such person's physician to withhold or withdraw life-sustaining treatment in the event of a terminal condition or permanent unconscious condition'. In comparison,

> *the legislature also recognizes that a person's right to control his or her health care may be exercised by an authorized representative who validly holds the person's durable power of attorney for health care.*
> **70.122.020, Washington State Legislature, http://apps.leg.wa.gov/rcw/default.aspx?cite=70.122&full=true#70.122.020**

If all the criteria for drawing up living wills are met, they should serve as valid evidence for giving a direction as to either what treatment to accept or what treatment to refuse (*Nursing Times*, 1999). Two consultants may give consent on behalf of an incapacitated patient in an emergency (Department of Health, 2001). Family members should be consulted only to establish the patient's best interests but not give consent on behalf of an incapacitated patient. If family members are not happy with a decision made by clinicians, they have no right under the law to overrule that decision but can seek a judicial review. Doctors, however, do not have to follow these directives if this is not in keeping with their training and their conscience; they are entitled to seek a second medical opinion if they disagree with the proxy.

In an emergency, healthcare professionals are duty-bound to act in the patient's best interests. The basic principles of beneficence, non-maleficence and fairness are applicable. These are also part of articles of the Human Rights Act 1998.

THE DOUBLE-EFFECT DOCTRINE AND PALLIATIVE CARE

Following the greater good or double-effect doctrine which accepts death as an unintended outcome, a positive act such as analgesia control (which is legitimate but may hasten the death of the patient) is lawful. Another example is

193

termination of pregnancy where the mother's life may be at risk. This doctrine originates with Thomas Aquinas, who is credited with introducing the principle of 'the double effect' in his discussion of the permissibility of self-defence which is applicable to palliative care as the intent is to control pain, though effectively shortening life through respiratory depression.

- *Killing one's assailant is justified, he argues, provided one does not intend to kill him.*
- *Aquinas observes that 'nothing hinders one act from having two effects, only one of which is intended, while the other is beside the intention'.*

Summa Theologica, II-II, qu. 64, art. 7, http://www. newadvent.org/summa/3064.htm

Accordingly, the act of self-defence may have two effects: one, the saving of one's life which is the desired outcome, and the other, undesired, is the unfortunate killing of the aggressor. This principle was first developed in the following case.

R v Bodkin-Adams [1956] Crim LR (UK) 365

An elderly patient suffered a stroke and the doctor (who happened to be a substantial beneficiary of the victim's will) decided to increase the opiate analgesic and the patient died. It was held that he was not guilty of murder if the first objective of medicine, restoration of health, was successful and if the practice was backed by a responsible body of professionals.

Healthcare professionals have a duty of care in law and under the ethical principles of beneficence and non-maleficence to ensure that patients have adequate and appropriate pain control and not to overmedicate a patient. Their primary aim should be to achieve the right balance for pain control. In the above case, it was held further by Lord Devlin that 'a doctor can do all that is proper and necessary to relieve pain and suffering, even if the measures he takes incidentally shorten life' as a side effect. The greater good principle would apply. The World Health Organization defines palliative care as follows:

Palliative care is an approach which improves the quality of life of patients and their families facing life-threatening illness, through the prevention, assessment and treatment of pain and other physical, psychosocial and spiritual problems. The goal of palliative care is achievement of the best possible quality of life for patients and their families.

Houses of Parliament Health Committee, 2004

If a patient is in pain, it can be difficult to ascertain their true needs if their declared request is an indication of a preference for 'euthanasia', saying they would like to 'end it all' or if, in fact, this may be an indication of their frustration and an expression of pain. It is possible that as soon as the pain is relieved, a patient will be a very different person and they may express a wish to be discharged home and/or to live a little longer. The nurse then faces a dilemma in ascertaining the patient's needs.

It is possible that a patient's wish to 'end it all' may be motivated by unbearable pain and/or poor pain control, or simply because they miss a loved one who has died before them. If the pain becomes intolerable, then they may see death as the only way out and a welcome relief.

THINKING POINT

Peter, an 87-year-old man, is a retired accountant, in the advanced stages of lung cancer with secondary metastases in the spine. He has been happily married for 69 years. Although not religious, he is known to have humanist sympathies, with no declared religion. He is now very drowsy with brief wakeful spells, when the pain becomes worse. He is unable to respond to conversation. He at times seems to be aware of the presence of his family and responds to his 86-year-old wife's voice. He had apparently informed one of his four sons, Y, that he had no wish to live in view of his condition with unbearable pain. The son, claiming to represent his father's wishes, insists that antibiotic treatment for a chest infection should be stopped. Some family members, however, disagree and demand that because of their cultural and religious beliefs he should be treated aggressively until the very end (even if there is no clear evidence of positive to his long-term prognosis). The patient himself is unaware of the ensuing dispute. The multidisciplinary team consensus is in favour of keeping the patient pain-free and comfortable.

1. Consider the role of the nurse.
2. What are the patient's best interests, and what difference would a living will make in this case?

The courts in the UK are clear about their reluctance to extend the law on euthanasia as is clear in the following case.

A National Health Service Trust v D **[2000] FCR 577**

This case considered the right to resuscitation of a 19-month-old severely disabled child. The medical staff decided not to give him active treatment due to an expected short life expectancy.

Held: It was held that 'the court's clear respect for the sanctity of human life must impose a strong obligation in favour of taking all steps capable of preserving life, save in exceptional circumstances'. The court took the view that withholding life-prolonging treatment did not breach Article 2 of Human Rights Act 1998, and that the primary consideration should not be the views of the family members or friends of the patient. Any clinical decision on the course of action to be followed should be based on the patient's best interests. Mr Justice Cazalet observed that 'there does not appear to be a decision of the European Court which indicates that the approach adopted by the English courts in situations such as this is contrary to Article 2'.

The court also acknowledged that the relevant consideration in treating the patient was not the doctors' views but the patient's best interest in relieving pain symptoms, albeit knowing that the side effect would be the hastening of death.

THINKING POINT

Consider the case of Tony Bland and compare and contrast this with the case of Diane Pretty.

CROSSING THE RUBICON – TOWARD A SLIPPERY SLOPE

Torts law and delict (Scots) law make no distinction between active measures and passive omissions, which may result in harm and breach of duty of care for a user or patient to have grounds for action in tort. It is relatively easy to establish a 'fiduciary relationship' between nurse and 'user' as this is based on trust. The cases of *Donoghue* v *Stevenson* [1932] UKHL 100 and subsequently *Caparo Industries* v *Dickman* [1990] defined the duty of care for nurses to ensure that the patient is not harmed by their actions or omissions. The difficulty for a victim of clinical negligence is that they must meet the 'hurdles' before they can succeed.

Difficulties may be posed in the clinical decision-making process and in setting a precedent when dealing with grey areas and the danger of 'crossing the Rubicon', hence the need for a judicial review by the courts, when a client lacks mental capacity or competence (see Tony Bland case: *Airedale NHS Trust* v *Bland* [1993] 1 All ER 821 HL; see Brazier, 2011). When conflicts arise, judges, who make decisions during judicial reviews seeking clarification on end of life decisions, must take into account the morals of society, which shapes their own ethical considerations. The law is not always clear-cut and a lot depends on whether there is some agreement with family members on whether to continue treatment. With any decision that allows the end of life, it is possible that some will see this as cheapening life, which must be preserved at all costs, while some may consider this a human right to be allowed to die with dignity.

On the other hand, criminal law is very clear on the elements of murder. The mens rea (criminal intent) can be established as well as the actus reus (guilty act). This will not be the case when withdrawal is the only option, if it is agreed by the multidisciplinary team that in the patient's best interests, further treatment would be futile, 'both medically and ethically, in the face of overwhelming disease' (Cohen, 1993, p. 52).

R v Shipman

Kathleen Grundy, an 81-year-old widow, who was an ex-mayoress of Hyde, respected and trusted her GP. She had followed him when he set up his solo practice and shortly before her death had even considered making a £200 donation to his practice fund. She was found dead on 24 June 1998. On Monday, 31 January 2000, the jury at Preston Crown Court convicted Dr Harold Shipman of murdering Mrs Grundy and 14 others.

Estimates of the number of people killed by Shipman range from a conservative 76 to over 1000. It is possible Shipman murdered more people than any other lone person in history. How?

The question that arises is 'how could this happen?' and there are no easy answers. Contributing factors might be the trust invested in doctors and healthcare professionals by their patients, and inadequate monitoring and poor systems of work within the health service and its professional associations.

http://www.the-shipman-inquiry.org.uk

Finally, it is useful to describe briefly how euthanasia has been received in other countries. Australia's Northern Territory passed the Natural Death Act 1988, which came into effect in July 1996, allowing euthanasia. It was in operation for less than a year (when four people were allowed to commit physician suicide) before being repealed by the federal government of Australia. In the United States, all states apart from Oregon do not allow physician- or other-assisted suicide. The Netherlands is of particular interest with more liberal views on euthanasia. It has strict guidelines with conditions to be met as follows:

(a) *The request must come from the patient. It must, in addition be free and voluntary.*
(b) *This request must have been a considered and persistent one.*

(c) *The patient should be suffering intolerably … there should be no prospect for improvement.*

(d) *The decision to end the patient's life must be one of the last resort having considered whether there is any less drastic alternative.*

(e) *The euthanasia must be performed by a doctor who has beforehand consulted with an independent doctor who has experience in the area of euthanasia.*

Davies, 1998, p. 352

The Dutch practice of euthanasia was formalized by legislation in 2000 to allow both physician-assisted euthanasia and other assisted suicide. Official figures showed a significant increase (from 16 per cent to 41 per cent of deaths) in euthanasia between 1990 and 1995 (Hendin, 2002, p. 2). The level of Dutch tolerance of euthanasia is demonstrated in the following case study:

Case study

In 1985, a doctor was charged with being implicated in about 20 deaths in a nursing home, without the knowledge or consent of the victims. He was found guilty and sentenced to a year in prison but, following an outcry against the severity of the sentence, the verdict was overturned on a technicality. He was then awarded the equivalent of US$150,000 damages by a civil court.

From Pollard B, Euthanasia Practices in the Netherlands, www.catholiceducation.org/articles/euthanasia/eu0014.html (accessed 9 September 2005).

The Dutch system has been criticized for failing to protect vulnerable patients and to address patients' choice and their right to autonomy, by failing to obtain proper and informed consent prior to euthanasia in more than 1000 cases (Hendin, 2002). The worrying factor here is that it is almost impossible to tell the real levels of such cases, as this is difficult to monitor, and to establish doctors' compliance with the guidelines and monitoring can be difficult. Similarly, other European countries such as Switzerland and Belgium have followed suit in legitimizing physician-assisted euthanasia.

The Select Committee on Medical Ethics (Walton Committee, 1994; House of Lords, 1993–94, paragraph 260) drew a line on morality, which they felt reflected the feelings of the majority of the UK public, and refused to extend the law by 'crossing the line which prohibits any intentional killing, a line which we think it is essential to preserve'. They suggested further that it was important that the move to block the legitimization of 'intentional killing' was seen 'as the cornerstone of law and the social relationships' (House of Lords, 1993–94). Where there is a lack of clarity or dispute, a judicial review should always be sought in order to safeguard patient rights. The law as it stands in the UK is based on the rule in *Airedale NHS Trust* v *Bland* [1993], where Lord Goff (at 870–871) observed that artificial feeding and hydration should only be discontinued when the condition was deemed to be permanent and in the patient's best interests. He went on to demonstrate his dilemma in balancing continuing treatment against stopping:

> *But it is not lawful for a doctor to administer a drug even though that course is prompted by humanitarian desire to end his suffering, however great that suffering may be.*

Furthermore, there is a need for balancing the patient's needs for pain control and their interest in being put through what can only be seen as burdensome treatment, and

> *so to cross the Rubicon which runs between, on the one hand, the care of the living patient and on the other hand, euthanasia actively causing his death, to avoid or to end his suffering. Euthanasia is not lawful at Common Law.*
>
> **Airedale NHS Trust v Bland [1993]**

If physician-assisted suicide were lawful in the United Kingdom, there would be real difficulties for doctors in determining or ascertaining motivation for a patient's request or potential agreement to 'euthanasia', which could be linked to depression. A potential conflict of interest would be possible where family members would disagree with clinical judgements doctors could legally 'assist' the patient to die.

THINKING POINT

Consider why pathways related to end of life decisions may be necessary. What is your view on care pathways such as the Liverpool Care Pathway?

In terminally ill patients, depression often fluctuates with pain, as well as altering the perception of the pain and subjective views of the future. The desire to die has been found to decrease over time in terminally ill persons (Chochinov et al., 1995). Specifically, the wish for euthanasia or PAS changes over time in a large proportion of terminally ill patients, and decision instability is particularly associated with depressive symptoms (Emanuel et al., 2000).

Statement from the Royal College of Psychiatrists on
physician-assisted suicide

It is difficult to establish the number of cases of euthanasia, although UK research involving general practitioners has suggested a figure of 584,791 deaths in England, Wales, Scotland and Northern Ireland. The most significant areas were alleviation of symptoms with possible life shortening (32.8 per cent) and non-treatment decisions (30.3 per cent). No voluntary euthanasia was recorded. Some have suggested that since its initiation as many as 453 people including 30 from the United Kingdom have been given assisted euthanasia through Dignitas, in Switzerland (LifeSite, 2005). The challenge facing organizations such as Dignitas is that it may not be easy to establish the patient's motive, before facilitating suicide, in that the motivation for ending life may be other than an intolerable suffering due to a medical condition and/or pain as in one case reported by Leidig (2005).

Not so long prior to the issuing of the Director of Public Prosecutions guidelines in England and Wales, 17 cases had been recorded by the Police in 2009–10 where complaint had been made about 'assisted suicides', while there were over 100 cases of Britons known to have ended their lives in Switzerland with assistance from Dignitas (CPS, 2010). The DPP guidelines do not apply to Scotland, which follows its own criminal law system.

Following the ruling of the House of Lords, Deborah Purdy in *R* v *DPP ex p Purdy* [2009] UKHL 45, the Director of Public Prosecutions (2010), aimed to clarify the law by issuing guidelines:

> *The policy is now more focused on the motivation of the suspect rather than the characteristics of the victim. The policy does not change the law on assisted suicide. It does not open the door for euthanasia. It does not override the will of Parliament. What it does is to provide a clear framework for prosecutors to decide which cases should proceed to court and which should not.*

CPS, 2010, http://www.cps.gov.uk/publications/
prosecution/assisted_suicide.html

Difficulties remain in the interpretation of the guidelines, where there may be a need to balance interests of the patient and those of family members and society. The patient's best interests should be at the centre of decision-making. The difficulty is establishing those 'best interests' may be problematic, as it may be felt that the person asking to die may be under considerable pressure or indeed clinically depressed.

The DPP guidelines have been further interpreted in the so-called 'locked-in syndrome' cases, the Tony Nicklinson and Paul Lamb cases, and they have so far failed to persuade the courts to change the law. The first person was deceased at the time of the appeal but represented by his family members.

Lord Justice Toulson introduces the two cases (paragraphs 1 – 4):

> *These are tragic cases. They present society with legal and ethical questions of the most difficult kind. They also involve constitutional questions. At the invitation of the court the Attorney General has intervened. (Para 1)*
>
> *Put simply, the claimants suffer from catastrophic physical disabilities but their mental processes are unimpaired in the sense that they are fully conscious of their predicament. They suffer from 'locked-in syndrome'. Both have determined that they wish to die with dignity and without further suffering but their condition makes them incapable of ending their own lives. Neither is terminally ill and they face the prospect of living for many years. (Para 2)*
>
> *Barring unforeseen medical advances, neither Martin's nor Tony's condition is capable of physical improvement. Although they have many similarities, there are some differences in their condition.*
>
> *There are also differences in the orders which they seek and the ways in which their cases have been presented.*
>
> ### *Tony Nicklinson v Ministry of Justice, AM v Director of Public Prosecutions and Others, High Court (Administrative Court), 16 August 2012*

CONCLUSION

Similar to healthcare professionals, judges may also face a dilemma in managing end of life decisions. There are often grey areas and complex clinical decisions, which are fraught with difficulties, and with ethical implications. Some judges have wrestled with their own ethics and morality.

> *The conclusion I have reached will appear to some to be almost irrational. How can it be lawful to allow a patient to die slowly though*

painlessly over a period of weeks from lack of food, but unlawful to produce his immediate death by a lethal injection, thereby saving his family from yet another ordeal? (Furthermore) I find it difficult to find a moral answer to that question. But it is undoubtedly the law.

Lord Browne-Wilkinson, Tony Bland v Airedale NHS Trust [1993]

Healthcare professionals, on the one hand, should act as representatives of their respective professional bodies and as advocates for vulnerable users. Occasionally, a conflict of interests may arise, as they wrestle with their conscience. The courts, on the other hand, have the opportunity to bring in changes by the back door by widening the interpretation of the legislation as intended by Parliament. The European Court of Human Rights may strike down any UK judgements that appear to contravene human rights legislation.

The role of ethics is to provide frameworks that are based on custom and human knowledge, which is fallible and has been subject to change at different times in history. Is it possible then that as a society we in the UK are becoming more and more indifferent to the value of human life and turning a blind eye to our innate conscience? As we have seen at the beginning, some philosophers like Kant (1724–1804) believed that ignoring our 'categorical imperative', which he believed to be our moral compass. Individual choice to commit suicide may however be perceived by some as immoral. The utilitarian view would make end of life decisions on the basis of usefulness to the majority in society rather than the best interests of the patient; thus, there is a possibility of rendering the concept of 'individual autonomy' redundant and meaningless and leaving some patients vulnerable. This could mean the easy way out.

There is no clear evidence that in countries where euthanasia is legal the link between depression and requests for euthanasia is taken into consideration. The ethical values of any given nation are influenced by moral philosophy and religious values, which may influence decisions; 'these are remarkably durable in the sense that their influence spans over the centuries' (Elford, 2000, p. 13). Values that may conflict even within a given society or internationally are difficult to change overnight. There is so far no persuasive evidence to convince the public and the healthcare professional bodies in the UK that the interests of the patient would be best served by widening the category of patients eligible for euthanasia. So far, the UK Parliament does not support changing the status quo. One dilemma facing any healthcare professional involved in end of life decisions is that, even in the case of a patient who has the capacity to make a decision, they may never be able to say with certainty whether or not a request for 'euthanasia' is a cry for help.

A balance should be struck between how best to serve the patient's interests while fulfilling the healthcare professional's own personal conscience as well as following professional guidelines (within the constraints of the law). Finally, the Law Commission on Mental Incapacity suggested:

> *One of the principles on which the Commission has proceeded is that people should be encouraged and enabled to take those decisions which they are in fact able to take. This principle embraces anticipatory decision-making by the person while competent in order to make arrangements for his or her future incapacity.*
> **Law Commission, 1995, paragraph 1.12**

There may be real difficulties in family members or a healthcare proxy or deputy accurately reflecting the wishes of the patient if they themselves have vested interests in inheritance, which is a motive in criminal law. Lord Joffe's (2005) failed 'Patient Assisted Dying Bill' was one attempt by a private member in the House of Lords to change the law by legalizing euthanasia with a provision for opting out for conscientious objectors, as well a chance for a competent patient's considered decision. With no answers, the debate on end of life decisions goes on and the moral dilemmas remain.

REFERENCES

Aquinas T. *Summa Theologica*, II-II, qu. 64, art. 7. 1225–74. http://www.newadvent.org/summa/3064.htm (accessed 2 October 2013).

BBC News. 27 June 2000. http://news.bbc.co.uk (accessed 4 September 2002).

Beauchamp TL, Childress J. *Principles of biomedical ethics*. New York: Oxford University Press, 2008.

Beigler P. Should patient consent be required to write a do not resuscitate order? *Journal of Medical Ethics* 2003; 29: 359–63.

BMA. *Advance statements about medical treatment: code of practice with explanatory notes*. London: BMJ Publishing Group, 1995.

BMA. *Withholding life prolonging medical treatment: guidance for decision making*. London: BMJ Publishing Group, 2000. www.bma.org.uk/ap.nsf/content/withholdingwithdrawing. (3rd edition, 2007.)

BMA. 2003. www.bma.org.uk/ap.nsf/content/home (accessed 15 January 2007).

BMA. *Guidelines on treatment decisions for patients in persistent vegetative state*. Revised December 2006. http://www.bma.org.uk/ap.nsf/Content/pvstreatment#ref (accessed 1 October 2006).

BMA. *Decisions relating to cardiopulmonary resuscitation. A joint statement from the BMA, the Resuscitation Council (UK) and the RCN*, paragraph 13, p. 19. London: British Medical Association, 2007. www.bma.org.uk (accessed 10 November 2007).

Brazier M. *Medicine, patients and the law*. London: Penguin, 2011.

Butterworths. *Butterworths' student statutes*, 2nd ed. London: Butterworths, 2000.

Campbell A, Gillett G, Jones G. *Medical ethics*, 4th ed. Oxford: Oxford University Press, 2005.

Cohen S. *Whose life is it anyhow?* London: Robson Books, 1993.

Crown Prosecution Service. DPP guidelines on euthanasia. CPS, 2010. http://www.cps.gov.uk/publications/prosecution/assisted_suicide.html (accessed 7 October 2013).

Davies M. *Medical law*, 2nd ed. London: Blackstone Press, 1998.

Department of Health. *Consent – what you have a right to expect: a guide for adults*. 2001. www.dh.gov.uk/en/Policyandguidance/Healthandsocialcaretopics/consent/consentgeneralinformation/index.htm (accessed 10 March 2013).

Dimond B. *Legal aspects of pain management. British Journal of Nursing* monograph. Dinton: Quay Books, 2002.

Director of Public Prosecution. Policy for prosecutors in respect of cases of encouraging or assisting suicide. 2010. http://www.cps.gov.uk/publications/prosecution/assisted_suicide_policy.html (accessed 10 October 2013).

EC Human Rights Commission. 1991. Quoted by the Church of Scotland. *Social work euthanasia, a church perspective*. Edinburgh: St Andrews Press, 1995.

Elford RJ. *The ethics of uncertainty*. Oxford: One World, 2000.

General Medical Council. *Withholding and withdrawing life prolonging treatments*, paragraph 16. 2002. www.gmc-uk.org (accessed 20 August 2013).

General Medical Council. Guidance to good medical practice. 2006. www.gmc-uk.org/guidance/good_medical_practice/index.asp.

Hendin H. *Practice versus theory, the Dutch experience*. Houston, TX: International Association for Hospices and Palliative Care, 2002. www.hospicecare.com/AOM/2002/mar2002article.htm (accessed 20 August 2007).

House of Lords. Paper 21 of 21-1, paragraph 260. 1993–94.

House of Lords. *Report of the select committee on medical ethics* (vol. 1 - report). HMSO, London, Session 1993–1994 (printed 31/01/94). https://www.gov.uk/government/uploads/system/uploads/attachment_data/file/272006/2553.pdf.

Houses of Parliament Health Committee. 2004. www.publications. parliament.uk/pa/cm200304/cmselect/cmhealth/454/454.pdf (accessed 15 November 2013).

Kant I. *Fundamental principles in metaphysics of morals.* New York: Liberal Arts Press, 1785.

Kendrick K, Robinson S. *Their rights, advance directives and living wills explored.* London: Age Concern, 2002.

Keown J. *Euthanasia examined, ethical clinical and legal perspective.* Cambridge: Cambridge University Press, 1997.

Kubler-Ross E. *On life after death.* Berkeley, CA: Celestial Arts, 1991.

Law Commission. *The Law Commission report on mental incapacity.* LC231. 1995. www.lawcom.gov.uk (accessed 2 December 2012).

Leidig M. Dignitas is investigated for helping healthy woman to die. *BMJ* 2005; 331: 1160.

Levack P. Live and let die? A structured approach to decision making about resuscitation. *British Journal of Anaesthesia* 2002; 89: 683–86.

LifeSite. Swiss euthanasia group Dignitas opening British office. 2005. www.lifesite.net/ldn/2005/oct/05101103.html (accessed 13 June 2009).

Lord Joffe. *Assisted dying for the terminally ill*, vol. II. HL Paper 86-2. 2005.

Morgan P, Lawton P. *Ethical issues in six religious traditions.* Edinburgh: Edinburgh University Press, 1996.

NHS Direct. Online Health Encyclopaedia. 2002. www.nhsdirect.nhs.uk (accessed 12 February 2012).

NHS Executive. *Resuscitation policy.* HSC 2000/028. London: Department of Health, 2000.

Nursing Times. Nursing Times essential guides: living wills. London: EMAP Healthcare, 1999.

O'Mathuna P. Responding to patients in the persistent vegetative state. www.xenos.org.org/ministries/crossroads/donal/pvs.htm (accessed 4 October 2013).

Pollard B. Euthanasia practices in the Netherlands. www.catholiceducation.org/articles/euthanasia/eu0014.html (accessed 9 September 2005).

Royal College of General Practice. Matters of life and death: helping people to live well until they die – general practice guidance for implementing the RCGP/RCN end of life care patient charter. 2012. http://www.rcgp.org.uk/clinical-and-research/clinical-resources/ (accessed 18 September 2013).

Royal College of Physicians. The permanent vegetative state. Review by a working group convened by the Royal College of Physicians and endorsed by the Conference of Medical Royal Colleges and their faculties of the United Kingdom. *Journal of the Royal College of Physicians of London* 1996; 30: 119–21.

Royal College of Psychiatrists. Response to assisted dying for the terminally ill bill. 24 April 2006. http://www.rcpsych.ac.uk/pressparliament/collegeresponses/physicianassistedsuicide.aspx?theme5print (accessed 5 June 2010).

The Shipman Report. http://www.the-shipman-inquiry.org.uk (accessed 10 October 2013).

Teichman J. *Social ethics, a student's guide*. Oxford: Blackwell Publishers, 1996.

Viney C. A phenomenological study of ethical decision-making experiences among senior intensive care nurses and doctors concerning withdrawal of treatment. *Nursing in Critical Care* 1996; 1: 182–87.

Winter B, Cohen S. Withdrawal of treatment. ABC of intensive treatment. *BMJ* 1999; 319: 306–8.

10 IMPACT OF PATIENTS' RIGHTS ON CARE

INTRODUCTION

The final chapter aims to provide the reader with an opportunity for reflection on the impact of human rights legislation, and other policy (on patients' rights). Morals of any given society may also affect morals for nurses and how they care for patients; nevertheless, the law must prevail, hence the limited reference to ethics in this final chapter. Professional values should reflect the values of any given society and also make a positive impact on the quality of care delivered.

The National Health Service (NHS) Plan (2000) aimed to improve the patient's welfare through the following principles:

- Redress over cancelled operations
- Patients' forums and citizens' panels in every area
- New national panel to advise on major reorganization of hospitals
- Stronger regulation of professional standards

How far has nursing come in order to meet these expectations?

FROM PATERNALISM TO PATIENT-CENTRED CARE

It could be argued that for doctors the now largely obsolete or updated Hippocratic Oath's 'most basic principle was that a doctor must always cure patients, but never harm them' (Science Museum, 2013). This had aimed to underpin the biomedical model of care (which preferred to focus on restoration of a patient's biological functioning) but not so much the psychosocial aspect, giving a patient their own individuality and autonomy. Most medical schools worldwide no longer require doctors to swear the Hippocratic Oath; rather, they adopt some of the principles in their own codes of practice.

Patient preferences of a paternalistic model were supported by research by Arora and McHorney (2000), who reported that, given the choice, 69 per cent of patients preferred to leave decision-making to their doctor (and presumably the nurse). It is possible that a paternalistic decision-making (carried out by doctors or nurses) could leave vulnerable patients open to abuse by a few healthcare professionals. From a paternalistic perspective it could nevertheless be argued (albeit fallaciously) that the caring relationship could be based on factors such as absolute trust or fear and conversely the patient's vulnerability. This would be based on the assumption that the clinician always knows what is best for their patients. This model does not leave room for patient engagement. In nursing, Florence Nightingale as the founder of modern nursing recognized principles of ethics:

> *It may seem a strange principle to enunciate as the very first requirement in a hospital that it should do the sick no harm.*
> **Florence Nightingale (1860–1920)**

The NHS Constitution (2013) now requires patients to be at the heart of decision-making. This will be reviewed every 10 years.

Updated policy (and presumably) litigation may have changed a previously perceived view of the benevolence for 'grateful' patients who would not be expected to assert their rights and be 'difficult' by asking questions or complaining. This could have been based on a 'mystical' professional code which was revered if not feared by the patient. Patients today are now generally more questioning – and rightly so. Litigation is more a reality, and things are very different, with the patient at the centre of decision-making and questioning more decisions about their care.

This would mean that the ethical principles such as patient autonomy and informed consent are respected. In paternalism, there was no room for a partnership with patients concerning decisions about their own treatment. Paternalism was synonymous with blind 'trust' in doctors and other healthcare professionals such as nurses. The problem, however, was that without any guarantees of patients' rights, that trust could be breached when making clinical decisions.

The modern view of this relationship needs to consider the patient's holistic needs and sees nursing as now based on

> *the use of clinical judgment in the provision of care to enable people to improve, maintain, or recover health, to cope with health problems, and to achieve the best possible quality of life, whatever their disease or disability, until death.*

> **Royal College of Nursing, 2003**

Most patients are now much more aware of their human rights and litigation is a reality. It may be more difficult for healthcare professionals to safeguard a vulnerable patient who may lack mental capacity for decision-making. Nursing has come a long way and should provide holistic treatment or care for the user. Peplau's vision may now be realized as she defined nursing as a 'human relationship between an individual who is sick, or in need of health services, and a nurse specially educated to recognize and to respond to the need for help' (Peplau, 2004, p. 6).

Where the law is unclear the nurse must always consult senior professional colleagues and the multidisciplinary team in acting 'in the patient's best interests'.

Modern nursing has emerged as an autonomous profession in partnership with medicine. We have moved away from a largely dependent profession subservient to medicine, thus reinforcing a notion that only doctors were qualified to make decisions on treatment – patient or multidisciplinary involvement was not considered important. In the past, the doctor played the crucial if not exclusive decision-making role while leaving nurses to carry out the doctor's orders.

In the paternalistic model, the patient, on the other hand, was probably not expected to voice any opinion or to be involved in decision-making. Before the Human Rights Act 1998, patients' rights may not have been recognized. Human rights were in danger of being ignored on the basis that the doctor knew what was best for their patients. Today, nurses are increasingly taking on medical (extended) roles, with the accountability that comes with them and playing a central part in the provision of care.

HUMAN RIGHTS AND LITIGATION

The emergence of modern medical science in the Western world also meant the development of treatment into hitherto unknown territory. An often quoted landmark American case on human rights, which though persuasive is not authoritative in the UK, defined a patient's common law rights:

> *Every person of adult years and sound mind has a right to determine what shall be done with his own body.*
>
> **Schloendorff v Society of New York Hospital 211 NY 125;**
> **105 NE 92 [1914]**

Since the implementation of the Human Rights Act (HRA) 1998 (in October 2000), patients have become increasingly aware of their human rights. Although it may not necessarily be linked, there has been an increase in complaints with the UK becoming a more litigious society. In 2005–06, there were 5697 claims of clinical negligence and 3497 claims of non-clinical negligence against the NHS, a small increase on the previous period, with £560.3 million having been paid out for clinical negligence claims for the same period (NHS Litigation Authority, 2007). The NHS Litigation Authority, which also monitors risk assessments claims while providing indemnity insurance for healthcare providers' organizations, with responsibility for the Clinical Negligence Scheme (CNST), Liabilities to Third Parties (LTPS) and Property Expenses Scheme (PES), received 10 129 clinical claims in 2012–13, which was a rise of 10.8 per cent on the 2011–12 period. Figures and this amount reflected a total of £46.9 million. The funding from the CNST does not include Existing Liabilities Scheme (directly funded by the Department of Health) and covers claims for incidents which took place before 1 April 1995. Medical negligence payouts have cost the NHS in Scotland more than £200 over the past six years, with the cost of hospital blunders set to rise further after a near-20% surge in claims being filed (Herald Scotland, 2013).

Human rights as provided in Schedule 1 of the HRA 1998 are the embodiment of the European Convention on Human Rights 1950, which originated from the Universal Declaration of Human Rights 1948, which was a declaration of the United Nations on 10 December 1948. The UK, in 1953, was one of the first countries to ratify the European convention, although this was not legally enforceable in UK courts until the passing of the HRA 1998. The statute took effect from October 2000.

The basic tenets of human rights are found in the HRA 1998, Schedule 1 (2013), and only those relevant to health care are summarized with some example of application to case law below. The articles of human rights (2–14) and only the relevant ones which are applicable to healthcare practice will be identified here, with one or two examples below.

Article 2: Right to life.

> 1 *Everyone's right to life shall be protected by law. No one shall be deprived of his life intentionally save in the execution of a sentence of a court following his conviction of a crime for which this penalty is provided by law.*

Article 3: Prohibition to torture.

> *No one shall be subjected to torture or to inhuman or degrading treatment or punishment.*

This article has often been relied on, with allegations of its breaches where poor care is identified with an example in the leading case which went to the European Court of Human Rights (ECHR).

McGlinchey et al. v the United Kingdom, application no. 50390/99, judgement of 29 April 2003

A woman known to have a heroin addiction (and also suffering from asthma) was sentenced to four months for a crime and subsequently imprisoned. While an inmate, she suffered severe heroin withdrawal symptoms which include nausea, vomiting and weight loss. She was seen by a doctor who on her arrival saw the patient and then advised the nursing staff to monitor her symptoms.

Nevertheless, the patient's condition deteriorated over the weekend. During this time, nursing staff did not call out a doctor, nor did they request for her to be transferred to a hospital. The following Monday morning she collapsed and required emergency admission to hospital, where she died.

Held: It was held by the ECHR that the prison service was in breach of Article 3 of HRA 1998 by failing to take appropriate steps to treat the prisoner's condition and relieve her suffering, and had failed to act sufficiently quickly to prevent the worsening of her condition.

This related to poor treatment decisions.

Article 5: Right to liberty and security. This may apply to detention unless this is under the Mental Act provisions or legitimate imprisonment.

Article 8: Right to respect for private and family life. This focuses on dignity and the patient's right to autonomy.

Article 14: Prohibition of discrimination. This may fall under the umbrella of the Equality Act 2010.

Aspects of law and human rights, the principles of human rights are usually described as absolute, limited or qualified (Department of Constitutional Affairs, 2006). To reinforce the classification of these articles please revisit the analysis in Chapter 1. Users with capacity should be allowed to make decisions which have an effect on their own treatment as well as their lives, especially those with continuing care needs (NHS Constitution, 2013).

Examples of public authorities who come under the jurisdiction of the HRA 1998 include local authorities, care commissioning groups, NHS trusts, or health boards, the police, prison and the Immigration Service. In reality, there are always difficulties for the patient in identifying evidence where their welfare is endangered by healthcare professionals' conduct. Most patients receiving health care are vulnerable and may lack physical or mental capacity. Patients may not have the energy to ensure that their rights are honoured and to fight against infringement of these rights, when recovery should be their primary concern.

> 6.3. In this section 'public authority' includes –
>> (a) a court or tribunal, and
>> (b) any person certain of whose functions are functions of a public nature, but does not include either House of Parliament or a person exercising functions in connection with proceedings in Parliament.

Human Rights Act 1998

The debate remains on why this key legislation does not apply to private organizations at present.

The post–Second World War era brought to the forefront the issue of human rights and how best they should be safeguarded, in light of those who had perished because of the abuse of human rights.

The Declaration of Human Rights 1948 in Geneva had recognized the need for protection of human rights in general, but especially had vulnerable people such as patients in mind. Owing to their physical and mental condition, many patients will fall into this category. Any person who is deemed to be a victim of a breach of human rights may bring an action under the articles of the HRA 1998. UK courts have a duty to apply this legislation, but a victim has the right of appeal to the European Court of Human Rights or they may lodge their case there instead if they so wish. It is recognized that the HRA has so far not managed to create a consensus of the law in specific areas (Mullally, 2006). What it has done is to generate a database of case law, which will be useful for victims of human rights' abuse. This resource will therefore facilitate the process of the application of human rights law (based on case law) in European Union member states.

The HRA 1998 has not diminished the substance of UK law in areas such as criminal law or employment law, but it has been able to benefit individuals in areas where interpretation of existing law lacked clarity or resulted in encroachment of human rights.

HUMAN RIGHTS, POLICY AND MORALS

The International Committee for Nursing links human rights with morals, with nursing having

> *four fundamental responsibilities:*
> *To promote health, to prevent illness, to restore health and to alleviate suffering. The need for nursing is universal.*
> *Inherent in nursing is respect for human rights, including cultural rights, the right to life and choice, to dignity and to be treated with respect. Nursing care is respectful of and unrestricted by considerations of age, colour, creed, culture, disability or illness, gender, sexual orientation, nationality, politics, race or social status.*
> ### International Council for Nursing, http://www.icn.ch/ about-icn/code-of-ethics-for-nurses

It is hoped that the Health and Social Care Act 2012 will make it easier to provide a holistic assessment and care, with its main aims

> *to establish and make provision about a National Health Service Commissioning Board and clinical commissioning groups and to make other provision about the National Health Service in England; to make provision about public health in the United Kingdom; to make provision about regulating health and adult social care services; to make provision about public involvement in health and social care matters, scrutiny of health matters by local authorities and co-operation between local authorities and commissioners of health care services; to make provision about regulating health and social care workers; to establish and make provision about a National Institute for Health and Care Excellence; to establish and make provision about a Health and Social Care Information Centre.*
> ### Health and Social Care Act 2012

At the time of writing, Scotland is undergoing a consultation process for similar legislation.

The Nursing and Midwifery Council (NMC) Code of Conduct (2008) requires nurses to safeguard the patient's welfare. From a legal perspective it is also clear that concerning patients' rights in the future, some cases may need to be tested in (through case law) some areas in order to ensure clarity. What is also certain is that human rights legislation has had a direct impact on NHS policy formation, as trusts must take on board its provisions in improving health care. One way this can be achieved is through education and training as well as by improving trust policies and guidelines in areas such as resuscitation and dealing with patients' property.

> *The government remains fully committed to the European Convention on Human Rights, and to the way in which it is given effect in UK law by the Human Rights Act.*
> **Department of Constitutional Affairs, 2006, p. 1**

In the world of litigation, the general public may now be seen as keen to capitalize on claims based on poor care. When considering patients' rights it cannot be overstated that it is essential that nurses are aware that patients do have rights and that should they suffer harm as a result of clinical negligence, they may be entitled to recover damages against them, in tort. The danger, however, is that their relationship may be surrounded by defensive practice, destroying any trust. It is difficult to justify this approach from the professional and ethical perspective, as care of other patients may be compromised where healthcare professionals are 'overtreating' and giving defensive medicine for a patient as a countermeasure against potential litigation.

It is better to manage care on the basis of risk management. Under the Health and Safety at Work Act (HASAWA) 1974, this means that any potential risks or hazards are reported and managed properly before a patient is harmed. This applies to both the employer (Sections 2–5; for example, Section 2(1) on ensuring the health, safety and welfare of employees while at work) and employee:

> *Section 7(a–b) It shall be the duty of every employee while at work:*
>
> *(a) To take reasonable care for the health and safety of himself and others who may be affected by his acts or omissions at work.*
> *(b) To co-operate with his employer or any other person, so far as is necessary, to enable his employer or other person to perform or comply with any requirement or duty imposed under a relevant statutory provision.*
> **Health and Safety at Work Act 1974**

The National Patient Safety Agency (NPSA) was established by the UK government in July 2001 for the purposes of coordinating the efforts of NHS trusts in the UK by reporting mishaps and problems affecting patient safety and thus allowing trusts to learn from any mistakes. The NPSA monitors the reporting of mishaps and also tries to 'promote an open and fair culture in the NHS, encouraging all healthcare staff to report incidents without undue fear of personal reprimand'. Since 1 June 2012, its key functions for patient safety were taken over by the NHS Commissioning Board Special Health Authority. Through its National Reporting and Learning System (NRLS), they collate reports nationally and make recommendations for improving practice. Furthermore, under health and safety duty of care is imposed:

> Every employer has a duty to conduct his undertaking in such a way as to ensure, so far as is reasonably practicable, that persons not in his employment who may be affected by the conduct of his undertaking are not as a result exposed to risks to their health and safety.

Section 3(1) of Health and Safety at Work Act 1974

While the NMC regulates the professional, the Care Quality Commission (CQC) regulates the providers to ensure that quality of care and that national standards are being met. The Royal College of Nursing, as well as being a professional body, also represents nurses as a trade union. The dual role was questioned by the Francis Report (2013) in respect of Stafford Hospital.

Accountability should be at the centre of care and all managers and professionals should be answerable for their actions.

> Recommendation no 2. –
>
> Putting the patient first
>
> The patients must be the first priority in all of what the NHS does. Within available resources, they must receive effective services from caring, compassionate and committed staff, working within a common culture, and they must be protected from avoidable harm and any deprivation of their basic rights.

Francis Report, 2013, p. 87

Taking the bigger picture on accountability means that from 2013, the Department of Health will hold the NHS Commissioning Board to account regarding improvements in health outcomes and corresponding performance indicators (Department of Health, 2013).

The evidence suggests that limited progress has been made in taking on board human rights in order to ensure patients' rights are respected and questions may still be asked, and as a society, we still have some way to go in recognizing patient's rights when caring for them. Common experiences of patients were cited as follows:

Not enough involvement in decisions
No-one to talk to about anxieties and concerns
Tests and/or treatments not clearly explained
Insufficient information for family/friends
Insufficient information about recovery

Department of Health, 2001

The NMC has issued guidelines for nurses and midwifes on raising and escalating concerns (NMC, 2010). Breach of patients' rights and abuse of vulnerable users within a domestic environment continue to be a concern for both children and adults, so the latest legislation to combat this is the Domestic Violence, Crime and Victims (Amendment) Act 2012 (Commencement) Order 2012, SI 2012/1432 (c. 54).

The 2012 Act extends the offence of causing or allowing the death of a child or vulnerable adult in section 5 of the 2004 Act ('the causing or allowing death offence') to cover causing or allowing serious physical harm (equivalent to grievous bodily harm) to a child or vulnerable adult ('the causing or allowing serious physical harm offence').

The majority of care that nurses and other healthcare professionals deliver is demonstrably positive and beneficial to the patient. However, occasionally a patient may experience a journey riddled with systematic failures, and their welfare is adversely affected by dangerous practice, near misses or never events; the latter is defined:

For the purposes of the survey a 'never event' is defined as

Wrong site surgery
Wrong implant/prosthesis
Retained foreign object post operation

**Royal College of Surgeons, 2013, http://www.rcseng.ac.uk/
patients/never-events-survey (accessed 12 October 2013)**

CONCLUSION

Since the inauguration of the NHS in 1946 it has become an established principle that all patients should receive free care at the point of delivery, with a mission to improve the quality of life through provision of universal health 'from the cradle to the grave'. The NHS Plan aimed to improve resources with 'the cash injection to boost capacity: 7500 more consultants; 2000 more general practitioners, 20,000 more nurses; 7000 more beds (particularly to boost intermediate care), investment in NHS facilities better healthcare provision by improving safety and recognising their human rights' (Department of Health, 2000). An example of an amalgamation of antidiscriminatory legislation (which is relevant to care) is through the Equality Act 2010, and this should make it easier to outlaw discrimination. Another example of promoting patients' rights now means that patients with mental capacity should be given a sufficient degree of information to make an informed choice on treatment.

Paternalism was seen as a by-product of medical science; we have nevertheless made progress in promoting the patients' rights. This belief may have been taken for granted as the norm not only by patients, but also by doctors, nurses and other healthcare professionals. Paternalism meant that patients were not party to nor were they expected to question medical decisions on their own treatment. Even with good intentions, there was always room for their human rights to be compromised. A nurse must safeguard vulnerable patients' rights, especially for those lacking capacity, by raising concerns with line managers and if necessary, escalating them (NMC, 2010), with the patient at the centre of clinical decision-making.

Nurses appreciate the significance and implications of scope of practice and the benefits of autonomous practice as well as raised expectations when working in partnership with the patient, the multidisciplinary team, as well as patient's next of kin and their friends. With autonomy of practice, however, comes accountability. This means that a nurse should be able to justify decision-making and nursing actions, while empowering their client. Accountability for nursing actions starts with the nurse's professionalism, as this is the basis of our relationship with the user. Given that professionals may be entitled to consider 'accountability to themselves' (perhaps as they reflect on the efficacy and justification of their nursing decision-making and actions), it is also clear that individual morality alone may not suffice to justify or define especially when things go wrong. In order to protect the patient, there is a necessary requirement for formal professional regulation, and accountability must start with the NMC, through professional colleagues/managers, the patient or user, the employer (under employment law terms of contract) and of course other branches of the law, such as health and safety law, criminal law or law of torts or delict.

In the majority of cases, everything goes well and the aims of nursing interventions are realized. Nurses should nevertheless acknowledge that, in spite of advances in medical science, evidence-based practice, and with the best intentions, human factors may prevail when things may go wrong. In this category should be included neglect and inadequate care, which may impact adversely on patients' health and safety. If harmed, the patient or their representatives are entitled to seek recompense for personal injury, with damages being awarded in litigation for clinical negligence. Patients' rights should be realized and at the centre of any decision-making. Nursing actions should be based on evidence-based practice. When any nursing frameworks or care pathways are identified for use, the nurse must be able to justify their use and outcomes, and demonstrate partnership with the user. They must always act in the patient's best interests.

REFERENCES

Arora K, McHorney C. Patient preferences for medical decision making: who really wants to participate? *Medical Care* 2000; 38: 335–41.

Department of Constitutional Affairs. *Making sense of human rights; a short introduction.* Crown, 2006. www.dca.gov.uk (accessed 30 April 2010).

Department of Health. *'NHS Plan' a plan for investment.* London: NHS, 2000. www.doh.gov.uk (accessed 8 June 2013).

Department of Health. *The expert patient: a new approach to chronic disease management for the 21st century.* 2001, paragraph 1.7. www.dh.gov.uk/en/Publicationsandstatistics/Publications/PublicationsPolicyAndGuidance/DH_400680 (accessed 16 November 2007).

Department of Health. NHS outcomes frameworks 2013/14. 2013. https://www.gov.uk/government/uploads/system/uploads/attachment_data/file/213055/121109-NHS-Outcomes-Framework-2013-14.pdf (accessed 24 November 2013).

Francis Report. Report of the Mid Staffordshire NHS Foundation Trust public inquiry. Executive summary. 2013. http://www.midstaffspublicinquiry.com/ (accessed 13 September 2013).

Herald Scotland. 2013. http://www.heraldscotland.com/news/health/revealed-213m-bill-to-nhs-in-negligence-claims.20271485.

International Council for Nursing (ICN). http://www.icn.ch/about-icn/code-of-ethics-for-nurses (accessed 20 October 2013).

Mullally S. *Gender, culture and human rights: reclaiming universalism.* Oxford: Hart Publishing, 2006.

National Health Service (NHS). The NHS plan. 2000. www.nhsia.nhs.uk/nhsplan/summary.htm (accessed 16 November 2007).

National Health Service (NHS). Constitution. 2013. Gov.org, https://www.gov.uk/government/publications/the-nhs-constitution-for-england (accessed 19 October 2013).

National Health Service Litigation Authority. 2007. http://www.nhsla.com/home.htm (accessed 20 July 2008).

National Patient Safety Agency. www.npsa.nhs.uk/ (accessed 12 April 2007).

Nightingale F. http://www.biography.com/people/florence-nightingale-9423539 (accessed 21 October 2013).

Nursing and Midwifery Council (NMC). *The code: Standards of conduct, performance and ethics for nurses and midwives.* London: Nursing and Midwifery Council, 2008.

Nursing and Midwifery Council (NMC). *Raising and escalating concerns.* London: Nursing and Midwifery Council, 2010.

Peplau HE. *Interpersonal relations in nursing: a conceptual frame of reference for psychodynamic nursing.* New York: Springer Publishing Company, 2004.

Royal College of Nursing. *Defining nursing.* London: Royal College of Nursing, 2003. www.rcn.org.uk (accessed 1 February 2007).

Science Museum. http://www.sciencemuseum.org.uk/broughttolife/themes/controversies/hippocracticoath.aspx (accessed 12 October 2013).

United Nations General Assembly. http://www.un.org/en/ga/ (accessed 1 July 2013).

INDEX